The British on the Costa del Sol

The 'British in Spain' achieved notoriety during the 1980s. As a group they were stereotyped as being made up of exiled criminals, drunken hooligans and inward-looking pensioners – unwelcome colonisers reconstructing their own insular 'little England'. *The British on the Costa del Sol* presents a more complex picture.

In this first book-length ethnography of the British expatriate community, Karen O'Reilly draws on history, social geography, tourism studies and theories of ethnicity and community to frame detailed interviews with British migrants themselves. What emerges is a rich account of who migrates, their reasons for migration and the day to day realities of expatriate life. While Britons migrating to Spain have not integrated into their host communities, neither have they colonised swathes of the Spanish coast. The author presents instead a marginal group occupying a liminal space between two countries and two cultures.

The British on the Costa del Sol is a lively and accessible account of an under-researched transnational community, and will appeal to social anthropologists and sociologists as well as to the general reader.

Karen O'Reilly is Lecturer in Sociology at the University of Aberdeen.

The British on the Costa del Sol

Transnational identities
and local communities

Karen O'Reilly

London and New York

First published 2000
by Routledge
11 New Fetter Lane, London EC4P 4EE

Simultaneously published in the USA and Canada
by Routledge
29 West 35th Street, New York, NY 10001

© 2000 Karen O'Reilly

Typeset in Bembo by
Florence Production Ltd, Stoodleigh, Devon
Printed and bound in Great Britain by
TJ International Ltd, Padstow, Cornwall

British Library Cataloguing in Publication Data
A catalogue record for this book is available
from the British Library

Library of Congress Cataloging in Publication Data
O'Reilly, Karen
    The British on the Costa del Sol: transnational identities and
    local communities/Karen O'Reilly
        p. cm.
    Includes bibliographical references and index.
    1. British—Spain—Costa del Sol—History—20th century.
2. Great Britain—Emigration and immigration—History—20th
century. 3. Costa del Sol (Spain)—Emigration and immigration—
History—20th century. 4. Immigrants—Spain—Costa del
Sol—History—20th century. I. Title.
DP302.C84 074 2000
946'.8—dc21   00–021537

ISBN 1–84142–048–4 (hbk)
ISBN 1–84142–047–6 (pbk)

For Trevor, for everything

Contents

Acknowledgements

Roger Goodman, of the University of Oxford, remains by far the greatest influence on this book. I owe him a huge debt of gratitude for teaching me anthropology, for training me in the 'arts' of academia, and for guiding, cajoling, supporting, advising, humouring and never bullying me through the three and a half years of my PhD. He has provided continuity and strength. Above all, he enabled me to write the thesis, and now the book, which I wanted to write, and I do not hold him responsible for any of its failings.

I am proud to acknowledge the help, encouragement and influence of the following professionals: Rob Stones, for taking me seriously in the first place, Richard Wilson, for keeping me going 'in the field' with his vigilant, challenging and warm correspondence, and Elizabeth Frances, for keeping my feet on the ground during the writing-up. But, nothing would have been achieved without friends. I especially want to thank Helen Hannick, Pauline Lane, Jackie Turton, Maggie (it's all part of the process) French, Ted Benton, Sean Field, David Forfar, Steve Hussey and David Lee for providing challenging debates, for reading and commenting on drafts, for emotional support, and for laughter. Special thanks to Carolyn Dodd for putting up with me and for putting me up so many times.

I would like to thank the Sociology department at Essex for their administrative support and help while I did the PhD, and the department at Aberdeen for giving me a lectureship, which meant I could write the book. The ESRC are to be thanked for their financial support in the form of a studentship award.

Numerous British migrants have generously allowed me to investigate their lives and to tell their stories. I cannot thank them sufficiently. They are too numerous to mention but, though I have used pseudonyms in order to respect privacy, they may be able to recognise themselves in the pages of this book. I hope I have done them justice. Special thanks are due to John and Anne Symonds, Cecil Roberts, Charles Betty, Hatti (A. Haitia), Joan Hunt, Keith and Maria Osborne, and to Kerrie for her friendship.

Finally, many, many thanks are due to my partner, Trevor, my daughters, Laura and Kelly, and the other 'children' in my family, Justin, Jemma and Jasie. Thank you for bearing with me, and thank you for being you. Here is the result of our hard work and your patience.

Karen O'Reilly
University of Aberdeen
January 2000

Map 1 The Spanish mainland
Source: Reay-Smith 1980: 19

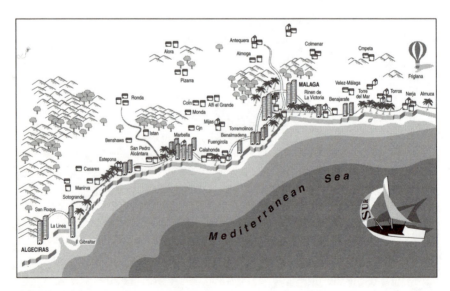

Map 2 Malaga province
Source: *Sur in English*

1 Introduction

The 'Brits in Spain'

When I first met my partner, Trevor, in 1988, he had a dream to move to Spain. He had been to the Costa del Sol on several occasions for holidays, once working there for a month, and had fallen in love with it. He took me to the area in which he hoped to settle, the Fuengirola area, and part of me could understand his desire. I too fell in love with the mountain views, Spanish fiestas and food, the warm winter sun, the holiday atmosphere, and the friendly Britons who had already settled there. After a few visits I wanted to move there too, but I had many fears and apprehensions. What would we live on? What would I find to replace my love of education and research? Would I miss my extended family and friends in England? I worried about my daughters' education: if they went to Spanish school would they cope well enough to be able to compete in the Spanish employment market? Would they be able to transfer their skills to England at a later date? Would they be happy? However, it was not an option we could take seriously for several years since we had neither the capital nor employment in Spain to fund such a move. I began to wonder how the many Britons who lived there had overcome such obstacles.

My interest in Britons in Spain thus activated, my intellect was also challenged by reports of the way in which Britons were apparently living in Spain; reports that suggested that many were not happy there, that they had made mistakes in the planning of their settlement abroad and now wished to return to Britain; reports of elderly people feeling lost and alone; reports that Britons showed no interest in the Spanish way of life nor in learning the language. I had been to Fuengirola enough times to have met several expatriate Britons and to know them to be extremely happy with their lives in Spain, and to be in love with Spain and the Spanish people. I was aware of no loneliness, ill health or unhappiness, and of no problems related to lack of integration or to isolation. I began to wonder what was going on, that reports could vary so much from what appeared to be the truth.

During the 1980s 'the Brits in Spain' became a phenomenon. Newspaper journalists wrote about them, television dramas and comedies were based on them, people talked about them. The tabloid newspaper, the *Sun*, wrote about their antics in the sun; the *Guardian* reported on their successes and failures. Radio programmes were devoted to the topic. Television documentaries reported on 'The British in Spain'. By 1992 there was a soap opera based on their experiences, which failed after only one year, but which had been expected to be a success to the extent that ten million pounds had been spent on the set. In the late 1990s the British in Spain continue to hit the headlines with the Consul in Ibiza denigrating the behaviour of his compatriots abroad, and football club managers embarrassing themselves during holidays on the Costa del Sol. But it was not only the Britons themselves who appeared to be a fascinating topic – not integrating, living lazy lives in the sun, having problems because they did not learn the language and drank too much alcohol, living like old colonials, wishing they could come home, having a wonderful time, all being old and poor, criminals or coppers – so many contradictory reports and messages were interesting in their own right. The phenomenon with which this book is concerned is therefore as much the popular representations of Britons who are living in Spain as the Britons themselves;[1] and the final part of this chapter (predicting the conclusions in Chapter 7) begins to unpack these stereotypes which tell us more about those who construct them than about those they pretend to describe.

Collective representations: 'the Brits in Spain'

In this section I examine in detail the collective representations of Britons living in Spain since they are the main relevance of this study. The phrase 'collective representations' is borrowed from Malcolm Crick, who borrowed it from Émile Durkheim, in order to include general, popular, non-scientific, non-analytical ideas, notions, images, assumptions and stereotypes about this group of individuals so often treated as one homogeneous group. Crick (1989: 308), writing during the early stages of the development of an anthropology of tourism, said

> It may seem derogatory to speak of collective social science representations rather than analyses. I do so to raise the issue of whether we yet have a respectable, scholarly analysis of tourism, or whether the social science literature on the subject substantially blends with the emotionally charged cultural images relating to travel and tourists.

I now raise the same issue in relation to British migration to Spain, which, as a pursuit, is so bound up with the hedonism of tourism that it lacks serious attention. When I initially told colleagues of my intention to research this topic, it almost invariably provoked laughter or derisory comments such as 'Oh, that's a good excuse for a year in the sun.'

As was once the case with the study of tourism, ambivalence, stereotypes and sweeping generalisations surround discussion about 'the Brits in Spain'. But, as Martin Hammersley and Paul Atkinson (1995) argue, there is no reason completely to discard common-sense knowledge about the world, just as there is little justification for treating it as unquestioningly valid 'in its own terms'. This common-sense knowledge should be worked with and examined in the light of new information. It is not possible to examine a phenomenon objectively until we face our preconceptions head on. Similarly, such common-sense knowledge is part of the world in which those studied construct their meanings and their reactions to the researcher. They shaped the assumed 'questions' which people were 'answering' when telling me about their lives, because they are what 'everybody knows' without thinking (see Spradley 1980). For this piece of research, these representations were all I 'knew' about the phenomenon under study before I studied it and, as such, are part of the research setting.

The British in Spain were, at the outset of my research in 1993, a phenomenon which had for some time been attracting the attention of the mass media and the general public, but not yet the academic community. Everyone I knew had something to say – an opinion to express, a question to ask, an assumption to challenge – about the British on the Costa del Sol and, of course, other coastal areas of Spain. Much of it was denigratory, but at times the comments seemed tinged with envy. Most thought the phenomenon would make a fascinating research topic. Many saw the behaviour and attitudes of the expatriates in terms of a problem; it is assumed they do not integrate, do not learn the language, spend too much time doing nothing and drink too much. It was implied that they don't take any interest in Spain or the Spanish way of life, that they spend most of their time in British bars, and that they buy British goods wherever possible. 'They have practically colonised the place, haven't they?' one woman asked. 'You should do some undercover work for the police while you are there', suggested a man who assumed that many of the British in the area are ex-criminals. 'It's one long round of beach parties and cocktail parties; I couldn't stand it for long', reported a woman whose friend lives in the Costa del Sol. One source of these images is experience; many British people have either taken a holiday in a Spanish resort themselves or know someone who has. Several know someone, a friend or relative, who has retired to Spain. Many of their opinions and assumptions have been formed partially from their own experiences and partially from talking to other people. However, this is a rather minor source; more important influences of popular representations are the media and literature.

The Britons who 'retired' to Spain had, by the early 1990s, appeared on our television screens in documentaries, holiday programmes, dramas, comedies, and soap operas, and in a range of newspaper reports and articles. A soap opera was launched on British television at this time: a soap opera which has now become famous for its huge costs and its failure more than for its content. *Eldorado* (a name which once conjured images of a golden, fantasy world) ran from June 1992 to July 1993. It was set in the Costa del Sol and depicted a British community of people who spent most of their time in each other's company, speaking little or no Spanish, drinking, socialising, and eating British food. The programme featured an ex (but still active) criminal, a suffering alcoholic, British bar owners, and a rather untalented entertainer amongst its migrant Britons. It was set in a complex of houses, shops, bars and a beach, apparently isolated from the rest of Spain.

In July 1992 Channel Four presented a two-part documentary titled *Coast of Dreams*, which was shown again in August 1994 (Touch Productions 1992). The programme reported on the experiences of British expatriates living in southern Spain. Both young and older couples were seen to be moving to Spain in search of their dreams. Newcomers to Spain appeared hopeful, excited, happy; they believed they had found the answer to life. More settled Britons appeared quite satisfied with the move and were aware of the envy of friends and relatives back home; but the younger ones, running bars in Spain, were having to work very hard and were not making their fortunes. They saw little of the sun and the beach and had little time for each other in their new lifestyles. Women, especially, seemed dissatisfied and disappointed. Older expatriates were depicted in the documentary as living alongside other migrants, knowing little of the Spanish way of life, language or culture, and not wanting to know more, and spending their days drinking and socialising. An interpreter from a local hospital talked of the way the British residents in Spain live in their little communities, dependent on each other for company and support, not speaking any Spanish and experiencing huge difficulties when faced with hospitalisation or illness. 'They forget when they come here that they will get older, that a partner may die and they will be left alone, that they may want to go home but they can't because they have sold everything there', she explained. A Spanish doctor spoke of the terrible problems these people have with alcoholism and liver disease: 'They live in ghettos, they have no idea of Spanish life, they just visit each other, and drink.' The programme also focused a little on the British tourists, who merely wanted a 'Blackpool in the sun'; everything that Britain can offer plus the sunshine. Little distinction was made between this attitude and that of the expatriates: 'They come here, they want to make their own little England in Spain', reported a Spanish woman. Retired Britons were shown socialising together, some speaking in crisp English accents, drinking gin and tonic, while Britons who had bought bars in Spain were shown spending time with tourists, enjoying the holiday atmosphere, the wine and the beer, and good English food. The two programmes together shared a general theme, depicting the difference between dreams and reality. They were individually titled: 'Paradise in the Sun' and 'Paradise Lost', and featured, simultaneously, the growth and decline of tourism, the development and subsequent disfigurement of the Costa del Sol, and the settling and unsettling of British expatriates. For the producers of these programmes these were clearly meant to be interpreted as associated concepts.

The British expatriates in Spain, and especially in the Fuengirola area of the Costa del Sol, have often featured in newspaper reports in Britain. The area has variously been labelled Costa del Bonk, Costa del Crime and Costa del Cop, by the *Sun* newspaper. Reports once focused on the number of criminals and, later, ex-policemen who live in the area. One report told how the bar owned by the famous bank robber Ronnie Knight, the criminal, is frequented by an ex-policeman, the cop, who once worked on his case. Some newspaper reports portrayed the British expatriates in southern Spain as better-off rebels who had chosen an escapist life in the sun. They were said to be living colonial lifestyles: 'First came the hardened expats, the colonials . . . They liked the look of Spain's sunshine coast: hot, relaxed, cheap, giveaway booze, close to the banks and shops and other home comforts of Gibraltar', reported the *Guardian* (Crampton 1993). Later 'news' depicts the British in the coastal areas living in ghettos, speaking very little or no Spanish, watching satellite television, shopping in Gibraltar for British goods, and drinking too much alcohol. In the *Independent on Sunday*, Ian MacKinnon (1993) described Britons living in ghettos, speaking *no* Spanish, buying fish and chips and British beer, and having little to do with the Spanish. John Hooper, in the *Guardian* (1993), said that 'the real-life inhabitants of Eldorado are forced to depend on satellite television for their home entertainment' since the guy who used to sell pirate video tapes has been caught; and Sarah Boseley reported in the *Guardian* on the same day that the expats 'have colonised the coast so much that the shops now sell Oxo cubes and British meat'.

Two reports which were published at around the same time, from Help The Aged (Mullan 1992) and Age Concern (1993), focused on the health and financial problems experienced by some elderly expatriates living in the coastal areas of Spain. At the time of the reports the peseta was strong against the pound, effectively devaluing British pensions and savings held in sterling accounts: 'Times are particularly hard for those people surviving on basic pensions', the Age Concern report argued (1993: 6). These reports were concerned that those who had moved to Spain several years ago were now older and possibly in worse health. They had discovered that the Spanish health service was lacking in home care and nursing provision, the system traditionally depending to a great extent on the family in times of need. With the British government refusing to pay supplementary or hardship benefits to expatriates, some were struggling to cope. The reports suggested these problems are exacerbated by factors such as the language barrier, isolation, loneliness and boredom. Newspaper journalism reflected and exaggerated these reports. Headlines appeared such as, in the *Daily Mail*, 'Life in the sun is not so hot for elderly' (Fletcher 1994) and, in the *Times Magazine*, 'Costa del Sunset' (Crampton 1993). The accompanying reports portrayed an elderly population for whom the dream of retirement in Spain had become a nightmare. 'If it weren't for the sun we'd go home tomorrow', agreed one elderly couple of whom the journalist said:

> They do not speak Spanish and have had endless trials with local bureaucracy. They miss their seven grandchildren. They have been shocked by

the cost of living. The interest on their savings from the sale of their house has fallen. The fall in the value of the pound . . . [has] hit their pensions hard. And, worst of all, their flat is not worth what they paid for it.

(Crampton 1993)

Furthermore, the expatriates themselves are implicitly to blame for their problems (see Skypala 1988); it is suggested that they did not 'go in with their eyes open' (Beard 1994) or that they 'fail to realise that a life in the sun cannot make up for illness, disability, bereavement and isolation' (Fletcher 1994). While newspaper reports focused on hard-up and unhealthy older expatriates, books written for people intending to visit or move to Spain's Costa del Sol warned readers to 'beware criminal Britons lying in wait for unsuspecting newcomers' (Hampshire 1995); and to avoid the pit-falls experienced by older, isolated and lonely Britons who thought life could be an extended holiday (Baird 1995; *Fodor's Spain 1994*; Voase 1995).

Reports about 'the Brits in Spain' continue to appear in our national news-papers and on our television screens, though perhaps with less frequency now than in the early 1990s. Nevertheless, the image remains of either upper-class, colonial style, or lower-class, mass-tourist style expatriates searching for paradise, living an extended holiday in ghetto-like complexes, participating minimally in local life or culture, refusing to learn the language of their hosts, and generally re-creating an England in the sun. The images may not be unitary but combine to construct a phenomenon with the above images and stereotype. Channel Five, for example, has been running a docusoap called *Viva España*, which features British expatriates living and working in Fuengirola. Radio One held its 1999 road show in Ibiza, where the Consul has expressed shame at the behaviour of his fellow nationals and where the entire European party scene now seems to be located. Occasional stories are told of wealthy celebrities living in the Marbella area, the California of Europe, while Costa del Sol criminals are still caught from time to time, and reported in the press.

Academic researchers, on the other hand, had shown little interest in this new migration trend, certainly by the early 1990s. Some academics had written on the topic as it impinges on or articulates with other issues such as ageing (Victor 1987), British home-owning in France (Buller and Hoggart 1994) and European migration (King and Rybaczuk 1993; Misiti *et al.* 1995). Others had begun to identify British migration to Spain as part of a larger and interesting phenomenon worthy of serious research; a phenomenon they labelled European International Retirement Migration (IRM) (Warnes 1991; Champion and King 1993). But the hypotheses, assumptions and conclusions made by academics prior to systematic research both mirrored and consolidated the collective representations addressed above to become part of the body of 'knowledge' about Britons resident in Spain. Prior to his team's research on IRM, Anthony Warnes (1991) drew on 'casual observation, impressionistic newspaper, radio and television accounts, and personal contacts' and on inferences made from studies of retirement migration within Britain, France and the US to suggest that migrants to Spain are attracted by the weather, the leisure opportunities and cheap property, and by the fact that British tastes and customs are catered for and English is often spoken by officials and locals. As for the characteristics of the group, Warnes hypothesised that migrants are likely to be from middle and upper occupational and income groups, to be property owners, pensioners, childless and usually in couples. Drawing on 'common knowledge and general observations', Tony Champion and Russell King (1993: 54) concluded that:

> aided by portable state and private pension schemes and by the general growth in wealth, increasing numbers of older people in Europe are moving on either temporary or near-permanent bases towards the Mediterranean 'sun-belt' . . . [T]he elderly migrants do tend to cluster in purpose built tourist and residential complexes with many services . . . very close by.

Champion and King accepted that, although they call the phenomenon retirement migration, younger Britons also migrate to provide services for this older migrant community. But many don't learn the language, don't assimilate the local culture, and end up in quasi-ghettos, they conclude. Assumptions such as these complement the 'collective representations' cited above of generally older British migrants, living in ghettos or colonies, speaking little Spanish, and, having been attracted by weather, leisure and low costs rather than by anything inherently Spanish, showing either disdain or disregard for Spain, its people and its culture (King and Rybaczuk 1993).

Recent research by academics interested in contemporary British mass migration within Europe tends to apply a 'problem' or 'policy-oriented' approach. Clues from research proposals and outlines lead the reader to conclude that migrants to Spain are mostly elderly; are suffering problems of ill health and poverty; are exacerbating, for host countries, problems related to ageing populations and mass unregulated migrations; or are colonising the areas to which they retire. Geography, gerontology, health studies, migration and tourism are seen as academic fields of inquiry suited to the research area. Findings of recent studies of IRM continue to imply that the majority of British in Spain are retired; however, these studies offer a more complex and sensitive analysis of issues of integration and lifestyle than were offered prior to research (see King *et al.* 1998; Rodríguez *et al.* 1998; Williams *et al.* 1997). An interesting finding which contradicts many images presented above, is that the second most important advantage of retiring to Spain which British retirees cited was the lifestyle of the Spanish people. Though language was seen as a disadvantage by these retirees, they were as likely to want to meet and get to know Spanish people as people of their own nationality. They were seen to want to integrate, but to find it difficult, and to want to adopt Spanish lifestyles while retaining some of their own (Rodríguez *et al.* 1998).

Thick description

This book represents a comparison of 'thin' and 'thick description', and owes a great deal to Clifford Geertz's introductory essay in *The Interpretation of Cultures* (1973). However, for this study the thin description is not purely the literal, meaningless description of an uninterpreted observation (as with Gilbert Ryle's 'rapid contraction of an eyelid' for a wink (cited in Geertz 1973: 7)), but is description which takes an action or event which may or may not be actually observed and which interprets and describes it in terms of what is already 'known' or presumed about a phenomenon. It is thin description only in as much as it is in opposition to thick description, which attempts to get to the bottom of what is going on by interpreting and describing the webs of significance in which 'man' is suspended and which 'he himself' has spun (Geertz 1973). Thin description, in this case, amounts to interpreting what we 'see' in terms of what we 'know'. It is thin in that it is not enriched with the complexity of significations which necessarily influence and are influenced by any situation. These descriptions in turn come to have a life of their own, as collective representations, which are handed down to us and which we accept, adopt and act upon (as with Émile Durkheim's collective representations, 1982), but which, little by little, we also adapt as new information is received. They become shared ways of thinking – constructions, which are not necessarily unitary but which form a body of 'knowledge' about a phenomenon. Academic literature, blended with fiction, plus emotionally charged sentiment and popular images together form this thin description or collective representations which, in the case of 'the Brits in Spain', remains uninformed by thick description (Beckford 1982; Crick 1989). Such thin descriptions are, in turn, often used to inform the hypothesis construction and 'problem' definition of social scientists' project designs. They become the focus for the scientist's gaze, especially for those who are advised: 'The first step in any study is to obtain a clear understanding of the definition and boundaries of what is being stud-ied' (Weller and Romney 1988). As Durkheim (1982) insisted, 'When . . . the sociologist undertakes the investigation of some order of social facts, he must endeavour to consider them from an aspect that is independent of their individual manifestations.' This aspect can be taken to be the phenomenon of the British in Spain; a phenomenon which includes some individuals and excludes others, and which lumps the included together under a coherent (sort of) set of ideas and collective representations.

Rigid hypothesis construction and strict research design confine a researcher, or social scientist, restricting her gaze towards what she assumes to discover and therefore precluding the possibility of discovering the unex-pected or the completely new. As Julian Pitt-Rivers argued in 1961, social anthropological analysis must always be preceded by description and problems must always be framed in such a way as to avoid attempting to fit new knowledge into ready-made theories and applying established concepts to 'foreign' ideas. The example he gives is class: instead of asking 'What are the social classes in this group?', one should ask 'What social distinctions are recognised in this society?' (Pitt-Rivers 1963: 34). For this book, my argument is that the representations of 'the Brits in Spain' are the relevance on which my study was based but do not form rigid hypotheses around which the research is designed. Hypotheses are constructed but are not rigid and are constantly reconstructed, while the research is in progress, using observations, experience and new information. This more flexible approach that I advocate (as have many social anthropologists before me) allows the focus of the research to move during its process. James Peacock (1986: xii), drawing an analogy with photography, advocates applying both a harsh light and a soft focus: 'Rather than focus narrowly on the object, anthropology blurs the boundary between object and milieu so as to include not only the object but also its background, sideground, and foreground.' However, this does not mean approaching a research topic with absolutely nothing to guide the research. Bronislaw Malinowski (1922) prescribed that ethnography calls for foreshadowed problems, not preconceived ideas, and William Foote Whyte (1984: 35) explains:

> I am not proposing that we enter the field with blank minds, leaving it to subsequent observations and experience to shape research plans. Striving for such a state of unconsciousness would be folly, but it is important to avoid the other extreme of becoming so fixated on a previously prepared and detailed research design as to miss opportunities to gather data about problems that may turn out to be more important.

Even a focused enquiry, informed by a prior review of the literature, need not preclude openness if an effort is made to 'suspend this outside knowledge' (Prus 1997). Using such an approach, this research project changed focus from elderly expatriates to migrants of all ages, and from permanent migration to many forms of fluid movement, including tourism. Traditional typologies of migration and the distinction between tourism and migration are thus challenged while the assumption that the British in Spain are mainly elderly and retired is confronted (see Chapter 3).

As a social anthropological study (if a methodology and epistemology determine into which discipline a piece of research falls), theorising remains close to the interpretations and to the particular study rather than appearing as abstractions from the study. This study has no theory to test; nor is it just a study of 'migration' or 'ethnicity' or 'community' or any other substantive topic into which many social scientists like to fit their research problems. I do not bring the study to a theory or topic; I bring concepts and theories to the study. As A.L. Epstein remarked (in 1978), concepts are developed to handle particular problems, but the concept developed will always have specific value for that problem and less so for other, similar ones. Throughout the text of this book theories and concepts are applied where they help to unravel the webs of significance or explicate complex interpretations, when they enable thick description; they are discarded at points where they fail to make things clearer.

In this chapter the concept of collective representations is used to describe the phenomenon being explored. Chapters 2 and 3 explore themes that occupy many migration studies: quantification, characterisation of a trend, types of migrant and push and pull factors. In Chapter 3 the opposing concepts of migration and tourism themselves are addressed and challenged by the existence of this fluid trend. Chapter 4 is descriptive but causes us to rethink the categories of elderly, crime and criminal, and associated meanings. Chapter 5 discusses ethnicity and identity, and draws on the concept of social spatialisation. Chapter 6 is concerned with community, exchange, informal economy and networks, and addresses the term 'ghetto'. The final chapter concerns itself with diaspora, transnationalism and post-colonialism. Concepts not only enable translation of a complex situation, they also 'enable us to transcend a plurality of contexts' (Prus 1997). A theorist might wish to take up themes from this study and apply them to a theory or concept, adapting and refining it with reference to insights offered by the thick description. I do not do that explicitly in this work because my concern has been to render confusing occurrences, behaviours and actions more readable, and not to test, adapt or apply a single theory to a case study. If I have been successful, I have made matters much clearer and yet more complex at the same time (see Geertz 1973: 29).

Methods of approach

The methodology most appropriate for this research 'problem' was that, often considered unique to social anthropology and influenced in great part by Bronislaw Malinowski (1922), of ethnographic research involving long-term participant observation. However, participant observation is a blanket term encompassing many and varied methods and techniques; in many ways it is more of a methodology, a theory about research which insists that people and actions cannot simply be observed, logged and counted but require interpretation, understanding and empathy. The actual techniques employed at different times were always dependent on the context of the situation; it was important to be flexible and for the methodology not to be too prescriptive. I spent fifteen months in Spain with my family during 1993 and 1994 and have returned to the area many times over the years since then. We chose Fuengirola and its surrounding villages of Mijas and Los Boliches as the place in which to study, for a variety of reasons discussed more fully in the next chapter. Fuengirola, in the Costa del Sol, could be considered the archetypal Spanish restort. In some respects it is just like any other

Spanish mass tourist area, but in many ways it is only like *some* other areas, and in some ways it is unique.

But I did not simply go and live as a British expatriate in Fuengirola; if I had done that I would have visited one or two bars, joined one or two clubs, made a few friends and only ever talked to a tiny minority of the population. I needed to discover what were the important areas of life, the important shared institutions, experiences, places, people and spaces for gaining a more complete understanding of the way of life. I spent the first few months spreading myself thinly, meeting as many people and visiting as many places as humanly possible. Later on in the research I selected a few venues and a few clubs for closer study. This involved omitting some areas of life; teenagers, for example, who are in a minority amongst Britons in Spain, were difficult for me to access using participant observation because of my own age. Similarly, the criminal underworld would have been fairly easy to infiltrate but potentially dangerous to me and my family.

The first point of contact was the bars. I called into many different expatriate bars, sometimes with my family and sometimes alone, and forced myself to talk to strangers. Bar owners often initiated conversation with the question: 'Are you on holiday?', prompting a response which led to a brief telling of our life stories in which it became established that I was a temporary migrant. On hearing a brief description of my research, customers and bar tenders alike would tell me of places I *must* go and people I *must* meet, thereby expressing what for them were significant people and institutions in British community life. Certain areas of life and certain experiences were of widespread consequence: certain clubs had huge memberships, certain people were notorious, and certain magazines and newspapers featured in all their lives (see Chapter 4). I knew I must focus on these, and become an established insider within a selection of clubs, bars, social groups and organisations. The English-language newspapers, many of which are written by expatriates for both tourist and expatriate readers, were invaluable sources of data, reflecting topics and issues of general importance. What they chose to report I could safely decide were matters of common interest. I could learn a lot from their tone and from their advertising.

Most of my time was spent being with and talking to British migrants, participating in and observing their lives, making mental notes which I wrote up at home, and conducting interviews. I joined the Royal British Legion and went to regular meetings. I worked voluntarily for the ecumenical centre, Lux Mundi, as a receptionist and helping at the weekly coffee mornings for British expatriates. I went to the Anglican Church coffee mornings and to the meetings of the Fuengirola and District Society, a social club for expatriates which holds coffee and games mornings. I did voluntary work for the hospice project, Cudeca, which at the time was fund-raising for its first hospice but was also doing some palliative care work. I found myself visiting a Swedish woman who later, very sadly, died of cancer. I helped a Spanish doctor on his reception desk for a while, and even taught some English to

Spanish adults for a short time. I befriended numerous British men and women of all ages, a Spanish woman and a Colombian family. Several of these have stayed in touch over the years.

Some authors have attempted to distinguish between the observing and the participating elements of participant observation, but it is a false dichotomy. The balance between observer and participant constantly swings during fieldwork so that at times I would be participating more and observing less while at other times I was more of an observer. For example, when my children finished school on the last day of the Easter term I welcomed them home as usual and we went out that afternoon to the beach. On the way we met some Spanish children who looked at us shocked and told us to hurry to the school: we were supposed to have gone to pick up the children's reports. When I got there I found myself listening to my eldest daughter's teacher tell me what a delightful child she is and how her Spanish has improved, while standing a little back from him so as not be sickened by the strong smell of alcohol he exuded, and trying desperately not to laugh at the stream of comments coming from children gathered around goading the teacher to speak to us in English (he was their English teacher as well as class tutor). At this point in time I was *participating* in life as a British expatriate with children in Spanish school. I was learning from experience and participation and not from observation or from any sense of being objective or distant. I *felt* what it was like to be confused by a lack of language ability and knowledge. I learned first-hand how unusual it was for an English woman to be attending this kind of meeting. Two important research methods were empathy and experience, and the two dichotomies of participant-observation and subjective-objective were critically challenged (see Powdermaker 1966, for more on this).

On another occasion I went to the disco with a friend. I let her decide where we went and when, and I made mental notes as she chose three bars to call in on our way, chatting to people she knew in each bar. We met her son and his friend at the disco at midnight. By this time I had consumed two alcoholic drinks and was getting more chatty myself. I was introduced to several teenagers at the disco and mingled into the group trying to observe ages, relationships and interactions. I took the opportunity to ask one group of teenagers what life in Spain was like for them, telling them briefly about my research first. As the evening wore on, however, I became more and more inebriated because my friend's son kept a bottle of vodka behind the bar from which we were poured generous amounts as soon as our glasses were getting low. Eventually, I was no longer able to ask any questions of anyone nor to observe anything objectively. At three or four in the morning I was escorted home by two young men who thought I needed help walking! I still had not stopped being a participant observer. I wrote up all my experiences in my field diary the next day and drew on them later when I was interviewing one of the young men I had met that night. It was definitely an advantage that I had met the friends he talked about and had seen the club in which he spends most of his nights, but at the time I had not been much of a detached observer. At another extreme, the day I sat in on a meeting of foreign residents held at Mijas Town Hall, and was introduced as a researcher, I was cast much more in the role of observer. However, since I was living and working in Fuengirola at the time, I was nevertheless a participant in some ways too. My observations and interpretations of the situation were necessarily filtered through my experiences as an expatriate or migrant trying to settle in Fuengirola myself.

Ethnographic research is essentially long term. More than a year 'in the field' is essential if the researcher is to participate in and observe one full year's events – even in surroundings comparatively familiar compared with the traditionally exotic and strange settings in which an anthropologist finds herself. My first few months in Spain were spent finding and becoming part of a community of people. During this settling-in period I was unaware of the various comings and goings in what turned out to be an important season for the community: the period of a huge temporary summer re-migration to the home country, consequential for those who were leaving as well as for those staying behind. When this time came around again, one year later, I was settled into my various roles within the community and could experience and observe the changes from several vantage points, as an insider. Spending a considerable length of time there also allowed people to get used to me, to settle down and to behave more naturally in my company. I was able to observe the processes of arriving and settling for newcomers, of seasonal change, and time-bound structures and institutions.

An essential component of participant observation is interviewing. Interviewing takes place all the time, in the form of general conversation and interaction and in more active, but opportunistic, questioning. However, more formal interviewing is often an essential tool. As recommended by J.H. Kemp and R.F. Ellen (1984: 231), varied interviewing techniques and styles were used according to the individuals, the situation, and the demands of research. Interviews were useful in different ways: gaining an individual's interpretation of a situation; opening up new lines of enquiry; testing hypotheses that were raised in the field; entry to cliques; interviewing key people; and when meeting representatives of official or formal bodies. Interviews often involved being told what people wanted me to know, rather than what they thought I wanted to hear. For example, those with an interest in welfare wanted me to record the problems some expatriates are facing; the 'field club' president wanted me to know how international and egalitarian his club is. Interviews led to the discovery of what people considered was important to show to the outside world. In taped, formal interviews of migrants I was given the official discourse, the shared myth of life in 'good Spain' which I discuss more fully in Chapters 5 and 6. Most individuals wanted me to know they had not made a mistake in moving to Spain, what a wonderful lifestyle they have, and how full and energetic their lives are. In this way they sought to dispel rumours they had read in newspapers and heard from visitors to the area, reacting to the collective representations discussed above. Participant observation, using both formal and informal interviewing, led to an interesting and valuable discovery of the many discrepancies and discontinuities between what was formally stated and what was informally expressed. On one occasion an interviewee completely contradicted herself the moment I turned the tape recorder off. She had insisted that she is never bored in Spain, that there is a range of leisure facilities and an endless supply of people to do them with. However, her friend arrived as we finished the interview and they both proceeded to bemoan the paucity of nice people to befriend and interesting things to do in Spain.

Ethnographers need to decide whether their research is overt or covert, but things are rarely so simple. As we met people for the first time in Fuengirola and they asked us about ourselves I felt compelled to tell the truth about my research rather than be discovered at some later date. This seemed much more ethical than letting people tell me things without their knowing I might take notes. However, participant observation is a difficult thing for those researched to come to terms with, and many people in this community seemed to prefer to forget I was doing research and to allow me to become covert in subtle ways. The owners of a bar I frequented almost daily assumed that my visits were a break from my work rather than part of it: 'Are you taking some time off again, Karen? Have you done much writing today?' I was asked. Interviewing British migrants in Spain called for careful and subtle questioning since many people had become suspicious of reporters and journalists who, they believed, had misrepresented them. Additionally, many migrants were not officially registered; some were not declaring income or savings for tax purposes, others were claiming benefits from the British government to which they were not entitled, several cars were not registered, and a few individuals were actually 'on the run' from the British police. I do not want to give the impression that all Britons in Spain are clandestine or criminal, but there was suspicion by many that I might represent the British government in some form in order to capture the few. It was necessary to maintain a subtle balance between overt questioning, assurances of my independence as a researcher, and covert questioning. A period of more active research on my part was often followed by rumours that I was 'from the DSS' or a tax inspector. When I attempted to conduct a survey (see Chapter 7), and later when I tried to take some photographs for my research, I was obviously reminding my researchees that I was studying them and they often seemed uncomfortable with this. The role of a participant observer can be as ambiguous for the research subject as for the researcher.

Before I went to Fuengirola I tried to envisage what my role would be within the community. I imagined I would work at the local Spanish school, teaching English on a voluntary basis, and perhaps would join some social clubs and groups. W.B. Shaffir *et al.* (1980) say choosing a participating role is very important, but in the event my roles were often chosen for me or were the result of circumstance rather than design. They were usually determined by gender, but also by age (an important variable in this community). Sometimes the role of researcher was enough, most often it wasn't: I was asked if I would like to model in a fashion show; I volunteered to work in a charity shop but this was misconstrued and I found myself visiting terminally ill cancer patients; I volunteered to help in the charity work of the ecumenical centre (helping expatriates in times of trouble) and found myself making coffees each Thursday morning; I let someone know I had a word processor and ended up designing the menus for their bar; I offered to work as secretary of one of the clubs and was turned down. A lot can be learned from the way people classify and treat the researcher; allowing myself to be slotted into roles became another research tool. For example, I realised I would have to achieve status in this community and that it would not necessarily be granted as a conclusion of anything I had done in the past (see Chapter 6). Similarly, a great deal is learned from the experience of being in the role itself, which is adopted both internally and externally (Coffey 1999).

Anthropological methods textbooks prescribe a learning of both the linguistic and cultural language of the group under study. 'Researchers must demonstrate to the actors that they can talk as they talk, see as they see, and do as they do' recommends Holy (1984: 30). But at the same time, 'we should not become so obsessively concerned with empathy that we overlook the possibility that objectivity may at times be reduced by over engagement' (Goward 1984: 88). I noticed that over a period of time my dress sense, my accent, my behaviour and interests all were gradually and subtly modified to enable me to fit in: I learned not to attempt serious discussions in 'fun' contexts; I learned to want to stay in Spain forever; I bought a pair of gold-coloured sandals and discarded the casual (scruffy?) clothes which had been more befitting of a university setting; and I even learned to appreciate 'Old Time Music Hall' entertainment. However, I experienced severe role ambiguity – a feeling that I was not being true to my self. In trying not to affect the direction of conversations or the outcome of situations and in trying to let people categorise and socialise me into their way of life, I often felt I had denied my own self (see Coffey 1999). When a group of people in a bar were discussing the case of James Bulger (a child who had been brutally murdered by two young boys in Liverpool, England) and were loudly expostulating that the murdering boys should be killed themselves in the same way as they had killed the 2 year old child, I felt very strongly about and against what was being discussed. I found it difficult to stay quiet, but felt I needed to in order not to influence the conversation or its outcome too much. I also felt I would learn more about what people think and feel by appearing ignorant or innocent and by listening well, than if I was loud and opinionated. But at times I felt I never got truly close to people because they never knew the real me. I felt that it was essential to remain emotionally an outsider to avoid being drawn into what I sometimes saw as a blind commitment to Spain. I sometimes felt lonely and homesick, but did not feel I could tell anyone this, since the accepted mode of being was to be content and to denigrate modern Britain. However, coming to terms with such restrictions on one's behaviour can be methodologically significant, leading to an increased awareness of shared culture and implicit meanings: feeling as a precursor to understanding. Experience also opens up new avenues of research. Hence, at the onset of my research I had no idea I would eventually be reading literature on community, informal economy, diaspora and nation.

The chapters

Modern anthropological studies of migration attempt to combine a structure and action approach to their field of study. They try to understand historical, international, inter-community, and interpersonal constraints on actors as well as allowing for the actors' creativity and, in turn, the impact of their decisions and actions on newly emergent social and political institutions (Buechler and Buechler 1987). Chapter 2 thus locates the migration of the British to Spain, and especially to the coastal resorts, within its historical context and within the geographical context relevant to this study. It also begins to come to terms with the actors' own rationalisations of their actions in first making the move, revealing the problems with traditional explanations based on economic push and pull factors, while acknowledging the relevance of external forces and constraints.

Chapter 3, in the tradition of thick description, begins to make the picture more complex and yet also begins to unravel some of the threads of meaning for migrants. It examines some main concerns of migration studies, with quantification and characterisation of trends, and finds the migrants both difficult to quantify and to fit into preconceived categories of migration or tourism, permanence or sojourning, retirement versus work, and old age versus youth. In an attempt to characterise the trend, it is easier to describe the migrants in terms of what they are *not* than in terms of what they are.

Chapter 4 refers back to the collective representations of the British in Spain discussed above and asks how the migrants themselves choose to portray their lives and their lifestyles in Spain. It describes important features of life in Spain for the British migrant and raises themes that are revisited throughout the book. This chapter depicts timeshare touts and ex-criminals living alongside elderly migrants, who are living life to the full. It describes a life of leisure, escapism and fresh beginnings but also of loneliness and insecurity.

Chapter 5 examines the ethnic and other identities of the migrants and establishes that an ethnic group, as perceived from the outside, does not always identify as ethnically distinct and does not always intend to construct boundaries based on ethnie. Identities are contextual and historically formed as well as created in interaction. For the British migrants to Spain, who have little daily interaction with Spanish people, an identity as residential tourists, as Britons who have visited, enjoyed and stayed, is more pertinent than a strongly ethnic identity. They have no wish to construct an oppositional identity while the Other is a Spanish people they respect, admire and wish to emulate.

Chapter 6 describes the construction of an 'ethnic community', not in terms of ghettos and not only in terms of symbolic boundaries, but as a symbolic inclusion based on a shared identity as British but different. The British community in Spain is characterised in terms of informal activity – networking, exchange and volunteering – most of which occurs on the margins of mainstream Spanish society. This forms a boundary of inclusion which enables migrants to settle and to stay, and to achieve status and belonging. But, rather than being ethnically discrete, the community that is often evoked contrasts itself with British society and aligns itself with imagined Spanish traits and lifestyles.

Chapter 7 examines the legitimacy of the labels 'colonials' and 'expatriates', challenging the implicit suggestion that this is a powerful group. It then explores the reactions of the migrants to experiences of discrimination and exclusion by the Spanish community. Finally, beginning to conclude the themes of the previous chapters, Chapter 7 depicts a community betwixt and between two cultures and two worlds; a community of British nationals who uncannily reflect Britain's ambivalent and changing relationship to the Other.

The Brits in Spain: a British phenomenon

The British in Spain are not an identifiable group of individuals, since people are moving back and forth all the time. Some migrate temporarily, some more permanently. Some are returning to Britain to live there again, while new migrants are each week setting out to start a new life in the sun. In Chapter 3 I identify this migration as a trend, as a movement of people which is historically specific. It is also a movement that can be characterised in terms of retirement, residential tourism, elderly migration, and as a movement of lower-middle and working-class people. However, not all migrants are old, retired, working class, nor even expatriate migrants. This is a *British* movement to which I refer: although members of other nationalities are migrating in similar patterns, their ethnic identity, their culture and their residence patterns differ in form to the migration of the Britons. In fact these are not just expatriates or immigrants, they are Britons, just as those who construct negative representations of them are often Britons.

Thus we begin to unravel some of the popular representations discussed earlier, the soap opera, the newspaper reports, the documentaries, the gossip, in short, the public interest (see O'Reilly 2000b). The best-selling books written by Peter Mayle of his life in Provence, *A Year in Provence* (1989) and *Toujours Provence* (1991), although 'ostensibly about the author's country of destination' are best seen as 'myths for the English', suggests Alan Aldridge (1995: 420). In the same way, the representations of the Britons in Spain, as constructed by Britons in Britain (but mostly England), are telling of contemporary British society and social change, as are the actions and attitudes of those migrants themselves. The behaviours and attitudes of the British migrants to Spain (as discussed in Chapter 7) reflect contemporary and historical British ambivalence to the outside; British nationalism, if you like. In addition the criticisms of these migrants reflect contemporary British culture and way of life, but more importantly they highlight the relationship between ideas and social change. Elite, travelling Britons are nowadays supposed to immerse themselves in, learn about and appreciate the otherness of other cultures rather than ignore, exploit, teach or look down on them. In literature, we have moved from the colonial mode of cultural translation, which assumes the inferiority of the other culture, to the anthropological mode, which 'displays respect for the source language and its culture' (Aldridge 1995: 426). In race relations, popular racism has been superseded by anti-racism. In tourism, mass tourism has given way to travelling and the search for 'the real'. But the Britons who migrate to Spain's coastal areas are, apparently, stuck in the mass tourist mode. The area in which I did field-work, as well as other areas in which Britons have settled in large numbers, are known as mass tourist areas. They are the areas to which the package tour companies continue to direct large numbers of visitors each year. What these areas signify to many people in Britain is 'tourists'; our attitudes to and ideas about the British who have settled or visit there are linked to notions and judgements about the modern tourist.

'The term "tourist" is increasingly used as a derisive label for someone who seems content with his obviously inauthentic experiences', says MacCannell (cited by Crick 1989: 307). A tourist in the modern age of mass tourism is associated with commercialism, the inauthentic, the trivial, the buying of signs rather than reality. Tourism itself is linked in the mind to the destruction of culture, the loss of the 'real', and the spoiling of the natural environment. Holiday packaging, directed in a large part to Spain's resorts, relieved tourists of the burden of decision-making; 'providing them with an "environmental bubble" to prevent confrontation with anything alien at all' (Crick 1989: 327). The image of this sort of traveller is one who is not concerned with the culture of the people or the area to which he/she is travelling, but is hell-bent on hedonism, spending, freedom and indulgence. This view of the tourist as narrow-minded, as opposed to the 'traveller' who wants to explore, to immerse oneself in the culture and real environment of the unexplored Other, is summed up by Paul Theroux (1992) when he says 'Tourists don't know where they've been . . . Travellers don't know where they're going.' But it's not just tourists that we can't take seriously; the whole phenomenon of tourism is so bound up with hedonism and pleasure that even sociologists and anthropologists have in the past found it difficult to take the subject seriously. As I said earlier, when I announced my intention to study the British in Spain, colleagues could not resist making jokes and derisory comments. More recent researchers, in the fields of geography, social policy and sociology have only been able to approach the topic since it became defined in terms of the elderly, retirement, tourism and the environment, or in terms of migration and poverty; in other words they were able to approach it as something serious as opposed to the frivolous and trivial.

Mass tourism and its tourists are now all bound up with images of over-development, exploitation, pollution and decay as intellectuals, religious organisations, radicals within the countries themselves, and more recently sociologists and anthropologists draw attention to tourism's more adverse sociocultural consequences. This has been picked up on by the mass media and reports have appeared depicting crowded beaches, pollution and decay, overcrowding, high-rise blocks and construction sites. Modern tourist brochures and travel programmes suggest travellers look inland for the 'real'. Spain's own tourist board, meanwhile, is trying to encourage visitors back to its shores and its rural areas by changing its now negative package holiday image. The tourist herself is even associated with bad behaviour: 'the behaviour of so many tourists is . . . deeply offensive to the people among whom they stay', says Crick (1989: 328).

The British abroad, especially, have received bad press in recent years as football supporters have been thrown out of countries for violent behaviour and package holiday-makers have reportedly misbehaved under the influence of too much alcohol. There was arguably a moral panic in the 1980s as these British representatives of our once-great nation were considered to reflect decadence in British society as a whole. Many Britons now apparently try to dissociate themselves from the image of the superficial, fun-loving, lower-class tourist. As I was writing this a radio presenter on my local radio station announced the results of a survey of what the British like to do abroad. One recurring response was that they like to pretend not to be British! In amongst all this we have the Britons in Spain – residential tourists, frivolous, hedonistic, eschewing the real authentic experience for the unreal, fun experience. Representative of the remnants of racism and ethnocentricity in our society, and of the lower-class traditions of mass and package tourism, their behaviour, to aspiring 'higher-class' people, is doubly offensive. The better *class* of tourist or traveller now seeks a cultural experience, an immersion in as opposed to insulation from the culture and environment being gazed upon (Urry 1990). Those who continue to take package holidays to sights of mass tourism are implicitly poorer, less discerning and lower in both intellect and 'class'. Those who are moving to Provence, like Mayle, are both intellectually superior to the non-discerning mass tourists, and are wealthier, middle-class travellers as opposed to working-class masses migrating to Spain's spoiled coasts.

Class in Britain continues to be ubiquitously tied up with notions of superior breed and intellect and therefore 'high culture', as well as with the traditional occupational and wealth classifications. The major division is one between the lower/working and the middle classes. This major division persists in the popular mind despite the attempts of successive governments to disguise it, especially John Major's aspirations towards a classless society. This major division, with its grey areas in between, is represented most articulately in the national newspaper industry, with the more left-wing and intellectual *Guardian* newspaper directly contrasting the (more) right-wing, anti–intellectual and working-class *Sun* newspaper. While the *Guardian* accuses the British migrants of living in a bubble, of not integrating and of regretting their poorly planned decision to move to Spain, the *Sun* is identifying with these fun-loving nationals and sensationalising their marginal, liminal status as criminals, cops or sexy sun-seekers. At the same time as the *Guardian* represents the intellectual and discerning traveller, multiculturalist, anti–racist individual, the *Sun* represents the 'naturally' nationalist, touring, fun-loving British masses. While acceptance of the outside exists alongside nationalism and euro-scepticism, anti-racism can be seen as an intellectual movement directly challenging the more natural and uncultured racism of the masses.

The language of racism and of 'racial rejectionism' tends to naturalise its subject (Bonnett 1993). It draws on scientific evidence, especially Darwin's theories in the *Descent of Man*, to support established views that non-western or non-white peoples are not only discrete species but are also much farther back than us on the road to civilisation. However, the dissemination of knowledge about the atrocities of Nazi German racial cleansing led to a public and scientific rejection of racism. Meanwhile scientific theories now abound challenging the notion that different peoples can be classified into discrete racial groups or typologies with attributable, typical cultural traits and intelligence quotas. Anti-racism and multiculturalism have evolved as a response to and rejection of racism. 'Within Britain multiculturalism has been associated with a model of society as a mosaic, a tapestry of equally valued but discrete cultures' (Bonnett 1993: 33). Multiculturalists both explore and celebrate the existence of different cultures, traditions and ways of life. Multiculturism has been criticised for perpetuating the notion of discretenesss but in the language of culture rather than race. A multiculturalist ideally immerses herself in 'the culture', in 'the field' (Aldridge 1995; Bonnett 1993). He or she does not so much gaze upon the exotic Other as observe 'the imponderabilia of actual life' (Malinowski 1922). The image of a reified culture, static and discrete but accepted and even interpreted, replaces the more biologistic notion of race. For the middle-class Briton, travelling becomes almost a collection of other cultures seen and understood, but perhaps still implicitly looked down upon. This is evident in the attitudes of the Britons in Spain towards the indigenous Spanish, who are seen as being stuck in the past and sharing a static culture. Anti-racism, on the other hand, is a more intellectual approach to the critique of racism. Anti-racists believe that racism can and should be educated out of people by challenging and changing their attitudes (Bonnett 1993: 37). As a result of this movement, during the 1980s in Britain some local education authorities, especially in areas with 'multiracial' populations, introduced training and education aimed at increasing awareness and eradication of racism, known as Racism Awareness Training Programmes. But while some Britons were made aware of their racist and rejectionist attitudes, others just changed the rhetoric. Race and immigration have repeatedly surged back into the headlines and on to the political agenda under the language of nationalism, while drawing on an image of Britain's small and overcrowded island (Hudson and Williams 1989). For many Britons, rejectionist sentiments were clothed within popularist myths of 'the ordinary Briton' and 'the nation' (Bonnett 1993). Fears that our little island would become overcrowded and that our national identity and integrity would be lost in a sea of alien culture if the flow of immigrants were not stemmed found little appeasement from the rhetoric of anti-racism. Anti-racism became associated with the left and with intellectualism. It was then easier to dismiss such rhetoric as the ramblings of 'the loony left'.

Whilst racism as an expressed sentiment has been rejected, the rhetoric of ethnicity has in some ways replaced it. Ethnic identity, or identification with nation state, with shared origins and imagined blood or kinship ties, is still seen as natural and primordial. The continuing importance of ethnic attachments in spite of mass migration, multiculturalism and mass communication has been explained by many authors in terms of the power of primordial attachments, kinship, blood ties and affection (Epstein 1978; van den Berghe 1981; Yinger 1986). Ethnic attachment is natural, biological and emotional. It is about identification with a common 'us' against a common 'them'. For every 'us' of ethnicity there must be a 'them', an opposition group. In the intellectual, cultured, anti-racist rhetoric, this 'them' must be accepted and understood. It is, however, unfortunate that this 'them' can rarely be seen to share territory or origins or affective ties with 'us', and therefore will always naturally be in competition with us. But the protagonists of anti-racist or multiculturalist movements prescribe that we overcome these powerful urges: culture must therefore conquer nature, even human nature. The lack of integration or the persistence of discreteness amongst Britons travelling abroad is thus indicative of uncultured, uncritical but natural racist and isolationist tendencies. Britons in Spain are accused of colonising, not because they are like the old elites of Great Britain but because they are seen not to have learned the language and the lessons of multiculturalism. They are denigrated as residential tourists who have not learned, as better 'class' people have, to appreciate the richness of other cultures. But this multiculturalism itself retains a superior and elitist view of the discrete, static, even backward other. For the aspiring elites, these migrants symbolise all the adversities of mass tourism, and its association with cheapness, crassness, and the lower classes. Those Britons who have not learned to appreciate the cultures and differences of others are uneducated, undiscerning, ignorant lower-class people.

The Britons in Spain, on the other hand, have internalised the multiculturalist approach to the other and believe themselves to acculturate and even integrate to some small extent. They even take trips inland to search for the 'real', authentic and unspoilt Spain; and they eschew the behaviours of the mass tourists who descend on the area each summer (see Chapter 5). Their view of Spain and the Spanish, though, is very much a socially constructed one, as much tied up with notions of tourism and holiday, with nostalgia and elite images of backward cultures as reflecting any 'real' Spain. They retain the legacies of British Empire, believing themselves to be superior and more advanced (see Rodríguez *et al.* 1998). They realise they need to integrate within Europe just as they realise that Britain is less powerful than it once was and needs the alliance of other nations. But they also retain the little Englandism, the isolationist tendencies, the island mentality and the 'natural' racism or nationalism of *Great* Britain, while denying that they do: they do not call their community an ethnic or expatriate one, but (when it is referred to) an international one, denying both its existence and its discreteness. They eschew contemporary British culture as spoilt, expressing no desire to go home, yet in many ways they have gone 'home' to traditional community values and traditional British culture.

2 Setting the scene

As Floya Anthias (1992) has pointed out, in order to understand migrants' experiences and identities, it is essential to contextualise the migration, to consider the history, both personal and general, of the movement. Causes or reasons for migrating, as proffered by the migrants themselves, can help us to begin to understand who moves and why, but more importantly they can reveal crucial insights into experiences and behaviours of migrants once they have migrated. But every decision to migrate is an individual decision heavily influenced by external factors and constraints. In many ways the history of this migration trend is the history of tourism, but it also the singular histories of both Britain and Spain, and the history of the relationship between the two countries. This history is continuous, it has no definitive point of departure and no end. This chapter examines historical, contributory and related factors in, rather than causes of, this migration at the national and local levels, as well as examining individual justifications for migration.

Reasons for migrating to Spain

Population geographers and migration specialists have traditionally sought to classify the reasons for migration as either push or pull factors. However, for some large migrations, such as those to California and Florida in the 1930s and 1940s, economic forces were insufficient explanation; these migrants were seeking a better quality of life, and were attracted by sun, sea and scenery more than economic factors (Robinson 1996; also see Ullman 1954). Now, at the start of the twenty-first century Britons and other northern Europeans are migrating to southern European coastal regions for apparently similar reasons. However, who can say that their reasons are not also economically driven? Clearly, the history of the migration trend, the political, economic and social conditions, have been factors which have eased or impeded migration, but a great deal can also be learned from the stories individuals tell about their reasons for migrating. The people who populate the pages of this book have mostly migrated to Spain during the 1970s to 1990s, with a massive influx occurring during the 1980s. So what were the reasons these people gave for migrating? When I met British migrants for the first time, conversations followed a typical pattern: they would ask me if I was there on holiday, I would reply with a short description of my research, and they would then proceed to tell me why they were there as migrants. This usually involved telling a personal story, and if the person was sitting with others, a group discussion often ensued in which the participants enthused about life in Spain generally.

Continuity and change

For many of the migrants I spoke to, moving to Spain had a sense of continuity about it. They had usually had some contact with the area, through frequent visits either as tourists or to visit family and friends who had already settled there (see Rodríguez *et al.* 1998). However, making the move more permanent tended to signify a break in continuity, often marked by an event in Britain. Wiseman and Roseman (1979) in their research on elderly migration in the US noted a similar phenomenon, and described these sorts of factors as 'trigger mechanisms'. Some people in Spain described how their businesses had failed or they had been made redundant, and how this had *triggered* their decision.

John and Adrian, for example, were both in their late fifties when I interviewed them. Having visited Fuengirola many times on holiday, because they could 'be themselves in Spain, with no-one condemning them', they migrated to Spain when John was made redundant. They live together on John's redundancy money, which they hope will last until they reach retirement age and can draw their pensions. They can live more cheaply and more freely in Spain, they said.

Another couple, Lillian and Tommy, both lost their jobs prior to moving to Spain. Tommy's sister lives in Marbella and they had visited her several times before deciding to move to Fuengirola (because it is cheaper than Marbella) when Tommy had an accident at work which resulted in his being no longer able to do the job. This happened not long after Lillian had been made redundant, so neither had anything to keep them in England any longer – except grown-up children. Lillian and Tommy have been together since 1970, though both are still married to someone else. They suggested that this might also have tempted them to move away.

For some migrants the trigger factor took the shape of personal tragedy such as a divorce, or a death in the family. June was 75 when her husband died unexpectedly. She was devastated at the loss of a partner with whom she had shared almost fifty years of her life and, though she had lived in the same village for over thirty years, when her children started to fight over who should look after her and began dictating to her about how she should spend her money, June decided to move far away. She went to Fuengirola to visit a friend, to think things over, and decided to stay. She went home to sort out the details and within three months had settled in Fuengirola as a permanent migrant. Her children were bewildered, she told me.

For others a less personal event such as a series of house burglaries in their area had signalled that they should leave. A younger couple I met on a walking expedition talked of the degradation of their neighbourhood in Wales as the trigger to their migration. 'I was getting sick of it', Mary told me. 'All you ever heard about was break-ins and muggings, and then people are getting so miserable these days back home. We just had to get out.' Pete, her husband, had been wanting to move to the Fuengirola area for several years but couldn't persuade Mary to leave her family. Finally, the rising crime rate in *her* home town provided the push that *he* was hoping for.

When another couple, June and Trevor, who own a laundry in Los Boliches (a village to the east of Fuengirola, and part of the same municipality), told me about moving to Spain, they also said the real trigger had been the extent of crime in their area in Scotland. 'It was just one thing after another', June told me, 'then when our neighbour was mugged – twice! – well, we just said that's enough!' June and Trevor have got a daughter who was then 11 years old. 'We didn't want her growing up in all that', Trevor said.

Those who had never been to Fuengirola before migrating there were in the minority. Many of these had lived much of their lives out of Britain working for transnational companies, the diplomatic service or in the armed forces, and had made a conscious decision to retire somewhere which offered what both Britain and Spain can offer and was also near to home. The closeness of home, and the possibility to fly back to see relatives, and for relatives to be able to visit, were important factors to several people.

Edward, for example, who was in his nineties when I interviewed him, had lived in South Africa, Nigeria and India during his life. When he came to retire he tried living in England but hated it, so he came out to Spain. It is warm, there are plenty of British to keep you company, and it is near enough to fly home regularly, he told me. Besides, his wife suffers from arthritis and the doctors told her that if she didn't move somewhere warm she might not last another winter. That was five years ago, he said. As I talked to him, Edward's wife, Ellen, was at the doctor's with a friend. She had gone with him to help him out, because the friend spoke no Spanish and Ellen did. Ellen was 85 years old at the time, but she had once worked as a nurse in Spain and so was fluent in Spanish. It was her idea to move to Spain when they could not settle to retirement in Britain.

Push and pull factors

Reasons or *post-hoc* justifications (because 'reasons' are often exactly this rather than actual causes) that people gave for migrating to Spain can be separated into two distinct categories: those that say negative things about life in Britain and those that say positive things about life in Spain. The negative things about life in Britain can then be separated into personal and general events or changes and were often articulated, as discussed above, as decisive factors in the move. However, other than the trigger factor, people could usually list several things about Britain which caused them to decide to 'get out'. 'England is so depressing these days. It's cold and grey, and everyone is miserable', one young women insisted when I asked her why she had moved to Spain.

At the same time, these push factors were often balanced with pull factors: those positive things about Spain which drew them to the country. These in turn can be separated into 'natural' resources, including the climate and the landscape; things offered by the settled migrant British community, such as social clubs, leisure opportunities and a welcoming community; and things offered by the Spanish community, such as respect for children and elderly, friendliness, warmth, security and a slow pace of life. Malcolm and Linda moved to Spain when Malcolm took early retirement from the military. They have lived in several different countries but settled on Spain for several reasons. I asked what it was about Spain that attracted them and Linda said enthusiastically, 'the people, they are so friendly; and the climate . . . and the pace of life, being able to take your time over things – everyone is in such a hurry in England these days; the *ferias* and fiestas; and having time.' Malcolm added, 'Everything takes longer here . . . and we like it that way. This is what we wanted from retirement – to relax more, to get up later, spend more time together . . .' He spoke slowly and softly as if underlining his words with this soft emphasis. During another conversation Malcolm ventured to suggest that actually what attracts people to Spain has little to do with the Spanish: 'As long as there is the sun and the slow pace of life, we could be anywhere in the world.'

Another ex-military couple, Peter and Mary, told me that Spain (or Fuengirola at least) is relatively free of street crime and muggings and is therefore a safer place for both young and old. 'Children play out until midnight here, and no-one is worried. And what is so wonderful is that you see the big kids and the little ones playing together, and the boys and girls.' Lillian and Tommy added some of these positive things to their list of reasons for moving. 'The slow pace of life here is a big attraction', Tommy told me. 'Life here consists of doing nothing . . . Everything takes longer here, you don't do anything much but the day's gone before you know it. If you can achieve one thing in the day you should be proud of yourself', he said. 'Yes, it's no good trying to rush anything here, you will just end up frustrated', Lillian confirmed.

One evening I attended a Royal British Legion dinner and dance. My partner and I were seated at a table with three other couples and a single woman, who, as expected, asked us how long we had been in Spain and if we lived there permanently. Upon hearing about my research, they talked endlessly about why they had left Britain and why they loved Spain. They moaned about the poor weather in Britain, enthused about the relaxing pace of life in Spain, told me excitedly about the cheap leisure opportunities and the numerous social clubs in Fuengirola, and agreed between themselves that the Spanish health service is very good and treats older people better. 'You are not cast aside when you are old here, like you are at home', said Anita, the single woman. 'In Wales I am sure the elderly wait longer to see a specialist than the young do.'

For older people the attractions of Spain over Britain include advantages to health of a good climate and the opportunity to be active, both because you can spend more time outdoors and because there are more clubs to join. Many also cite Spain's relative cheapness as an advantage; you can get more for your money, they would tell me. A lot of this is to do with the exchange rate between the pound and the peseta, but crucially, the things that make life enjoyable – wine, beer, cigarettes, eating out, leisure activities – are cheaper regardless of the exchange rate. For young single people the attractions of Spain are obvious. There is more to do, the sun shines more, which means there are more hours in a day, people are happier and more free. I met several young people involved in the timeshare business and others working as couriers for whom this kind of work and Spain together offered fun, sunshine, laughter and a feeling of freedom. They contrasted this with work life in Britain, which they saw as 'dull, routine, boring and monotonous'. One young man, Ronnie, who returns each year to work the summer season, says that in Spain he does what he wants, sleeps with whom he wants, drinks what he wants, works in the sunshine, pays no taxes, then goes home to 'sleep it off'.

The anonymity is something that attracts a number of people (and perhaps ensures others can't go home again). Terry, who was working as an electrical repair man in Spain, told me he had got involved in petty crime in Scotland and came to Spain to hide. He wasn't in big trouble, he told me, but he could not afford to hang around. On the other hand, Sheila, who has been divorced twice and whose ex-boyfriend was causing her a lot of hassle in the UK, enjoyed the anonymity which enabled her to be whatever she wanted to be. She told me, 'No-one here knows about my past. I can start all over again and be who I want to be.' I never did find out what it was she did not want to be – it seemed irrelevant anyway.

Some people of course do not migrate fully to Spain (see Chapter 3). For these migrants the stories they tell about coming to Spain on a regular basis focus on the advantages Spain has to offer. However, their stories also include reasons for not moving to Spain more permanently. Phyllis and Stuart, who visit Los Boliches each year for six or seven months, told me that they would love to come to Spain to live but they would miss their family too much. Tim, a gay man in his forties, said he liked to come to Spain to be himself but he couldn't afford to live there permanently. More than one man told me he would settle permanently in Spain but his wife wouldn't leave her family and friends, and more than one woman told me she would love to live in Spain but was afraid to make the break.

An explanation of this apparent need for people to explain why they do not move to Spain more permanently might be found in the characterisation of migrants, *by* migrants, as maverick, brave, different, exciting and fun-loving people. 'You have to be brave to move here', one woman told me. 'All of us are a bit maverick, a bit unusual', another man said 'or we wouldn't do it.' Dan, who had just made plans to move to Spain permanently, told me on another occasion,

> It takes a little something extra; not everyone can do it. It takes a lot of intelligence to move here. It's not easy. The *Sun* makes us all out to be thick, but you couldn't move here if you were thick. You will meet so many intelligent people here. We have some very interesting conversations.

And Cyril, who retired to Spain with his wife in the 1980s, told me:

> Everyone says they would like to live here but not everyone does. It takes a lot of guts to do something like this. It's not just ordinary people, otherwise they'd still be in England. It takes that little something extra.

External factors: history and geography

While it might be interesting to discover the reasons actors give for their decision to migrate, we must not forget that these are often simply no more than *post-hoc* justifications, constructed from the perspective of the new context within which they have found themselves (see R. Cohen 1996). As Skeldon argues, a major problem in attempting to explain migration is

> post-facto rationalization; that is, people justify their migration on the basis of what has occurred since their movement, and it is extremely difficult to discern either what their reasoning or what their situation was during the lead-up to their decision to migrate.

> (Skeldon 1994: 3)

Ethnographers in the interpretative tradition are concerned with processes and concepts that address these; a historical perspective is therefore crucial. Every decision to migrate is an individual decision heavily influenced by external factors and constraints. The history and social geography of Fuengirola and other Spanish resorts have been crucial factors in the migration process, just as the flows of tourists to the areas have been crucial to their subsequent development for mass migration. Political factors have also played their part.

Spain as a country of immigration

Since the Second World War Spain has been first a country of emigration, then later a country of immigration. Part of the massive labour migration of the 1950s and 1960s included a huge south to north European migration. Indeed, 2.2 million Spaniards emigrated between 1960 and 1970 to what was then the rich north (King and Rybaczuk 1993). But things started to change in the 1970s and by 1975 Spain had 'turned positive', in that it had a net positive migratory balance (King and Rybaczuk 1993). Many were still emigrating, especially from the poorer parts of Spain, but these were now outnumbered by the immigrants, some of whom were return migrants and some of whom were arriving from economically less-developed countries of Africa, Asia and South America. Spain was unprepared as a country of immigration, and was slow to react. They were particularly slow to gather reliable figures on the numbers of immigrants, which was necessary prior to action and development of responsive immigration policies. As a result many illegal immigrants settled and remained undocumented.

In the 1980s immigration increased rapidly. Important flows came from European countries, from South America, from Africa (mainly Morocco) and from Asia (mainly Filipinos). The most substantial groups of legal foreign residents were (in order of importance) UK, Germany, Portugal, France, USA, Argentina, Morocco, Philippines and Venezuela. In 1989 there were 73,535 immigrants from the UK (as far as anyone could measure) and 9,020 from Venezuela (King and Rybaczuk 1993, figures from SOPEMI Report 1990). In the 1980s two-thirds of Spain's foreign residents were Europeans. Some of these flows are the cause of more anxiety than others for Spain: immigration from Africa increased fivefold between 1980 and 1992, for example, with Morocco accounting for 60 per cent of the increase (Solé 1995). The illegal migration of many of these Moroccan immigrants has caused some concern (Papademetriou 1994). The migration of British and northern Europeans, on the other hand, was not initially viewed as a problem, but its rapid growth is getting worrying. Montanari and Cortese (1993) predict that demographic growth, permanent migration, temporary migration and tourism, mean that the ethnic population of the Mediterranean countries, at least in certain periods of the year, will continue to grow alarmingly. Concern is being expressed about the effects of this massive annual influx of immigrants and visitors on water consumption, the treatment of waste, and the demands placed on natural and cultural environments (Jurdao 1990; Montanari and Cortese 1993).

It has been said that while some migrations might not be numerically significant at the national level, they can have significant local effects (Rodríguez *et al.* 1998). In the Fuengirola area this is certainly true of European retirement migration, which has significantly affected some areas. In the municipality of Mijas, for example, in the last census in 1991, Europeans accounted for over 11 per cent of the population and almost a third of those aged over 55 (Rodríguez *et al.* 1998). Visibly important European groups are those from the UK, Germany, Sweden, Norway, Finland, Denmark, Belgium and the Netherlands. Other very visible groups of immigrants are Moroccans and gypsies. More recently, locals in the Fuengirola area are becoming aware of the immigration of Russians, Japanese and Asians, who are spending money on property in the area, and of the increasing numbers of asylum seekers to the area, especially victims of the Yugoslav conflict (see Newland 1994).

The history of a trend

There are many historical and contemporary representations of Britons abroad other than those discussed in Chapter 1: Britons as colonials of the Raj; Britons as expatriates earning vast amounts in Dubai; the Welsh in Patagonia; Britons buying farmhouses in rural France and so on. However, the trend with which this book is concerned and which specifically relates to those labels, stereotypes and images discussed in Chapter 1 is both time and space specific. They relate specifically to the mass migration to, and settlement in, Spain's coastal areas and islands associated with mass tourism, a phenomenon which grew in importance in the 1970s to become a trend in the 1980s.

Some of the first contemporary British visitors to Spain were writers, backpackers and intellectuals enjoying the simple tranquillity of rural villages (Burns 1993a; MacCannell 1996). A few of them settled, carving out new lives for themselves. When Ronald Fraser (1973) interviewed local villagers for his study of a small Andalusian village, his interviewees included a number of 'foreigners' who had settled in *The Pueblo*. Amongst those who had settled in the 1950s and 1960s were a British diplomat, an architect, an author and his wife, and an artist turned silversmith. These 'professional' people had come from diverse parts of the world, from Britain, New Zealand, South Africa and Italy.

My research was concentrated in the Fuengirola area which, like many of the coastal areas now developed for tourism, was still a small fishing village in the 1960s (Kean 1994). Migration there by Britons began at least as far back as the 1960s, but those few stragglers making their way so far south were usually wealthier, upper-middle or professional class couples buying second homes to escape to and, occasionally, settling more permanently (Punnett 1990). Others were posted to the area for work with British or international companies. However, the number of British immigrants in Fuengirola at this time was still so small as to be insignificant (Lore 1994). Tourism had not yet reached its shores.

A 70 year old woman, Brenda, who had lived in Fuengirola thirty years when I interviewed her in 1994, told me of the enormous changes she had witnessed in the area:

There were only a few British, it was so quiet, nothing like it is today. And the Spanish, they would take their children out of school to help them in the market, to translate and to help them, 'cos they couldn't read and write you know. You see where these apartments are here [pointing] . . . well this is where the beach was, and this was the front, and around there, that was all green – and the river used to be full then, too.

Brenda had been 'forced' to migrate when her husband had been posted to the area with his company, and had never wanted to settle there, she told me. She had refused to learn the language and had spent all her time with the one or two other English wives she met. Her husband has since died and she has stayed on because Fuengirola now 'feels more like home' to her than Britain does, though she can still only speak a few words of Spanish.

A professional couple, John and Judith, who bought an apartment in Los Boliches in the 1960s were proud to tell me of the changes they had witnessed to the landscape and the social make-up of Fuengirola in the thirty years they had been visiting.

There were none of these big blocks in those days; none of this was here, and none of the people, it was a tiny fishing village . . . and the Spanish were poor, and most of them were illiterate in those days. All us Britons knew each other in those days, and we would visit each other for drinks and for dinner. We were a small cliquey group, not like now. There are so many now, it's impossible to know them all, and most of them are not really our type, you know.

Such tranquillity was set to change dramatically over the next decade: the adventurous travellers of earlier decades were to be replaced by tourists following well-worn paths to established destinations (MacCannell 1996). The increase in real disposable incomes of northern Europeans, the increase in leisure time and paid holidays experienced by workers across the social scale, and developments in transport which made travelling long distances cheaper and more comfortable, all help to explain the rapid growth in international tourism which sparked off, in Spain, a building boom of hotels and apartment blocks (Jenkins 1991; MacCannell 1996; Punnett 1990). Tourism, by the late 1960s, was no longer the preserve of the wealthy and privileged, it was a mass phenomenon with Spain as a favourite destination (Burkart and Medlik 1974). The number of foreign holidays taken world-wide swelled from 25 million in 1950 to 330 million in 1989 (Punnett 1990).

Malaga, 30 kilometres east of Fuengirola, now familiar as a historical and busy town rather than a tourist spot, was famed as a winter resort at the turn of the century and was actually one of the first tourist areas. It was not until the later 1960s that mass *coastal* tourism emerged as the country's fastest expanding industry and small villages like Fuengirola were rapidly developed and exploited as areas of tourism (Burns 1993b). The development and marketing of all-inclusive package tours was critical in this growth of mass tourism and its Europeanisation during the 1960s and 1970s (Shaw and Williams 1994). This phenomenon grew to the extent that by the late 1960s more package tours were being taken by north Europeans than any other type of holiday. It was especially big business for the United Kingdom, where over the space of five years tour operation developed into a competent mass industry which was able to offer entire holidays often for less than the cost of a scheduled flight. During this period a holiday abroad joined consumer society's demand for the good life, along with the car and television (Burkart and Medlik 1974). Mass tourism is a form of mass consumption and tends to be highly spatially polarised. It tends to result in the creation of entire cities or towns 'built solely for consumption' (Shaw and Williams 1994). The Mediterranean regions were notably affected, and new resorts such as Fuengirola and Torremolinos could not remain unchanged. As Lanfant (1995: 5) says:

> With tourism, what enters a country is not only passing tourists but also the apparatus of tourist production, a model for planning development and all the incentives which lead a society down the road to change under the influence of . . . a 'dynamic from without'. Economic and cultural strategies become progressively bound together with the aims of the tourist industry. Imperceptibly the place becomes determined by external forces and reconstructed from a tourist point of view.

During the 1960s American loans and reforms within Spain enabled an industrial boom, which, assisted by this growth in tourism and by remittances from half a million Spaniards working abroad, led to a period of economic growth, the rate of which was the highest in the world (Facaros and Pauls 1992). Spain, often considered backward by its European neighbours, was beginning to catch up with the rest of Europe. However, few Britons actually settled or bought property in Spain until after the death of the Spanish dictator, General Franco, in 1975, which led to the removal of many disincentives. General Franco, a monarchist at heart, chose Juan Carlos I as his successor, little suspecting how dramatically he would change the country by dividing it into autonomous regions nor how effectively he would bring in a democracy that would prove more conducive to prospective immigrants.

I met a small number of Britons who had lived in Fuengirola since the early 1970s. 'Peter's Place', considered to be one of the oldest British bars in the area, was opened in 1975, and the owners were still living there. Charles and Ellen had retired to the area in the 1970s, when they were both in their seventies themselves. Mary moved to Fuengirola in 1976 with her parents. She is now in her forties, speaks fluent Spanish, and runs a boutique in the next village. Her parents, however, have moved back to Britain.

The 1970s were troubled times in Britain; relative to the rest of the world the economy was in a decline the extent of which led to the label 'the sick man of Europe' (Pearce and Stewart 1992). Unemployment grew at an alarming rate from 1 million in 1975 to 3 million at the beginning of 1983. Paradoxically, at the same time both living standards and incomes were rising; the sale of consumer durables rose dramatically; and the growth in holidays abroad was phenomenal (Bedarida 1991). More and more Britons visited Spain's coastal areas and islands each year as tourists, some staying longer, returning, and eventually buying businesses and homes there (King and Rybaczuk 1993). According to some commentators, there were two main reasons for this migration: Britons were moving to Spain either to retire or to make money (Davey 1990). For others it was a consumption-driven migration: a second home abroad became the ultimate consumer aspiration; 'a new phase in the development of the affluent society' (Svensson 1989: 1; see also Buller and Hoggart 1994).

In 1972 moves towards a Europeanisation of the relationship between Britain and Spain began with Britain joining the Common Market. This was strengthened when Spain joined what was then the European Community in 1986. Over subsequent years European and Spanish legislation have coincided to make it easier for Britons (and other Europeans) to purchase property, to reside, to work and to move freely within Spain.

During the 1980s, Spain's administration began actively to encourage foreign investment in Spain and foreign purchase of land and property in order to compensate for the very seasonal and regional nature of tourism, which brought such a downward spiral in incomes each winter (Jurdao 1990; Valenzuela 1988). Land and property was cheap in Spain compared with Britain (and other northern European countries) and developers capitalised on this new market, building cheap, high-rise, often poorly constructed blocks of apartments in an unregulated fashion in many of the most popular resorts (Davey 1990). Urbanisations (new, densely concentrated developments of small and larger villas) sprang up in a spontaneous and often unplanned manner in and around these same resorts (Jurdao 1990; Pearce 1995).

In the early 1980s increasing numbers of Britons, following a pattern set by the Germans (Svensson 1989), began buying holiday homes and retirement homes in Spain's coastal areas. Britain experienced strong economic recovery from 1983 onwards through the mid-1980s (a boom that was received more optimistically by the general public than the specialists (Pearce 1995)), coupled with a massive growth in the property market and an accompanying increase in expendable wealth of many traditionally lower-class and lower-middle-class individuals. This meant that for the first time many more people had money to spend on second homes, which, with the lengthening of holidays from work or on retirement, they could visit for longer and longer periods. Others were able to sell properties in Britain, making huge profits with which to buy first homes[1] upmarket in a cheaper

Spain, buying themselves a higher standard of living to retire to, or buying themselves an income in the way of small businesses serving the tourists and newly settled communities of expatriates. This was at a time when both the service industry in general and self-employment were on the increase back home, and when autonomy at work and entrepreneurialism were both key themes in Thatcher's Britain. During the mid-1980s the exchange rate fluctuated at around 200 pesetas to the pound sterling, reaching 220 pesetas to the pound at one point in 1985. Tourists were, by now, flocking to Spain in large numbers and, attracted by the low prices, good exchange rates, the sun and sea, and the increasingly welcoming infrastructure of the tourist areas, they began to consider Spain as a place to live. In Fuengirola, and places like it, many Britons became aware of the employment opportunities so many British tourists provided, and started to set up services: car hire, bars, restaurants, laundries, letting agents and, later, estate agencies. Individuals began to settle in the area in search of work within these industries with their beautiful surroundings and seemingly relaxed way of life. Valenzuela (1988: 46–7) reports:

> In 1986 alone foreign investments in real estate and housing totalled 195 billion pesetas . . . Investment in the larger cities is speculative and comes from international firms, but in the tourist zones it involves individuals investing their savings in a dwelling, initially for seasonal use but ultimately as a place for retirement.

The development of an area for tourism frequently provides amenities from which the more settled community can benefit: residents already living in the area, as well as those who decide to move there more permanently, can take advantage of a better provision of public transport and higher standards of provisions for shopping and entertainment than the area would normally have been able to provide (Burkart and Medlik 1974).

Many went to retire and many, disturbingly for some, were elderly. A trend which began in the 1970s grew at such an alarming rate in the 1980s that it prompted Francisco Jurdao to wonder if certain European countries (as well as Japan) were exporting their elderly, and with them the problems associated with ageing populations, to Spain (Jurdao and Sanchez 1990: 20). According to their figures, the area surrounding Fuengirola, the municipality of Mijas, has 94 purpose-built tourist developments (*urbanisaciones*), in which live 12,000 foreign nationals. Regardless of the census figures mentioned earlier, these authors estimate that in 1990, actually as much as 70 per cent of the population of the municipality of Mijas was foreign, and 50 per cent of those were British. In 1998 an English-language newspaper, the *Entertainer*, quoted a figure of 600,000 English-speaking foreigners living in southern Spain. These are purely estimates though; official figures do not accurately reflect foreign residence for various reasons (Williams *et al.* 1997, also see Chapter 4).

In the later 1980s tourism in Spain, especially in the familiar resorts, began a decline which by the end of the decade appeared to be threatening the economy (Shaw and Williams 1994). The effects were eased by the 'residential tourism' of many northern Europeans, discussed above, which had been successfully encouraged in the tourist areas. In addition, the Spanish Tourist Authority determined to change Spain's image of package, cheap holidays in the sun and to promote 'cultural tourism' in an attempt to attract the more discerning visitor in search of culture, quality and natural beauty rather than sun, fun, leisure and pleasure (Marvin 1990; *Sur* 1994; Valenzuela 1988). This had three main purposes:

1   the tourist industry would be revitalised;
2   this more discerning visitor would hopefully spend more money than the package tourist; and
3   redirecting what Urry (1990) calls 'the tourist gaze' away from the coast and toward inland Spain would ease the problems associated with tourism's geographical concentration (Punnett 1990).

Later still, the Spanish Tourist Board announced, as one of its main priorities for the further development of the sector, the need to encourage tourism from non-European markets, especially the US and Japan (EC 1995).

At this time a recession in Britain together with the slump in the property market abated the flow of Britons who had previously been able to sell at huge profits in Britain and buy more cheaply in Spain.[2] By the early 1990s, when the peseta gained strength against the pound sterling for a time, Spain was not such an attractively cheap option. For example, at one point in 1993 the exchange rate dropped to 167 pesetas to the pound sterling. At the same time interest rates on capital held in sterling accounts were falling. 'Retirees' who had made the move and were living on British pensions in Spain, or on capital invested in sterling, began to feel the pinch; their money was suddenly not worth as much as it had been a short while ago. This prompted the response and reports from charities for the aged in Britain mentioned in Chapter 1. At the same time the Spanish introduced several new taxes which negatively affected foreign property owners (Mellado 1993) and future sales of Spanish property (Svensson 1991). Many bars and businesses in the Fuengirola area began to fail due to the drop in custom in the form of tourists and seasonal visitors, and several immigrants had to return to Britain. There is possibly, now, a return migration in process (Svensson 1991).

However, people were and are still moving to Spain and to Fuengirola, although many are now renting property rather than purchasing, at least initially. Some migrants feel they have 'had their fingers burned', while others are more cautious than their predecessors as a result (Hay 1993). The peseta is currently weaker again against the pound, so that migrants are comparatively wealthy again (for now) and Spain appears as a cheap option for retirees, for purchasers of property or businesses, and for would-be tenants. The coastal areas, with their settled foreign communities and their organised infrastructures, with the sun all year round and the promise of better health and wealth, are still attracting large numbers of migrants in the form of visitors and settlers (Pascual Vegas 1993). The European Union is now overtly encouraging 'residential tourism':

> The idea of freedom of movement is being enhanced to ensure that people of any age can travel from one part of the Union to another perhaps for very long periods. This is particularly relevant for older people who have retired and who may wish to spend many months in parts of the Union other than their original home (because the weather is better or the cost of living lower, for example). In effect, this amounts to protracted periods as tourists.
>
> (EC 1996)

Furthermore, they insist, this market is set to grow as Europe's population ages. But, there is no mention of migration, or settling permanently, though this is clearly an implication.

Fuengirola

Fuengirola presents a combination of images, many of which can be summed up in the contrasting symbols of an idyllic Andalusia and the spoilt Costa del Sol coastline. It has become in many ways synonymous with British migration to Spain, mainly as a result of the fact that many reports in the media were directly reported from Fuengirola and Los Boliches: the notorious criminal Ronnie Knight and the infamous London Pub are prominent features; recent drug busts reported in the national British media involved individuals we met or knew of from the Fuengirola area. Many of the collective representations discussed in the preceding chapter emanated from the Fuengirola area of the Costa del Sol. The Channel Four documentary, *Coast of Dreams*, was filmed in and around Benalmadena, between Fuengirola and Malaga. *Eldorado*, the BBC soap opera, was filmed in the countryside behind and on the beach just along the coast from Fuengirola, and drew some of its cast from the local community. Many television and press reports discussing the British in Spain centre on Fuengirola and the surrounding area, especially Los Boliches – a region at the eastern end of Fuengirola, physically and symbolically separated from the main town by a dry river bed.

The Fuengirola area is believed to have a high concentration of foreign residents compared with other areas of Spain (Baird 1995). These 'foreigners' include Germans, Finns, Swedes, Norwegians and Americans as well as Britons. Mijas, a little village in the mountains behind Fuengirola and extending down along the coast west of Fuengirola, is considered to have the greatest number of British and other foreign residents (*Fodor's Spain*

1994; Kean 1994).[3] I settled on the Fuengirola area for research for these reasons, and because we had contacts there, knew it to be well populated with Britons (see Kean 1994; King 1992; *Fodor's Spain 1994*), knew there to be a close British community in Los Boliches especially, and knew there to be many British businesses and social clubs in the area. The Fuengirola area differs from other close towns also thought to have large numbers of British residents. Although there is no research to support it, the general consensus in the area is that Torremolinos, to the east, is a cheaper area for holidays and for buying property, attracting younger and less well off migrants while Marbella, to the west, is a more affluent area, attracting 'the jet-set' and earning itself the label 'the California of Europe'.

Fuengirola is situated in Spain's Costa del Sol between Malaga, to the east, and Marbella, to the west. From Malaga airport it is a 30 kilometre drive westwards, on the renowned N340.[4] Originally named *Suel* or *Sohail*, it is overlooked by the Castillo de Sohail on a hill west of the town – a castle of controversial origins, possibly first constructed in the tenth century (Anderson 1992). Before 'suffering the ravages of tourism and over-development' it was, depending on the commentator, either a typically Spanish, sleepy, fishing port whose locals lived peaceful, settled lives (King 1992; Ortega 1993), or a poor and scruffy village on an unwanted stretch of coast 'where people eked out a miserable life' (Kean 1994: 60).

According to David Pearce (1995), 'some of the world's most intensely developed coastal tourism is to be found along the Mediterranean coast'. 'The coast has sold its soul to the devil' (*Let's Go* 1993). Fuengirola is a prime example. The municipal area has been developed to such an extent that the 'old town' is surrounded by high-rise blocks and new urbanisations; original residential areas are overrun with hotels and tourist accommodation (Jurdao 1990). The town, as it is now, is over-populated and is saturated with bars, supermarkets, restaurants, cafes, discos and so on, many owned by foreigners. Legislation to save the destruction came too late for places like this, says Peter Davey (1990). It is 'artificial and hermetic' (Luard 1984); 'tacky' (Baird 1995); 'dull and cheap' (*Fodor's Spain* 1994).

Alternatively, Fuengirola is a healthy, thriving, busy little town, on a sunny piece of coast surrounded by magnificent mountains and pretty white villages. It attracts thousands of tourists a year in the form of young couples, families and older people from within Spain and from international locations, especially Britain. Residents and tourists alike can enjoy the close proximity of rural, 'traditional' Spain as well as the many amenities offered by a modern, cosmopolitan tourist resort (King 1992; Reig 1995).

Fuengirola is in the province of Malaga, in the autonomous region of Andalusia. It is often said that all of Spain is in Andalusia: 'the image of Spain is the reality of Andalucía' (Stradling and Vincent 1994). Andalusia is white villages nestled on hillsides; narrow streets; olive groves; window boxes overflowing with geranium blossom; goats roaming majestic mountains; old men chatting outside cafés in the dusk of an early winter's evening; flamenco and fiestas; Moorish castles; sun-soaked beaches; and endless blue skies (Lloyd 1992; Luard 1984; Stradling and Vincent 1994). The closest white village is that of Mijas, in the mountains just behind Fuengirola, a well-known tourist spot which has retained some of its 'authentic village atmosphere' (*Fodor's Spain 1994*); alternatively it is 'as traditional an Andalusian village as Malaga airport' (Ritchie 1994: 52).

Stretching from Almeria province in the east to Huelva in the west, Andalusia is an area of hot summers and warm winters. In the southernmost part, the Costa del Sol, shielded by the Sierra Nevada mountain range, offers approximately 3,000 hours of sunshine a year. Summer temperatures here range from 20 to 40°C, and winter temperatures from 9 to 20°C (Davey 1990; Marvin 1990).

As has been shown, most of what is written about Fuengirola, the Costa del Sol and Andalusia is emotive. Whether Fuengirola (and towns like it) is over-developed into a concrete jungle or is a busy modern town with a rural backdrop, or is indeed all of those things discussed above, depends on interpretation. This is how I described the myriad juxtaposed images I encountered in my early days of fieldwork:

On our second day in Fuengirola we went for a long stroll along the paseo and around some of the back streets of the town to orient ourselves. We had visited the area in the past but had not paid sufficient attention to where all the British bars and the shops were, etc.

Fuengirola is a coastal town 30 km west of Malaga in the Costa del Sol. It has a population of about 47,000 people (doubling in the summer). It was once a fishing village (until development in the 1960s) and it still has a port and a strong fishing community. It is surrounded, in the distance, by little villages of white-washed houses and, more closely, by several urbanisations or mini-housing estates with their own bar, laundry, swimming pool, residents' associations and shops.

The town itself is a mixture of the old and the new, the traditional and the modern, side by side; of hotels and villas; of supermarkets and corner shops; of Spaniards and foreigners. Along the beach you will encounter fishing boats side by side with sunbathing tourists, sun beds and *tapas* bars. There is the marina with some very big and expensive yachts, then the port where the fishermen land and auction their catch each day. Away from the beach there are tourist souvenir shops side by side with the greengrocer and the ironmonger; business centres offering lessons in computer programming side by side with café bars and small restaurants. Everything one might need, it seems, is within walking distance.

Several of the bars and some businesses advertise in English – is this because they are English owned or are they attracting the English-speaking customer I wonder?

(Field notes, June 1993)

3 Migration

A great deal of the discussion around migration in Europe is polemical, and focuses on problematic or potentially disruptive waves of immigration from the east or the south to the wealthier north-western European states. In order to get some sort of control over these flows, figures are sought, trends are characterised and future trends are predicted. Though it is becoming increasingly difficult to distinguish between economically and politically motivated migrants, refugees, especially in the wake of events in the former Yugoslavia, are considered the biggest threat to stability. Other migration trends – especially like that of the British to Spain, which is not always even permanent and is difficult to separate entirely from tourism – receive much less attention. In the tradition of mainstream migration research, this chapter attempts to characterise the trend of British migration to southern Spain.

European migration research

Since the mid-1980s interest in migration has been revived within Europe. The main triggers of concern have been: (a) the fall of the Iron Curtain and political and economic disruption in Eastern Europe, both threatening an influx of immigrants into Europe and (b) 'racial' tensions within Europe, which question the harmony of ethnic pluralism and implicate persistent ethnic discreteness as a cause of conflict (Fassman and Munz 1994). In the 1990s in Europe, migration is a hot topic. Mass migrations, emigrations, and immigrations affect the population size, structure and character of a nation, as migrations alter the course of history (Castles and Miller 1993; Champion and Fielding 1992). The now familiar spectre of ethnic cleansing threatens to result in recurring flows of asylum seekers into western states at a time when racism and xenophobia are on the rise in Europe generally. Individual governments are again concerned that massive influxes of immigrants into their countries will compete for capital and over-stretched resources. For many, 'migration' has become synonymous with 'social problems' (Anthias 1992, Collinson 1993; Fassman and Munz 1994).

One of the most pressing and potentially destabilizing political challenges facing western Europe (and in a wider sense the whole OECD area) in the 1990s is the influx of refugees and migrants. Western states seem to act as magnets attracting hundreds of thousands from the Second and Third Worlds.

(Overbeek 1995: 15)

The rhetoric is indicative of the fears: nations prepare for tidal waves, invasions and crises. Governments concerned to monitor, predict and regulate migration, especially *immigration*, demand research which can help them find effective policies to control and manage the flows (Champion and King 1993; Martin 1993; Miles 1993). Migration is therefore a national policy issue.

Trends in migration are a cause of concern in almost all OECD countries, even though they are not all in the same situation. Southern European countries like Spain, Italy and Portugal are seeking to control fresh waves of immigration . . . Accelerating migratory flows and rising numbers of prospective immigrants also mean that tighter control of flows is needed in order to make migration policies more credible and integration policies more effective.

(SOPEMI 1993: 13)

Although population moves have occurred since the dawn of history, from the mobility associated with hunting and gathering to recurrent flights from natural disasters (Cohen 1996), migration, according to much of the rhetoric from within Europe, is deviant from the implicit norm of stability and stasis. We are encouraged to think of the migrants themselves as deviants, as the cause of disruption and chaos (Benmayor and Skotnes 1994a: 4). Much of this disruption is considered attributable to ethnic diversity. In 1992 alone several catastrophic events – race riots in Los Angeles, neo-Nazi onslaughts in the former German Democratic Republic, war in Yugoslavia – were explained with reference to mass migration and the problems of ethnic mixing (Castles and Miller 1993). Migrations thus demand integration policies.

New migration trends within Europe, such as the migration of increasing numbers of Britons to southern Spain, are a special challenge to governments since they often involve groups (such as retired people) and forms of mobility (which are sometimes very flexible) which have until now not attracted much attention and are therefore little understood (Buller and Hoggart 1994; Champion and Fielding 1992; Champion and King 1993; King *et al.* 1998; Rodríguez *et al.* 1998). At the same time European countries are now experiencing a differentiation in migration trends which they need to begin to conceptualise, since various types of migration affect their population structure at any one time (Collinson 1993). However, these contemporary, intra-European migrations are less threatening to the integrity of an imagined pure ethnic nation state (see Skeldon 1994) than are the in-migrations of poorer peoples from either the east or the south, and accordingly these migration trends have received less attention (and probably funding) from within Europe.

As a result of national concerns, migration research is often associated with demographic change and focuses its attention on quantification, trends, macro study, and predictions (Kearney 1986; Pooley and Whyte 1991; Robinson 1996; also Collinson 1993; Fassman and Munz 1994; OECD 1993; Salt 1992). Indeed, assessing international migration trends and growth is essential to Europe's security and stability, insists Vincelli (1994). The first step to the monitoring and control of a trend is the collection of sets of statistics (Anthias 1992) and so one of the first things a study of European migration often attempts is quantification. All generalisation requires quantification. Even more qualitative research, aimed at understanding and explaining migration, often seeks a quantitative base (see, for example, Skeldon 1994).

However, as we shall see, migration trends are often notoriously difficult to quantify. This is especially true of refugees, whose interest is sometimes best served by being undocumented, but is also true of other trends such as that of northern Europeans to southern European Mediterranean countries for retirement (King *et al.* 1998). Social surveys generally use migration 'trends' or 'movements' as the units of analysis as opposed to individual migrants (Warnes 1992); hence, as well as collecting statistics, researchers distinguish between mass movements by characterising trends. Specific trends then attract more attention than others: south–north and east–west population movements are seen as cause for more concern that their counterpart north–south and west–east moves. Similarly, migration into Europe has received far more attention than migration within Europe. But trends are not only described in terms of the direction of the movement. Part of the process of monitoring and controlling population movement and change is to typify migration, sorting different trends into different categories, based on sets of criteria. Studies of migration thus often begin by posing certain questions: the who, where, why, and for how long of migration studies (Champion and Fielding 1992; Collinson 1993; Pooley and Whyte 1991). Distinctions are then typically based on types of migrant and on migration motivations, but this is particularly problematic for groups such as the British migrants to Spain, who are, as I will show, very difficult to quantify and who cannot easily be characterised in terms of migration motivations or push and pull factors.

One need only think of the word 'immigrant' and the concepts, issues and images this conjures up to understand how certain approaches to migration have dominated research. Europe became an area of immigration between 1945 and the 1970s and now even southern states are experiencing in-flows. Labour migration, refugees, asylum seekers and more recently family reunion migration have been the main focus for studies of European migration (Salt *et al.* 1994). There has in fact been a shift in migration flows, whereby the predominance of guest worker migration into Europe in the 1960s and 1970s has been overshadowed by the movement of illegal immigrants, asylum seekers and skilled labour (Champion 1995). Accordingly, labour in-migration has long been the predominant theme but more recent research on migration into Europe has focused less on labour demand and more on return migration and refugees; and, more recently, emigration by highly skilled professionals has received some attention (Buller and Hoggart 1994). For Dirk van de Kaa (1993) the specific types of migration affecting Western Europe towards the end of the century, apart from economically motivated migration in general, fall into the following categories:

- family reunification
- political discrimination
- return to country of origin
- gypsies
- internal conflicts and upheavals, including the victims of ethnic cleansing.

Other migration trends receive scant attention by both researchers and by the mass media in general. If they are too small to be called a trend, then they are unlikely to be noticed at all by geographers, demographers or governments, even if they are picked up on by the media (as with British migration to Spain). Even though, as King *et al.* (1998) note, few migration specialists now assume that the only important movements are the economically motivated ones, moves such as international retirement migration (a growing trend, especially from the north to south European countries, and a facet of British migration to Spain) remains under-researched.

Other than the work on retirement migration of Russell King and his colleagues, one is led to assume that migrants, generally, tend to be young. Indeed, initial migrants in most trends are typically young males in search of work or refuge, with women and children typically joining later. Even European out-migrants tend to be young, unmarried and male (King 1993). For Europe at least, the migration of older people is almost unknown except as internal migration or retirement to the seaside. As discussed earlier, a few commentators have begun to notice a new trend of older people moving to southern Europe on retirement and accordingly have begun to use a new label of north–south elderly or retirement migration (Boissevain 1994; King *et al.* 1998; Misiti *et al.* 1995; Rodríguez *et al.* 1998; Williams *et al.* 1997). This is the category most used for British migration to Spain, even though estimates have shown that just half of the migrants here are aged over 50 (Williams *et al.* 1997).

In attempting to characterise trends, research has traditionally concentrated its attention on what are known as 'push, pull and network factors' (see previous chapter). Push factors impel people to leave the country of origin and include such things as political oppression, poor living standards and low economic opportunities. Pull factors attract them to a different place and include a demand for labour, the opportunity for higher living standards and political freedom. Network factors cover family reunion migration where, typically, a young male who initiated the migration is later joined by his family; and the opening up of opportunities in the host country by migrants on behalf of friends and family who join a network of migrants. Such explanations of migration are essentially ahistorical and actor-oriented, disregarding many wider, structural factors. The focus is on what motivates the migration. Collinson (1993), for example, offers four broad categories of migration motivations associated with political and economic push and pull factors. The British in Spain are not characterised by commentators in terms of a certain motivation but the implicit suggestion is that the main factor is one of pull: attractions in Spain draw the migrants who are not forced either economically or politically to leave their country of origin. It has already been shown, in the previous chapter, that this trend does not fit easily with any of these typical characterisations. Both attractions of Spain and disaffection with Britain were important, but trigger factors in the lives of each individual were also crucial. Many migrants work, but this is not a trend motivated purely by economic factors (though the fact of Spain's cheapness compared with Britain is relevant). Networking is a relevant factor, as migrants are attracted to an area where others have already settled, but this is not the same as a network migration in which families join earlier migrants once they have settled and can provide for them (see Rodríguez *et al.* 1998 for more on reasons for moving to Spain).

Migration is often opposed in the literature to tourism and to less permanent moves to other places. Ideally, 'tourism denotes the temporary, short-term movement of people to destinations outside the places where they normally live and work' (Burkart and Medlik 1974: v). It is this temporary, short-term character of tourism which distinguishes it from migration, which, in turn, represents a long-term population movement with a view to taking up permanent residence (Burkart and Medlik 1974: 40). Although, for some authors, business travel and conference attendance are tourism (Smith 1978), tourism is more often defined as a temporary break from normal routine and life. It is defined more by what it is not than by what it is – it is *not* home and it is *not* work; it is a change of scenery and lifestyle, an inversion of the 'normal' (Graburn 1978; Smith 1978; Urry 1990; Voase 1995). 'Migration', on the other hand, implies a more permanent change of residence, as opposed to touring, visiting or sojourning, which always imply an intention to return home. Anthony Warnes (1991: 53) suggests that for demographers, migration is a 'permanent' change of residence, with permanent commonly being taken as six months. For sociologists too 'migration involves the (more or less) permanent movement of individuals or groups across symbolic or political boundaries into new residential areas and communities' (*Concise Oxford Dictionary of Sociology* 1994), whereas for geographers, migration is the 'permanent or semi-permanent change of residence of an individual or a group of people' (*Dictionary of Human Geography* 1994). Many authors agree that the term is ambiguous, but it seems there is consensus as to the fact of some degree of settlement or permanence on the part of the migrant.

However, things are never so simple. For Pooley and Whyte (1991: 3)

> migration is an imprecise event which can include anything from a short-distance move within a small community to emigration to the other side of the world, and from a move to a new location for only a few days, before the migrant travels elsewhere, to one that lasts for a lifetime.

Clearly, within this definition, migration can include those who have no intention to settle or become permanent. Perhaps within the term 'migration' we need to distinguish between that which is permanent and that which is less so; between migrants, sojourners and tourists. According to the World Tourism Office, 'tourism includes all travel that involves a stay of at least one night, but less than a year, away from home' (Shaw and Williams 1994: 5). This definition quite clearly overlaps with migration. The thesis that there is a continuum between tourism and exile (Battisti and Portelli 1994) seems more reasonable, since no-one can seem to decide where one starts and the other stops. But even for Battisti and Portelli (1994: 38), 'the traveller' is someone who goes home. In the end it is not so useful to try to distinguish absolutely between categories but better to be sensitive to a group's internal categories and self-ascriptions.

Cohen (1996) warns that appearances can be deceptive: illegal immigrants may pose as tourists; visitors may overstay and settle more permanently; more permanent settlers often retain a desire to return home eventually. Writers distinguishing between migrants who intend to remain in their new place of residence and those who see their stay as temporary have used the term 'sojourner' (Brein and David 1971; Klein 1990; Skeldon 1994; Siu 1952; Uriely 1994). This is a useful concept in certain situations, as a direct comparison with permanent migration and as a reflection on an individual's orientation towards one or other place. Apart from the discussions around migrants, sojourners and tourists, some European research has acknowledged that more flexible forms of migration exist, such as seasonal visiting and peripatetic residence (see Warnes 1991). Studies of migration in developing countries, on the other hand, tend to conceptualise seasonal, circular, oscillating and return population flows. They often refer to these temporary moves as circulation (see, for example, Chapman and Prothero 1985).

The British in Spain: problems of quantification

In order to view British migration to Fuengirola as part of a larger trend, and to assess both its extent and significance for governments and policy-makers, quantification or informed generalisation is necessary. Several authors have recognised the problems of gaining 'hard' data on this recent trend in migration, either because little or no research has been done, or because official statistics in the various areas do not reflect the different migration types within the main trend (Misiti *et al.* 1995; Valenzuela 1988; Williams *et al.* 1997).

In October 1992 a symposium was held in Alicante to discuss the social and economic problems of older British people who have moved to Spain. It was attended by delegates from fifty-three Spanish and British governmental and non-governmental organisations and a booklet was subsequently published by Age Concern, England. It discusses problems with gauging 'the scale of the problem': 'Many delegates commented on the difficulty of ascertaining the precise numbers of elderly expatriates living in Spain' (Age Concern 1993: 9). The reasons given are that formal records do not distinguish between temporary and more permanent residence, and that many Britons are not registered as resident in Spain. However, the report concludes that 'the numbers of retired British people in Spain is significant', that is, large enough to be worthy of attention by charitable organisations and governments. Concentrating his attention towards elderly or retirement migration, Tony Warnes (1991: 56–7) states that:

> Existing sources for studying elderly migration to Spain are inadequate or defective. All available sources in the UK and in Spain only partially cover the phenomenon . . . Migrants to Spain are not registered in any systematic way by that country.

Clearly, a large number are undocumented: even the annual numbers of deaths of British citizens in Spain during the 1980s can be used as evidence that many more Britons must be resident in Spain than are recorded (Warnes 1991). In a discussion of retirement or elderly migration of northern Europeans to Spain, Russell King and Tony Champion report that 'the data to measure these age-specific international migration flows are extremely scanty' (Champion and King 1993: 54).

King and Rybaczuk (1993) identify three main sources of data on foreign immigrants in Spain: the Spanish census; statistics of those with residence or temporary stay permits; and statistics for those with work permits. None of these is satisfactory: some authors estimate that *legal* foreign residents only represent about 69 per cent of the immigrant population (Gonalvez-Perez 1990: 18, cited in Warnes 1991: 195). The Spanish census data are 'sadly out of date' by the time the census reaches publication; moreover statistics for those with work permits obviously exclude all those who do not have or need such permits.

If existing data on British migration to Spain are difficult to obtain and to trust, gathering new data is an even more problematic task because of the fluidity and unofficial nature of the population (Williams *et al.* 1997). There are various sources from which a researcher could attempt to collect data on

British migration to Spain but there are problems with each. European nationals spending more than six months of any year in Spain are obliged by law to register at the local police station as residents and to obtain a residence permit. However, for various reasons many British nationals do not register and, as a result, official Spanish records of 'residency' are an unreliable reflection of numbers of what should be a clearly defined group. But the reasons for not registering often tell us more interesting things about the group than do the figures that we might have obtained.

One reason for not registering is fluidity of movement. Many British migrants do not stay in Spain for a set time of either less or more than six months of the year. They may be in Spain for a short time, to return at a later date, or may not be sure how long they will stay. They may be resident in Spain for more than six months each year but not in one block, or may stay just a little over six months and feel the regulations do not really apply to them. Those who do expect to stay longer than six months find the process of applying for and gaining residence permits an expensive, time-consuming and bureaucratic nightmare. Then, acting as a further deterrent, there is always the possibility that the permit will be refused and the person will be asked to leave the country within a few days. As the following quotes demonstrate, gossip circulated within the community about British people who had applied for residence permits and had been refused for one reason or another.

> I had some friends who applied for residence and they were refused, and they had to get it so that the boy could go to school, but they had to go back to England in the end, the boy and Marie, without her husband because he couldn't go back there because he left debts behind. In the end they could have got the boy into school without residence permits but they didn't know that and once they had applied they had to go through with it.
>
> (Liz, thirties)

> I knew a couple in their seventies who've lived here twenty years, then they thought perhaps they should apply for residence. They hadn't done it before. Well, they have to go home now because they've been refused – because they don't have enough money. His pension is not enough for both of them they say. It's ridiculous, they've been living here twenty years!
>
> (John, fifties)

With the threat of expulsion in mind, many residents who believe their situation is not a straightforward one (if only one half of a couple is receiving a state pension, for example) keep a low profile, hidden from the authorities, in the peaceful knowledge that there is little chance they will be discovered. Amanda (in her forties) told me: 'It's better to stay quiet. No-one knows you're here unless you apply, then they've got you, and if you haven't got enough money they can kick you out.'

Apart from being put off applying for residence permits by the threats of confusing bureaucracy, high costs and possible expulsion, some British migrants feel that as Europeans, and especially since 1992 signalled the free movement of people within Europe, they should not have to register and should be able to move freely within Europe without worrying about papers or bureaucracy. This attitude prompted the following comment in a book-let produced by the Department for Foreign Residents in Mijas:

> Yes, even now that Spain is a full member of the European Community, you still need a residence permit to live in Spain. 'Free Circulation' is not really free, even in other EC countries. All EC nations require some sort of residence document from their foreign residents, and Spain is no exception.
>
> (Ayuntamiento de Mijas 1993)

Many migrants have been attracted to Spain by what they imagined was a laid-back, relaxed approach to life. Part of what attracts them to Spain is the holiday spirit and the feeling of freedom: needing to register, to sort out papers and to be legally visible contradicts this experience of freedom and escape from routine offered by the idea of an extended holiday in the sun. And there are, of course, as discussed in the next chapter, those who have more straightforwardly escaped to Spain, either because they have broken the law or because there are individuals or a lifestyle from which they wish to escape. These individuals do not want to be found or discovered and so have no intention of alerting the local Spanish police to their presence in Spain.

It would, in fact, be very difficult for the Spanish authorities to prove how long a person had been staying in Spain, and therefore required a permit, since there are no records of the few border checks which now take place. Only those migrants running a registered or visible business; those who are formally employed; and those officially 'looking for work' are documented and are therefore compelled to register with the police as residents. There are also financial disincentives to registering: many residents do not have suf-ficient income to qualify for a resident's permit (the requirement in the Province of Malaga, at the time of writing, is actually higher than a British state pension); while non-resident migrants currently receive tax-free inter-est on capital held in Spanish bank accounts (see Betty and Cahill 1995). As a result, temporary migrants, many retired migrants, and many younger peo-ple who are working either illegally or informally, do not appear on police records.

Since one cannot rely on police figures on residence, another possible avenue would be to refer to the local census data held by the councils in Fuengirola and in Mijas.[1] However, the figures that these have of foreign residents in their areas are admittedly grossly inaccurate, to the extent that when I requested data, council officers in Fuengirola and Mijas handed me the figures apologetically. The Fuengirola council, for example, had 987 British nationals on its figures in 1992, but one local official estimated that there were at least ten times this number of Britons living in the area. A Colombian woman I met in Fuengirola was researching for a postdoctoral degree in Economics at the University of Malaga. Having developed an interest in the economic activities of foreign, especially British, migrants in the area, she attempted to collect data on British residence in order to conduct a survey. I went with her to the council offices in Fuengirola and Mijas. Councillors admitted that it was impossible to trust their census data and advised my friend to give up on her idea. One councillor told us that when the census is carried out 'suddenly all the British go back home, it is impossible to find out whether they use property they own for holidays or for residence'. Even reference to regularity of rubbish collection or electricity use, for example, would not suffice, since the foreigners will say someone else was using the property, he told us.

Another possible data source is the British Consulate in each area, but once again figures are unreliable. Britons residing in Spain were, at the time of my research, encouraged to register with their local British Consulate, but this is not a requirement (Creffield 1995). Many migrants I spoke to were unaware of the existence of such a register, and others had not bothered to register. As a result, unless they had cause to use their Consulate for any reason − if their passports were lost or in times of legal difficulties, for example − they were never recorded there as living in Spain. In addition, those who were registered with the Consulate, but subsequently left Spain, did not usually inform the Consulate of their change of residence. The number of British property owners in Spain has been offered by some of the more popular books on living in Spain, as a guide to the size of the British expatriate population there. However, this figure is spurious since a vast number of property owners in Spain use these as holiday homes whereas many expatriates, in Fuengirola at least, are tenants rather than owners. There are numerous expatriate and foreign national social clubs in Fuengirola and the surrounding area which could provide clues as to numbers of migrants going to or residing there (see Sleater 1993). However, these figures do not generally reflect essential differences between temporary and permanent migrants, and in addition many people may be members of more than one club, while others may not join a club or society at all.

There follow some examples of estimates of numbers of Britons in Spain. They demonstrate the variation between estimates but also give some clue as to the extent of British migration to Spain and to the Fuengirola area in particular. The main problem is one of incomparability of sources: each estimate refers to a slightly different group of individuals; ranging from foreign nationals in Spain to Britons in the village of Mijas. The best anyone can offer is a range of figures from various sources and an acknowledgement that, in terms of size, the migration trend is significant (King *et al.* 1998), important (Rodríguez *et al.* 1998) and consequential (Mullan 1993), and that the effects locally are substantial.

For the whole of Spain, according to C. Bel Adell (1989), there were 46,914 British residents in Spain in 1986 and 73,535 in 1989. According to European Commission figures, 86,000 Britons were living in Spain in 1991. In 1993 the Consulate in the Costa Blanca suggested a figure of 25,000 for retired Britons living in his area alone (Age Concern 1993). In 1995 D. Creffield reported that, according to British Embassy estimates, 300,500 Britons were living in Spain. Another source gives 50,000 Britons (retired and otherwise) as the estimated figure for the Costa Blanca again; while 100,000 Britons apparently live on the Costa del Sol (Damer 1995).

Various reports estimate there are now between 100,000 and 300,000 British, and approximately one million foreign nationals (Lore 1994) living in Spain as a whole; whereas back in 1986 apparently one million foreign nationals owned property in Spain's coastal areas (Valenzuela 1988). In June 1999 the *Entertainer* reported that there were 600,000 English-speaking foreigners living in southern Spain. Social scientists Francisco Jurdao and Maria Sanchez hazarded a guess that over 25,000 Britons were living in Mijas in 1990, a village whose total population at the time numbered only 36,000 (Jurdao and Sanchez 1990)! On the other hand, 34,000 Britons were registered with the British Consulate in Malaga as resident in the Malaga province in 1993. At the same time the British Consul, Michael Bartrum, told me he estimated that 20,000 Britons were living in the village and coastal areas of Mijas. According to the census figures collected by Mijas council in 1994, there were then 6,379 British residents and 136 Irish living in the municipality. An interesting figure is one from Mijas council, again, which quotes 21 per cent of the voters on the electoral role for the area in 1994 as being British.[2]

In Fuengirola, as discussed earlier, the local 1991 census figures show only 987 Britons as resident in an area with a population of approximately 47,000 residents; a population which, incidentally, doubles in the summer months due to the massive influx of visitors. Local officials and commentators, on the other hand, offer estimates of between a few hundred and a few thousand Britons actually resident, but not always registered, in Fuengirola (see Elliott 1993). This issue of how many are resident at different times of the year is a crucial one, particularly for the local officials and businesses who have to prepare for and cope with seasonal flows that affect the supply of services, the extent of custom, and other things such as security and crime control.

Some migration specialists have begun to recognise the importance of 'local effects' of what might otherwise not be significant trends. British migration to Spain has significant local effects, not only in terms of the retirement migration which has drawn the attention of some researchers (King *et al.* 1998; Rodríguez *et al.* 1998) but also the temporary and permanent migration of younger and working groups. Chapter 4 goes some way to describing the impacts of this migration at the local level, but further research is clearly needed before the trend can be quantified.

To summarise, many British migrants are undocumented for one reason or another. Many pensioners are claiming British pensions which are still paid into British bank accounts. Moreover, younger, working migrants sometimes work informally within the British migrant community. It is not surprising therefore that existing data in Spain and Britain on employment, tax, pension or state benefit payments, and even data on residence or home ownership, do not accurately reflect the fluidity or extent of British migration to Spain. Existing official data on the British migration to Spain are difficult to trust because (a) the migrants are often fluid in their behaviour and (b) many of the more permanent migrants either fear expulsion or do not desire to be registered as official residents. Attempting to collect quantitative data illustrates the complexity of this migration trend and reveals the suspicions members of the community feel towards bureaucracy and control.

I was unable to collect quantitative data using questionnaires (see Chapter 7), but quantitative conclusions can be drawn from qualitative and sensitive research which focuses on one geographical area and one social group over a period of time, using intensive ethnographic methods. Such conclusions, though admittedly not directly generalisable to other areas, challenge the assumptions made by the general public and by academics intending to research this migration trend, as I discuss in the following sections. I was also able to compile a database on 259 people, using participant observation and interviews and recorded by me in code in order to protect identities. It includes data on sex, age group, residential status (discussed below), property ownership and retirement. No individual under 18 is included. It is important to note that the database is *not* statistically representative of British migrants to Fuengirola, since the sample was not drawn randomly. It does serve, however, to demonstrate variation between migrants, and is used to give an idea of the large numbers of migrants who do not fit neatly into typologies or stereotypes formed by other authors and commentators (see Tables 1 to 4). However, it should be remembered that any attempt at quantification will result in a skewed picture, since those most difficult to log have certain traits which are very different to those who are documented.

Forms of mobility

Most commentators on the British in Spain have distinguished between expatriates and tourists. However, academics who have talked or written about the phenomenon are aware that there are different forms of migration but are confused as to the variation; they tend to distinguish simply between visiting, tourism and residence. Sean Damer (1995), for example, focused his attention on expatriates 'living permanently abroad', while many media reports distinguished straightforwardly between those living in Spain and the tourists (see for example Crampton 1993; Fletcher 1994). In particular *The Coast of Dreams* depicted those who had gone *to live* in Spain; who had chosen to extend their two weeks' holiday to a life in the sun. Champion and King, in their discussion of European migration, identified a new trend in retirement migration of northern Europeans (especially Britons) to the Mediterranean 'sun belt'. They hypothesised, prior to research, that these elderly migrants move either temporarily or on a near-permanent basis, and that many are seasonal visitors 'dividing their year between the foreign retirement home and their country of origin' (Champion and King 1993: 54). Later, Russell King and his colleagues have been forced to admit that residence patterns are so fluid that the very concept of 'permanent place of residence' is inadequate: 'An understanding of the spatial patterns of residence will increasingly require space and time dimensions', they conclude (King *et al.* 1998: 100).

With the focus again on elderly migration, the report from Age Concern accepts the existence of different forms of migration to Spain and distinguishes between those 'who own holiday accommodation which they may visit for a fortnight a year, seasonal visitors who may spend the whole winter in Spain and people who are fully resident and who see Spain as their permanent home' (Age Concern 1993: 9). Manuel Valenzuela (1988), in a discussion on mass tourism to Spain, distinguishes like many others between tourists (who visit), seasonal visitors and permanent settlers. Warnes (1991: 56) is plainly aware of the flexibility of this migration trend which, he says, shows 'every gradation from a one-week holiday to a household changing its only permanent residence' (see also Williams *et al.* 1997). However, Warnes generalises his discussion to one of migration, which, he says, is more or less permanent, and to seasonal residence, which for him is not the same as migration. Rodríguez *et al.* (1998) skirt over the issue and concentrate their research on 'retirees' in Spain. Though their questions were clearly directed at migrants, to qualify for inclusion in the study one only needed to be resident in Spain for more than two months of the year.

As I began fieldwork in the Fuengirola area, it soon became plain to me that I could not continue to talk in terms of 'expatriates' and 'tourists', as if all migrants were either permanent or not.

> This morning I went to the hospice shop to volunteer for work. Pauline said they would not need me until after September. 'It's very quiet at this time of year, until October, really; people come back then and we get busier. It's a bit quiet just now. They come back for six months, well some come for only three months now because it's not a cheap place to come any more, to Spain. Of course, some don't come until January. They'll wait and have Christmas with their family, and it's not worth renting somewhere and then leaving it empty over Christmas', she said.
>
> (Field notes, July 1993)

Pauline lives in Spain all year round, but not all British migrants are either residents or tourists.

> 'Those two over there, they live here', the barman told me in a loud voice, as a sort of introduction to two women sitting nearby. They were sitting fairly close to each other and one said to the other, 'I'm going home for a month, so I'll phone as soon as I get home, but don't tell anyone else will you?' The other replied, 'Oh, I didn't know. We're going home too, until September, so we won't see you till then.' They knew I was listening to them and did not seem to mind. They started to talk to me then.
>
> (Field notes, September 1993)

A typology of migration to Spain

Migration seems to be quite peripatetic in this situation, but can be loosely formed into 'ideal types' which attempt to capture the experiences of the migrants themselves. I developed a typology based on a combination of an individual's sense of commitment or orientation to one or other country and on amount of time spent in one or other place of residence.[3] Like other commentators, I identified three main groups among the British in Spain: the residents, the visitors and the tourists. But the migrant groups are sub-divided thus:

- Full Residents
- Returning Residents
- Seasonal Visitors
- Peripatetic Visitors.[4]

Full Residents I identify as individuals who have moved to the area permanently. They generally see themselves as living in Spain and often state that they have no intention to ever return to live in their home country. Individuals in this group would fit comfortably into the category of 'migrant' as used by demographers, sociologists and geographers. Many own property or a business in Spain, while others rent their homes there. Many are retired but an equally large number are working in Spain. This is a numerically significant group, with an average age possibly in the forties. Of the 259 individuals included in my database, 167 were Full Residents; 86 of these were male and 81 female (Table 1). A total 48 of the 167 Full Residents were retired (Table 2). A majority, namely 96 Full Residents owned the property they lived in, while 71 lived in rented accommodation (Table 3).

Returning Residents are resident in Spain as regards home, orientation and legal status.[5] This group is made up of a majority of retired or economically independent individuals who, although they usually consider they now live

Table 1 Numbers of migrants by sex and residential status

	Full Residents	Returning Residents	Seasonal Visitors	Peripatetic Visitors	Total
Male	86	22	8	11	127
Female	81	32	8	11	132
Total	167	54	16	22	259

Table 2 Retirement by residential status

	Full Residents	Returning Residents	Seasonal Visitors	Peripatetic Visitors	Total	%
Retired	48	53	13	14	128	49
Not retired	119	1	3	8	131	51
Total	167	54	16	22	259	100

Table 3 Property ownership (in Spain) by residential status

	Full Residents	Returning Residents	Seasonal Visitors	Peripatetic Visitors	Total
Own	96	52	6	19	173
Rent	71	2	10	3	86
Total	167	54	16	22	259

in Spain, return to Britain each summer for anything from two to five months to escape the searing heat and overwhelming crowds of a Costa del Sol summer. Their return 'home' often provides the opportunity for these people to spend time with their families. Many of this group own homes in Spain, but a significant number rent property in the form of apartments and small villas. A number of them own a second home, or a 'mobile' home on a residential plot, in Britain, enabling their seasonal return, while others rely on friends and relatives to supply accommodation during their visits. According to the definitions discussed above, the individuals in this group are also 'migrants'. Of the 259 individuals in my database, 54 were Returning Residents. The average age of these 32 females and 22 males was in the seventies (Table 1). All except one were retired (Table 2). A total of 52 owned their property in Spain and two rented (Table 3) but I knew of many more Returning Residents who rented property in Spain and yet on whom I gathered insufficient data for inclusion in my database.

Seasonal Visitors comprise a large number of migrants who live in Britain but return to Spain each winter attracted by, amongst other things, low accommodation rentals, cheap leisure, the welcome of the established British community, and the health benefits of avoiding a harsh British winter. They are almost always retired individuals and couples who own property in

Britain and who may also own property in Spain (see Tables 2 and 3). Their winter stay can last anything from a couple of months to six months each year, and is not always taken in one trip: many return to Britain for the Christmas period, for example. The qualitative difference between this group and the Residents is in their orientation, which tends more towards 'home' than 'host' country. However, they generally have emotional ties and commitments in Spain and often spend enough time there for the visit to be much more than an inversion of what is their normal life or routine. Though their visit to Spain does not involve a clearly defined change of permanent residence, they are migrants rather than tourists. The average age of this group is in the sixties or younger.

Peripatetic Visitors, which make up the fourth group, usually own second homes in Fuengirola or the surrounding area, and visit when they can. This visiting may have no pattern or routine to it and may be dictated by business or work in either Britain or Spain, or by health, wealth or family commitments. This group has a lower average age than the Resident and Seasonal Visitor groups, possibly in the fifties or younger. The orientation of the members is often divided between Britain and Spain; with either country variously being considered 'home'. Because of business commitments, women are able to visit Spain more often than men. Commitments such as property, family, friends and work *in* Spain mean their visits amount to more than leisure, travel or tourism. Though I have labelled them as visitors rather than residents (since they usually do not have or need residence permits), they identify themselves as migrants rather than tourists.

Full Residents

Within these groups there is considerable variation. Let me introduce some Full Residents below. We will meet these individuals again later; here I will simply give a little of their backgrounds.

Cases

James and Anita, who are in their late fifties, are Full Residents in Spain. They sold their small house in Wales in 1988 and rented an apartment near the beach in Fuengirola. They insist they will never return to Britain. They both retired early owing to injury and receive disability pensions from Britain, which they supplement with income from casual work. They have some capital put by 'for a rainy day'.

Irene is single, aged in her seventies, retired and a Full Resident in Spain. She moved to Fuengirola in 1979 and bought a small apartment with the capital she had accumulated over the years. She has no property in Britain and never wants to live there again. She has been back once in fourteen years and hated it. She has no family in Britain. 'I'm practically Spanish now', she told me.

Andy is 22 years old. He moved to Fuengirola five years ago and is now a Full Resident, living there all year round. He works for a timeshare company and does some casual work as a waiter. His family all live in the north of England, but 'I didn't want to get like any of them so I got out. I couldn't never live there now', he told me.

Tom and Marie, in their early sixties, are both retired. Tom was a major in the army and was able to retire earlier than the state retirement age. They sold their home in Devon and bought a villa on the outskirts of Fuengirola where they have now settled permanently, as Full Residents. They love Spain and have no desire to return to live in England. They go 'home' occasionally to visit their grown-up children but they always 'long to get back'.

Ken and Mary moved to Fuengirola permanently when Ken was made redundant; Mary was in her late forties and Ken was fifty. They sold their home in England and bought a little bar with the proceeds. They invested the redundancy payment Ken received, hoping to use it as a cushion in lean times, but lost it all when the BCCI bank folded in 1991.[6] Their bar is successful and they hope to sell it within a few years, to retire early, and to spend their retirement in Spain. They only return to England for short visits.

Linda and Terry are both in their early thirties and Full Residents in Spain. They owned and ran three small businesses and a house in Scotland and sold them all in 1990 to move to Fuengirola and run a bar on the beach front. The bar was unsuccessful and they eventually sold it. They now work informally doing furniture removals, cleaning, bar work and odd jobs. They rent a large, bright apartment near the beach and insist they are blissfully happy. They never want to go back to Scotland, and neither do their two children.

Returning Residents

Returning Residents tend to be retired, but there are major differences in standards of living and activities within retirement.

Cases

Pat, in her early sixties, is retired from her usual employment and collects a state pension from Britain. She runs a small letting agency in Fuengirola, where she now lives for several months of the year. She owns a small apartment in Fuengirola and a small house in the north of England, to which she returns for the months of June to September. She considers Spain to be her place of residence, her home. She is a Returning Resident in Spain.

Alice and Edward are both in their early eighties. They have lived in Spain for nine years and own a large villa with its own swimming pool. They also have a house in the south of England to which they return for the summer months in order to see their families and escape the summer heat. In Spain, Edward runs a charity group and a bridge club and Alice works as a volunteer nurse. They love living there and have no desire to go back to England, at least not while they feel fit enough to look after themselves.

Robert had been a frequent visitor to Fuengirola for many years, so when he retired in 1993 he bought a small apartment near the beach and moved there for good. He sold his home in Scotland to pay for it. When I interviewed him he told me he intended to return to Scotland to stay with his daughter each summer for a few months while he rented his apartment to tourists. The proceeds from this would fund a good life in Spain for the rest of the year, he anticipated. He knew others who did the same and were usually very successful. He told me emphatically 'I love Spain, it is the best place on earth. There is nowhere else I would live now.'

Seasonal Visitors

I introduce below some Seasonal Visitors who visit Spain for the winter. However, there are also a few young migrants who can be classed as Seasonal Visitors, but who visit Spain during the summer season, when they can find work in timeshare or in the tourist industry. These migrants return home during the winter, some to jobs and some to live on the dole.

Cases

Derek and Jennie are retired, in their late sixties. The have been returning to Fuengirola every winter for eleven years. They rent out their home in London and use the proceeds to rent an apartment in Spain for six months. They say they have split lives – half in London and half in Spain – and they love both. Each year, by the end of the winter, they are ready to go back, but once they are home they start to miss their other life and their friends in Spain. They run a dancing school while they are in Spain, and enter several dancing competitions while in England.

Ted and Hazel are in their late forties and are Seasonal Visitors to Spain. They own a small guest house in the north of England which gets very busy through the summer but tails off during the winter months. So in the winter they pay a manager to run things for them while they spend five months in a cheap apartment in Spain, enjoying the break which they feel is their reward for working so hard all summer.

Glenys and Ted are retired and spend each winter in Spain, in a rented apartment near the centre of Fuengirola. During the summer months they live in a mobile home in England. They have a strong network of friends in Spain and a different set in England. 'We've got the best of both worlds', said Glenys, 'but I wouldn't come here to live. Oh no. Home is where the kids are, in England.'

Peripatetic Visitors

Peripatetic Visitors are a heterogeneous group.

Cases

Linda and Joseph are Peripatetic Visitors to Spain. They run a successful property development company in Ireland but 'go out' to Spain whenever they can. They own a large house in Ireland and have owned a luxury apartment in Spain for six years. Sometimes they visit Spain together but more often one of them will go while the other stays in Ireland to keep an eye on the business. They told me that they consider they live in Spain, even though they spend more time in Ireland. 'Home is where the heart is', Linda told me. They have no children.

George and Jessie are both older than the state retirement age but George still runs a large business in England. They own homes in Britain and Spain, visiting the one in Spain whenever possible. Jessie is able to go more often than George and takes every opportunity since she suffers from a debilitating illness which is greatly eased by the Spanish climate. Both George and Jessie consider that England is their home: that is where they truly live, but they have strong networks in Spain. They have three adult children, one of whom lives in Spain.

Alf is a truly Peripatetic Visitor with a life in each country. He runs a retail business which involves maintaining a relationship between Britain and Spain, and he spends one or two weeks in each country intermittently. He owns property in Fuengirola and would like to settle there permanently one day. He also has a wife in Wales and a live-in girlfriend in Spain. Alf is in his forties.

Tourists

This is an emic typology, reflecting migrants' own categorisations and conceptualisation of difference between them with regard to length of stay and feeling of belonging. Full Residents, Returning Residents, Seasonal Visitors and Peripatetic Visitors are all migrants because their intention and orientation go beyond seeing Spain as a holiday destination. They are migrants because they are not tourists. If tourism is always temporary and is defined in terms of what it is not (work, home and so on), then migration, for the migrants to Fuengirola introduced above, is something more than tourism or travel, more than an inversion of the 'normal'. On the other hand, tourists are a ubiquitous part of the British community in Spain, and many of the representations of the British conflate migrants and tourists into a single category. The crucial difference lies in their orientation to home. Whereas some Peripatetic Visitors consider 'home' to be in Spain, tourists identify as being in the area specifically for a holiday. They are not migrants. They might own a small apartment in the area and may return to it once or twice each year thereby building networks and relationships with members of the other groups of migrant, but their orientation is towards their country of origin. This group includes all ages but Fuengirola tends, these days, to attract young families and middle-aged couples rather than young, single tourists.

Word of warning about typologies

The five groups above reflect quantitatively significant general trends and qualitatively different orientations, which I identified within Fuengirola and its surrounding area. However, the categories merely enable concep-tualisation and are neither mutually exclusive nor fully inclusive. I have distinguished between migrants and tourists, as most commentators do, but have identified many different degrees of migration. I have distinguished between residents and visitors and, further, between Full and Returning Residents, and between Seasonal and Peripatetic Visitors. An individual can move from one to the other of the groups I identify by, for example, decid-ing not to return to Britain each summer and thereby moving from the Returning Resident group to the Full Residents; by limiting the winter visit to two months taken in two-weekly blocks, thereby being more of a Peripatetic Visitor than a Seasonal Visitor; by extending the winter stay into near-residence, and accompanying this with a change of orientation towards Spain as home; or by gradually spending longer in Britain at each home visit and thereby becoming more of a Seasonal Visitor to Spain than a resident there.

To clarify the situation further, it is necessary to point out that not every individual fits neatly into either one or other of the above categories: there are people spending time in Spain, as Warnes (1991) suggests, at any point along the continuum from one week a year to all-year-round. It is not always simple to tell where tourism stops and migration starts. Perhaps, as Battisti and Portelli (1994) suggest, there is a continuum between tourism and exile, with migration coming somewhere in-between, along which roles and out-looks overlap and reverse. Furthermore, distinction between categories is not a simple matter of self-ascription since a person who goes backwards and forwards might, like Linda, consider he or she lives in Spain; while some-one who spends more than six months of the year there, as Glenys and Ted sometimes did, might insist that their home is in England. The amount of time spent in Spain and the existence, or not, of an intention to return 'home' are not direct indicators of orientation. Some people I met in Fuengirola changed their minds as to where 'home' was several times dur-ing my fieldwork.

Consider Dave, for example. Dave was in his early twenties when I first interviewed him. He had moved to Spain with his parents in 1989, hoping to find work but he has only been intermittently successful, taking casual and temporary jobs and experiencing long periods of unemployment. When I interviewed him he told me, 'I am going back to England as soon as I can.

I can't wait. I've got a lot of friends here and all that, but it's so boring.' He felt England was his real home, and that Spain never could be. However, when I talked to him a few months later, Dave told me he was staying on in Spain after all. He had a job and was getting married! Six months later still, Dave moved back to England with his fiancée. Three years later, Dave is living in Spain again, without his new wife.

Although British migrants in Fuengirola had no labels for my groups of Full Residents as opposed to Returning Residents, and Seasonal Visitors as opposed to Peripatetic Visitors, most Britons identified in terms related to those categories. They used phrases such as 'I live here all year round'; 'We live here, but we go back for the summers'; 'They come out each winter'; 'She goes backwards and forwards' to distinguish between themselves. Labels which were used, on the other hand, reflected the more apparent distinction (which I discuss more fully in Chapter 5) between those who considered Spain to be their home and those who felt their home was in Britain. The terms 'expatriate' (Anglican Church 1993; Betty 1994; Elliott 1995; Holbrook 1993) or 'resident' (Elliott 1995; FADS 1994; SALVA 1993) were applied to those whose first home was in Spain (usually my Full Residents and Returning Residents); and the terms 'visitor' or 'regular' (FADS 1994; SALVA 1993) applied to those who visited regularly but whose first home was in Britain (my Seasonal Visitors and Peripatetic Visitors). 'Tourist' or 'holiday-maker' applied to a clear category of people who visited Spain for a short holiday. In reality, people move backwards and forwards, from one category to another, from one country to another, and from one orientation to another. Movement is extremely fluid and flexible.

Retirement or elderly migration?

Many commentators assume that British migrants in Spain's coastal areas, especially the Costa del Sol, are either retired or elderly, or both. Academics such as Champion and King (1993), King *et al.* (1998), Rodríguez *et al.* (1998) and Warnes (1991) focus their attention on what they term 'elderly' or 'retirement' migration. Researchers I met in the Fuengirola area, working in the fields of sociology, gerontology, social policy, and health studies,[7] were concentrating their research on the problems and experiences of elderly British migrants. The Age Concern report, *Growing Old in Spain* (1993), focuses only on older migrants. Spanish social scientists, Jurdao and Sanchez (1990), have published books about the mass migration of elderly Europeans to Spain's coastal areas and islands. Valenzuela (1988) acknowledges the existence of many retired foreign residents in Spain's coastal areas, while others make passing reference to retired British living in Spain, as if these were the only British immigrants (see Buller and Hoggart 1994; Misiti *et al.* 1995). Even travel writers assume that most expatriates in the Costa del Sol are retirees (Baird 1995; *Fodor's Spain 1994*; Hampshire 1995; Voase 1995). However, this case of British migration to Fuengirola highlights the problem of applying notions of 'retirement' or 'elderly' as unitary and exclusive categories.

The term elderly often implies a fixed life stage which usually, because of state legislation and policy, is taken by western authors to mean anyone aged 60–65 upwards. In his edited book on *elderly* migration, Andrei Rogers (1992) uses age to define his population – for him elderly equals people over the state retirement age for each country. This is problematic when talking of British migration, to Fuengirola at least, because this contemporary trend, albeit possibly age specific, does not solely refer to people over 60. Sometimes, especially in winter, when more Returning Residents and Seasonal Visitors and therefore more older migrants are spending time in the area, one might get the impression that this is an elderly migration trend. But, although the average age of migrants is above the average age for the populations of either Britain and Spain, I would estimate the average age of migrants to be in the fifties or younger, and certainly not elderly. This is because, although many migrants are older individuals, there are sufficient people in the forties to fifties age groups and younger to bring the average age to below what can be defined as elderly.[8] Of the 259 individuals on whom I collected data, 160 (62 per cent) were under the age of 60, and this was excluding children. In 1993 Ronald Elliott, an 'expatriate' himself, reported that 45 per cent of expatriates in Andalusia are under the age of 45 (Elliott 1993).

Full Residents, especially, should not be generally described as elderly. Many are younger: whole families have moved to Fuengirola to live permanently, some with very young children, and many teenagers and young adults migrate independently of their families. Attention given to 'elderly' migration alone will omit all these individuals and families. Indeed, the *Sur in English*, a widely read English-language newspaper for the English-speaking reader in Spain, claimed in June 1999 that the age of its readership is coming down as increasing numbers of working-age people join the community of retirees.

The use of such a label implies that the 'elderly' share certain characteristics in common. If the main criterion is one of age, then why not refer to the over-75s, for example, asks B. Bytheway (1995). Instead the term 'elderly' is used as a blanket term for old people, and, although for some it is a positive term denoting superiority, achievement and dignity – as in our 'elders and betters' – more commonly it has negative connotations. If it is not taken to imply a life stage such as retirement, or to chronological age, then the word tends to refer to a physical or mental state. It is then attended by negative, ageist stereotypes to the extent that 'we see elderly people only in terms of their diseases, disabilities and deprivations' (Fennell *et al.* 1988: 7). Elderly people are seen as a burden (Bytheway 1995), as dependent (see Speare 1992), and as frail (Holmes and Holmes 1995). Population redistribution which occurs as a result of something labelled 'elderly migration' will possibly be viewed problematically by the receiving countries, since their concern will be the demands an influx of elderly people will place on resources (Longino 1982; Speare 1992; Warnes 1991; see for example Jurdao and Sanchez 1990). The notion that the populations of many western countries are ageing is surrounded with pessimism without the added 'threat' of an influx of 'elderly' people. As N. Wells and C. Freer maintain (1988: 3):

> Sociodemographic trends justify society's concern about the impact of the growing number of older people, but for many the prospect of an ageing population is not simply about numbers, since their fears are greatly influenced by the prevailing images of old age. It is likely that when asked to think of an old person, most of us, whether professional or lay, are likely to picture a frail, bent person, slow to move and think and short of memory.

Retirement migration is a more useful term than elderly migration, and could reasonably be applied to two migrant groups: the Seasonal Visitors and the Returning Residents. These migration trends, with their flexibility and fluidity, are arguably associated with the freedom of retirement from work and its concomitant freedom from routine, and from the need to earn a wage. They are also associated with chronological age and with couples whose children have grown up and left home. These movements have almost certainly been fuelled by the growth in expendable wealth of northern Europeans, during the 1980s especially, and the ability to transport pensions abroad (Reay-Smith 1980). They are possibly a continuance of the tradition of 'retiring to the seaside' (see Karn 1977; Longino 1982).

Full Residents and Peripatetic Visitors, however, should not be characterised in terms of retirement migration unless the concept is adapted to include both voluntary and early retirement. Even then the groups should not be characterised solely in these terms since there are many workers in both groups. A significant number of Full Residents own, and work in, their own businesses – typically bars, restaurants, car hire firms, estate agencies and property management firms – serving the British tourist and migrant communities. Additionally, again challenging the concept of retirement migration, a significant number of younger, single Britons are migrating to Spain to work casually in the British-run businesses, to work informally alongside the British communities, or gaining more formal employment with the timeshare and holiday-ownership companies. James and Anita fall into this category: between them they do bar work, ironing, cleaning, painting and hairdressing; similarly Alan, who has tried working as a painter/decorator, as a shop assistant, and in timeshare sales.

Researchers should be aware that although many migrants are retired, this does not necessarily mean that they are therefore all of state retirement age. A major problem of associating the two concepts of 'retirement' and 'elderly' is that though both partners may retire when the man reaches retirement

Table 4 Retired migrants by age group and sex

	Retired females	Retired males	Total	%
60 and over	49	39	88	69
Under 60	22	18	40	31
Total retired migrants	71	57	128	100

age or a little earlier, the woman may still be considerably younger than the state retirement age. Many retired migrants to Spain have taken early retirement from professions or have unofficially retired to live on their capital; that is to say, they are younger than the state retirement age (sometimes being as young as in their thirties) but are economically independent. James and Anita, for example, the Full Residents I introduced earlier, retired in their fifties, and there are many other cases. Of the 259 people on whom I collected quantitative data, 69 per cent of the retired were actually aged 60 or over; 31 per cent were under 60 (Table 4).

Cases

Charles and Lucy, for example, who are both in their thirties, sold a lucrative business in England, bought a villa in Los Boliches, and invested the rest of their capital from which they take an income. Neither now works. They have two young children who attend Spanish school.

David, who is 48 years old, considers himself 'retired'. He was made redundant from an engineering job when he was 45, invested his redundancy money in shares, sold his house in Wales and now rents an apartment in Fuengirola. He collects a small income from his investments and makes a little extra 'doing the car boots' (buying second-hand furniture and household goods and selling them at the car boot sale each Saturday).

Retirement, also, need not mean inactivity. As I discuss in the next chapter, many older and retired migrants feel they are fully participating citizens in Spain, whereas they would have been marginalised or discarded if they had stayed home. Madge, for example, is 75 years old and a significant person within the British community in Fuengirola. She is a member of the Anglican Church council and of the Royal British Legion and is on the welfare committees of both. Since she speaks fluent Spanish and has worked as a nurse in Spain, she is often called upon to translate for people, to give medical advice, or to make phone calls for those who can't speak Spanish. She regularly makes the coffee for the church coffee mornings and she visits sick and disabled migrants. Madge has recently conducted a small survey of the provision of residential care for the elderly in Spain. She is considering helping to set up a residential care home especially for British migrants. Her life is full: 'I don't have time to get bored or lonely, I don't know how people have the time', she told me.

Gordon, who was 91 years old when I interviewed him at the Fuengirola and District Society (FADS) social, described his full and active life in Spain. He has lived in Spain for twenty-one years.

> I don't speak a word of Spanish; my wife does but I don't. I'm 91, I play bowls and I walk every day and I never use a stick. You could talk to my wife, but she's gone to the *ambulatorio* [clinic] to get some pills for someone. I don't know why she does these things, she could be there three hours. I don't know when she'll be back. Just 'cos she speaks a bit of Spanish. She's always trotting off with someone.

Gordon's wife is 85 years old. A week after meeting them I saw Gordon and his wife going for one of their walks; they were three miles from home.

To summarise, the British migrants to Spain cannot *solely* be defined as elderly, whether the term is meant to imply age, a fixed life stage or a physical or mental state. Certainly some are elderly, old, frail, bent, disabled, and many are over 60 years old; but none of the groups I have outlined above can be characterised in this way alone. Neither can they be characterised exclusively in terms of retirement, since many are clearly not retired, many are below state retirement age, and many are working in Spain (and some in Britain). Furthermore, the label 'retirement' should not be taken to imply inactivity or even end of life. Many retired migrants are living very active lives in Spain.

Work and migration

Full Residents

Full and Returning Residents, Seasonal Visitors and Peripatetic Visitors can be differently characterised in terms of the work they do now, the work they used to do and therefore their occupational class. Full Residents can be separated into three distinct categories: the fully retired, the retired who are still doing some work, and the working. The fully retired are a large and important group. They are of mixed class backgrounds. Take for example, Dolly, whose husband died two years before I interviewed her, who is very wealthy and who lives on her own in a luxurious apartment. She has a Spanish woman to clean her house and a Spanish gardener. Dolly told me she is of a 'higher calibre than most people round here'. Her parents were farmers and landowners in Ireland. She meets people for coffee and gateaux occasionally and likes to go to expensive hotels. Hotels are her hobby. But Dolly has few friends in Fuengirola. 'It's difficult to know who you can trust when you've got a lot of money, like I have', she explained.

Compare her with Fred, an ex-lorry driver, who lives on just his state pension. He has no residence permit although he has been in Los Boliches ten years; a basic British pension is considered insufficient means by the

Spanish authorities who need proof that a person can support himself or herself before they will grant residence permits. Fred lives on the twelfth floor of a dilapidated apartment block and wonders what he would do if the lift ever broke.

Some are younger, early retired, who had successful businesses and can afford to live off their pensions quite comfortably, such as Charles and Lucy, discussed earlier, who live off their capital investments. Others retired early from well-paid jobs and live comfortably on their pensions, such as Peter and Maureen, who were both officers in the Royal Navy for many years.

The semi-retired are another important group. They tend to be younger retired people who retired early with redundancy money, and who hope to make this last until they reach state retirement age at least, such as Tom, who is hoping he can stretch out his redundancy money until he reaches retirement age, and is doing some painting work and some bar work on a casual basis. Others were owners of their own businesses, such as Linda and Terry, discussed earlier, who have some capital but have to do odd jobs to supplement their income and preserve their nest-eggs.

Full Residents who are working full or almost full time are either self-employed and owning a business, self-employed and muddling along in odd jobs for other people, or working for multinational companies such as Dunnes or Iceland. The first group is very visible. There are many British-owned businesses in the Fuengirola area, including bars, estate agencies, property maintenance companies, garages, car rentals, book shops, second-hand furniture shops and even auction rooms. Some of these businesses are more successful than others, and some of the owners have been in the area much longer than others.

Cases

Len and Ada moved to Spain in 1982. They run a small bar in Los Boliches which is successful enough to have provided the means for them to live there comfortably. Most of their customers are tourists and Seasonal Visitors, and some residents. They bought the bar with redundancy money. They do not employ anyone to work in it; it is too small and they do not make enough money for that. They do, however, make enough to afford to visit England once or twice a year as well as have a holiday in another country (they favour Portugal and Greece).

Tina, who is engaged to be married to a Spanish man, runs a hairdressing business which is quite successful. She has mostly British customers and has managed to secure the custom of several Seasonal Visitors, so she knows if she has a bad summer that things will pick up in the winter. The Flamingo Bar, in Fuengirola, on the other hand, has had five different owners in the past ten years. None of these has managed to make the bar work for them. Each time I have visited Fuengirola over the past ten years I have met new bar owners who were not there last time, and have been told of others who could not make a go of it and have returned.

There are few (if any) very successful businesses run by British migrants that employ lots of people. The large businesses tend to be multinational companies (e.g. timeshare firms and superstores) which have not been researched as part of this community of British migrants. However, the impact of these companies is felt by the migrants as they sometimes provide a source of employment.

The self-employed people who have gone to Spain to try to make a go of it are generally from working-class backgrounds and have risked little in leaving home for a while to try their hand. Some of them are skilled crafts workers like Barry and Tony. Barry is a very skilled mechanic as well as a trained landscape gardener. He has no wife or children, and no other ties in the UK, yet he does have a flat to go back to if things don't work out in Spain. He had work in England, where he worked for a large property maintenance company, but having visited friends in Spain several times, he wanted to try settling there himself. Tony was a cabinet maker who had been making quite a good living in the UK. However, he said he could live comfortably in Spain by working just three days a week, as opposed to the five days a week he had to work in the UK. He and his wife thus moved to Fuengirola where they believed they could work less and live a better life. However, when we last visited Spain, Tony was struggling to find enough work and was looking around for other ways of earning a living. He didn't want to go home, but was worried it might come to that.

Others are less skilled, and just manage to get by. Mary, for example, was made redundant from her job as an office clerk while she was off sick with a long-term injury. She got very little redundancy money, certainly not enough to see her through to her retirement (she is only in her forties) and so she went to Spain to look for casual work in the bars. Mary is now scraping a living doing several odd jobs including waitressing, laundry work and some bar work.

Some are running away from bad debts or miserable divorces, like Megan, who went to Spain for a holiday and found she could get by doing odd jobs for people and so stayed on. She has been in Fuengirola eight years now. She worked as a chef in Wales. In Fuengirola she does some cooking for a small, British-owned restaurant, some cleaning for another couple, and has had a range of other part-time jobs to keep her going.

There are some formal employees, but this is a smaller, and less visible group. They tend not to become part of the migrant community. I did not meet or interview many of these workers. Some are working for timeshare, some are working for large companies, and some for smaller companies. However, Spanish social security payments are very high indeed, enough to make it quite difficult for a British migrant setting up a small business to employ someone on a formal basis. Some professional teachers are working in the international schools, and financial planning consultants employ a number of migrants. One person I interviewed was Rob, who works as a financial consultant in Los Boliches. His parents had retired to Spain a few years previously. Rob was feeling disillusioned with Britain and his wife was feeling disillusioned with her job as a teacher. When the opportunity of a job in Spain came up, Rob took it even though the income was half what he had been earning. He said he can live in Spain on less money and still have a better quality of life.

Returning Residents

Returning Residents, those who consider that they live permanently in Spain and yet who return to Britain each year for the summer period, are most likely to be retired and of or near retirement age. Many have occupational pensions and/or capital or investments which supplement the basic state pension. Many of them can afford to keep a home in both countries, or at least can afford the trip home and the cost of rent and bills and so on while they are there. Most of them are property owners in Spain at least. Some of them are poorer than others and these try to rent out their homes in Spain in order to fund the trip home, but most are from middle-class backgrounds and have good pensions from well-paid jobs.

Cases

Eddie and Elsie are not very well off, although Eddie was in the army and gets an army pension. They have bought a small apartment in Spain and they try to rent it out while they go home in the summer. They do not have a home in England and usually try to spend some time in rented accommodation and some time with friends or family. However, some summers they can't afford to go home and they have to stay and put up with the heat.

Terry, on the other hand, was a managing director of a large chain store and Joan was a personnel officer. They are now both retired and own a villa in Spain and a cottage in Scotland. They go back to Scotland each summer, to stay in their cottage, and while they are there some of the family come for a visit. They also own a large and comfortable motor home, and sometimes they spend part of the summer touring England and Scotland in this.

Seasonal Visitors

Seasonal Visitors are retired and tend to be comfortably well off. They usually own homes in Britain, which they may or may not need to rent out to fund their visit to Spain each summer. Most of them rent an apartment for their visit to Spain and some return to the same one each year. Once again, they are usually from middle-class backgrounds. However, Ronnie, whom we met in Chapter 2 and who works in Spain each summer, is a Seasonal Visitor who is quite different from the older, retired, majority who go to

Spain for the winters. He is also from a working-class background and is an unskilled worker in Spain.

Peripatetic Visitors

Peripatetic Visitors are a very interesting, heterogeneous group. They are often business-owners, and are usually sufficiently well-off financially to afford this peripatetic lifestyle, but there are some who just take the risk that they will find work in each country. Justin, for example, changes his mind periodically about where he lives. He intends to go to college in England one day, but tried it once and dropped out after the first term. He now often goes back to England for long periods, where he claims unemployment benefit, followed by extended periods in Spain doing odd jobs.

Characterising a trend

It is important that any characterisation leaves room for difference and variation: the richness and diversity of life. In Fuengirola there are child migrants and older migrants, there are poor migrants and wealthier ones, men and women. Some migrate in families, and some individually, some own property and some are tenants, some have moved to Spain permanently and some (though not many) want to go home. The migration trend with which this book is concerned is one that grew in importance during the 1970s and especially the 1980s (Bel Adell 1989; Jurdao 1990; Valero Escandell 1992). It is a very different migration trend to those that usually concern studies of migration and identity. It is neither strongly economic and voluntary in cause and motivation, nor economic and involuntary. It is neither strongly political and voluntary nor involuntary and strongly political, and so does not fit into Collinson's (1993) typology of migration. It cannot be characterised as labour migration, refugee migration or asylum seeking. It is essentially voluntary (though some individuals would dispute this personally) and perhaps mildly economic in motivation; but more than that, migrants are moving for a better way of life, to the sun, to a place they are familiar with and feel comfortable in, away from somewhere they sometimes feel less comfortable. However, migration cannot be characterised simply in terms of economically motivated push and pull factors. People fund this migration in whatever way they can, some finding this easier than others.

This is a north–south intra-European migration of predominantly white people to a predominantly white country. In Fuengirola, at least, it is a movement of predominantly lower-middle and working-class individuals in retirement (not necessarily at old age) or in search of work within the migrant community.[9] These migrants are either visiting or settling in large numbers in the coastal, tourist areas of Spain. The various migrant groups outlined above – the Full Residents, Returning Residents, Seasonal Visitors and Peripatetic Visitors – can each be characterised in slightly different ways with respect to age, retirement, mobility, orientation and class. Other Britons live in Spain. However, individuals living in rural and undeveloped areas, those working with transnational companies, and labour migrants throughout Spain are not part of the trend under discussion. I speak of a trend, a general tendency, rather than an identifiable group of individuals. The members of the group change constantly: some have lived in Spain thirty years, others visit for two or three winters and then never return. As a trend it is something that has been and is developing and changing constantly; unlike a 'process', this change is indeterminate and unpredictable.

4 A way of life

In this chapter I examine the collective representations of the British discussed in Chapter 1 in the light of themes that arose out of fieldwork. Several of the assumptions made about the British in Spain are challenged by the experiences of the migrants themselves, but, as is usually the case, the representations also have some basis in reality. The mass media, during the early 1990s, brought attention to the health and social needs of a frail, elderly population in Spain. However, the migrants themselves depict a healthy, happy lifestyle where elderly people are more active and more included than they would be back home. The media were also fascinated by the number of criminals supposedly escaping to Spain, with such attention resulting in the label 'Costa del Crime'. In fact there are a few criminals amongst the British in Spain and quite a lot of crime, but the relationship of the British migrants to crime is a complex one, and is all tied up with notions of escape and freedom. Timeshare is an important feature of life in Spain for the migrants which is not captured by the representations of them. The general lifestyle of the British, however, is something that commentators seemed fascinated with, and is worth exploring in some depth. Leisure is important to this group, but they are not quite 'hanging around in bars all day'. Club life and the life of organised social groups is very important, and voluntary work features quite highly. Alcohol is certainly a feature of life, but not in the ways implied. In fact the only real, but quite hidden, problems for the migrants are those of loneliness and isolation. It seems, as I discussed in Chapter 1, the stereotypes tell us as much about the British in Britain as the British in Spain. This chapter aims to tell the reader descriptively what life is like in Spain for many migrants.

The elderly

It has been shown in Chapter 3 that British migrants to Spain are not all elderly nor even all retired, though the representations of them focus on this aspect. However, the average age of migrants is above the average age for the populations of both Britain and Spain and there are quite a number of elderly migrants, especially within the Returning Residents and Seasonal

Visitors categories discussed in the previous chapter. Sensationalist press reports have tended to equate being elderly in Spain with loneliness, disability, ill health, poverty, or all of these (Boseley 1993; Fletcher 1994; MacKinnon 1993), and some members of the migrant community have contributed to these stereotypes. Concerned about the problems some older migrants are experiencing, they have made it their business to draw these issues to the attention of governments and aid organisations in Britain and, to a lesser extent, in Spain. However, their reports show that the 'problems' are not simply those of being elderly but are related to the decrease in value of the basic British state retirement pension (Brooks 1993); to the lack of integration of Britons into wider Spanish society and to poor language learning (Betty 1994); or to European Union regulations regarding the payments of Social Assistance and Social Security (Elliott 1995).

Migrants themselves seemed concerned to stress the benefits of life in Spain. Furthermore, as the following extracts from my field notes demonstrate, contrary to the images of old age discussed above, migrants in Fuengirola believe that they are enjoying a far more positive experience of ageing than they would have had if they'd stayed in Britain.

> Cyril is 63, Joan is younger. Noting my regular attendance at FADS socials, Cyril asked me if I get tired of 'old company' and when I said I didn't really notice, the conversation became centred around the theme 'age doesn't matter here'. Mary said 'If we were in England now, we would have to sit about and do nothing all day. We'd be useless.' Ann said 'It's the weather. You can go out much more, and no-one cares what you wear, and you're healthier, 'cos you walk more.'
>
> (Field notes, January 1994)

> After living forty years in Africa, I couldn't stand it in England', Alfred told me. 'I used to sit looking out onto the greyness with nothing to do but hope the weather will clear up.' He likes to play golf and can only do that here. 'In England I'd be too stiff', he said, shaking his head.
>
> (Field notes, February 1994)

Retirement for the British migrants in Spain does not equate with inactivity; there are numerous leisure activities in which they can take part and mobility is eased by the warmth. Older people can choose from a wide range of things to do, including joining the clubs and societies discussed below, working a little, and getting involved in voluntary work. Rather than being stuck at home doing nothing all day, wishing someone would visit them, they can become part of a community in which they feel valued. Many have important or influential roles in the clubs. Dick, who is 75, is chairman of his club and his entire organising committee are over 55 years of age. 'Old people here are just *people*', he told me, profoundly. Meg, who is in her sixties, runs the library and does the accounts for her club: 'You aren't discarded here when you retire, not like we were in Wales', she said. Madge, who was introduced in Chapter 3, is 75 yet involved in the welfare committees of two clubs. Even those who might not wish to take part in clubs and voluntary work can be more active because of the weather and the Spanish lifestyle. They can take leisurely strolls in the sunshine all year round, can play bowls, swim, or simply walk to their nearest café or bar where they can sit and chat with friends before taking a leisurely stroll home. It is the contrast with home that is so crucial. Alfred, a Full Resident aged 73, told me on another occasion:

> If I was there now [in Britain] I would just sit in my chair all day and get stiff and stuck there, like I see people my age. I would look out on all that greyness and I wouldn't want to go out for walks and that like I do here. Here I can call in a bar and have a chat with someone, and no-one minds that I'm old. In England old people aren't welcome like they are here, they should stay hidden.

Older migrants in Spain are healthier too, of course, thanks to the warmth and the opportunities for walking and fresh air. For many, this was one of the attractions of the area in the first place, along with the pace of life and the leisure opportunities (see Chapter 2). As Janet Mendel, an expatriate herself, reported in an article in a local English-language magazine. '*Jubilados* [in Spanish] means retired. It also means to be jubilant, and if you're one of thousands of expatriates happily retired in Spain probably you can see the connection' (Mendel 1993: 39). For the most part it is paradise, she enthused; statistics show older people generally stay healthier longer in this unstressful climate. She insisted that reports of loneliness, poverty and ill health are true but exaggerated. Other people told me how content the elderly migrants in Spain seem to be:

> After the meeting I managed to get talking to Ronald who is married to a Spanish woman and has lived here five years. I told him about my research and he said he often thinks about how they live here (the elderly British). He often had to interpret for them when they went to the doctors when he lived in Arroyo. I said that apparently some people feel very isolated if, for example, they lose a partner after moving here. He was very surprised. He has only come across older people who are really enjoying life, he said, 'And why wouldn't you? You wake up to the sun, and the mountains, and you go out and see smiling faces. They have problems, sure they do, like all older people, but the problems don't seem so big here. They are manageable.'
>
> (Field notes, July 1993)

It often struck me how different the elderly migrants in Spain looked compared with elderly people in Britain. They wore bright colours, suntans, shorts and T-shirts, lots of jewellery, and smiles. They looked fit and healthy. I was reminded of the film *Cocoon*, in which a group of older people discover a youth-giving swimming pool, inhabited by an alien, and start to roll back the years as they swim in it each day. The migrants were aware of a feeling of freedom from restriction on dress and behaviour. I overheard Joan, a Full Resident in her fifties, tell her new migrant friend, 'You can wear what you like, no-one takes any notice really. I couldn't dress like this back home, not at my age!'

There was a strong feeling that older people in Spain are an accepted part of mainstream society, not some marginal group, like they are in Britain. People in their sixties and seventies talked to me about 'the elderly' as if they were other than themselves. 'I don't like being around old people all the time', said one woman of 67 years, but in Spain 'old people and children are not segregated from society, not like they are in Britain.' There is less ageism in Spain, I was told. In fact, Don, a Returning Resident in his fifties, told me 'There's no stigma about age here, nor about class or anything. It doesn't matter who you are.' But more than this, the migrants believe that the Spanish both respect their elderly more than the British do, and take more care of them as they age. 'You see few nursing homes, 'cos the family does it all here', explained Alex. The health service are said not to dismiss elderly people the way they do in England. 'They give you all the same tests as they give younger people', said Barbie, 'and yet in England they don't bother with old people there.' In short, Spain is seen as a better place to be as you get older.

Crime and criminals

Many of the collective representations or stereotypes discussed in the first chapter depict the British in Spain as criminals on the run, and it is true to say that crime and criminals are a ubiquitous feature of life in Fuengirola, though this affects some people more than others. Although it now has new owners, while we were in Spain for the main fieldwork period, the notorious criminal Ronnie Knight owned and ran a bar called *Ronnie Knight's*. Many people I spoke to knew him well, and though I never managed to interview him myself, he did not keep a particularly low profile. Other notorious criminals live and work in the area. I spoke to more than one British resident who told me quite openly that he had spent some time in jail in the past. When I asked one man how he came to speak such good Spanish, he replied, 'I learnt it inside, love.' In my innocence, assuming this had all happened a long time ago in his youthful, wilder days perhaps, I asked if they teach Spanish in British jails and he laughingly told me he had been inside in Spain for three years, 'for drugs', and had just been out a week. We became quite friendly with another man who had recently been in jail in France for two years for smuggling cocaine across the border, and a woman resident I knew quite well has since been in a Spanish prison on a charge of suspected murder. One bar I frequented was also frequented by a small group of women whose husbands were in prison in Spain. They used to laugh about me joining 'the prison wives' meetings'. And one night when I was in a music bar having a dance with some of the locals, a woman I had met a few times told me her friend was very drunk and in a bad mood because her partner had gone back home to 'knock someone off'. 'It's 'cos her husband has gone back to England to do another job, you know, to knock someone off, that's why she's in such a state', she explained. It is the casual way in which you get to hear about such things that is striking.

Petty crime was something several people admitted to having been involved in before they came to Spain. More than one person I interviewed told me he or she could not return to the UK because when they left they had thought they would never go back and so they had not paid off all their bills, or they had run up such large overdrafts or debts that part of coming to Spain was to leave all that behind them. Some of the British residents were quite openly involved in petty crime in Spain. One night I saw a man trying to pass off counterfeit notes in a bar. The bar owners had recently invested in a note scanner and the woman who was serving scanned his note and dryly handed it back to him saying, 'I don't want this one. Give us another one.' She scanned that too and then proceeded to show everyone nearby how she could see that it was a forgery. The man who had tried to pass it off simply shrugged his shoulders and said, 'Well, I don't know what to pay with then. I've got a wad of them.' Someone else paid for his drink. No-one condemned him and he carried on drinking in the same bar that night and many others. On another occasion the same man was trying to sell items he had made of some beautiful wood. When I commented on the quality of the wood, he happily told me where he had stolen it from.

One woman I spoke to at length about life in Spain told me to let her know if I wanted any forged documents: 'There are illegal ways around all these things if you are prepared to do them', she said. She told me that in order to prove they can support themselves financially, in order to get res-idence permits, some people pass money around from one bank account to another using the same lump sum as capital for different people. She knows where you can get fake MOT (Ministry of Transport) test certificates. She told me of people who use the same number plate on more than one car, and she knows many people who are not legally resident and many who are working illegally: 'It makes you do it when it is so difficult to become legal and so costly.' A man in his seventies one night offered my partner Trevor a forged passport. He was showing off in front of the barmaid that he could forge any European passport and all he needed was two photographs. His wife has since been arrested in England for carrying forged passports and was given an eighteen-month prison sentence.

It seems that crime is just something you hear more about amongst some of the British migrants in Spain. Even those who would be unlikely to get involved in crime in the UK told me they did things in Spain that they would not normally do, such as driving their car without insurance and not paying all their taxes. A few were working for financial gain while claiming social security benefits from the UK, or were living on pensions and were earning a 'bit on the side'. Several people had no work permits, or were not legal residents, or drove their cars illegally on British plates and/or with no insurance; but they often felt that the laws were so confusing that they were justified in not always being legitimate (see Chapter 7).

Drugs offences are also ubiquitous amongst the migrants. Several teenagers I met or heard of were involved in illegal drug sales. Moreover, a number of bar owners were aware that their bars were being or had been used as meeting points for the drugs trade. One man told me he refused to have a telephone fitted in his bar for that specific reason (this was before the now widespread use of mobile phones, which has no doubt negated this prerequisite). Since I completed the period of intense fieldwork of 1993–94, I have made many return visits to Fuengirola and Los Boliches. Each time there are stories of people who have 'been in trouble'. A few people we knew have since been charged on drug-related offences and a number are in Spanish jails. One man we knew quite well was murdered in Britain recently. This was a big shock for us, but as usual was reported by friends in that nonchalant way in which these things seem to reach one's ears in Spain.

One of the explanations given for young people getting involved in crime is the desire to stay in Spain but the lack of work for them. Kath, a mother of two teenage girls, explained:

> It's so easy for the youngsters to get involved in crime. They want to stay, you see, but there is no work for them really, only timeshare. Then someone comes along and offers them some easy money, and then it's too late.

Full Residents of all ages get involved in crime when the legitimate means of funding their residence in Spain fail for various reasons. For example, Andy loves his life in Spain but his bar does not get enough trade to support him and his wife. He is now involved in a number of illegal activities which have grown out of a few small contacts.

But for all this, Spain is considered to be more crime-free than Britain, even now, with constant reports of increases in petty crime in tourist spots. The key word is safety: Spain is seen as safer for children, for the elderly, for single women. 'You see children playing out in the street here when it's well after dark, sometimes until the early hours, and most people will tell you there is less rape and mugging and that. More opportunistic crime perhaps, but less rape and murders', said Jan, a Full Resident and a young mother. 'It's much safer to walk the streets here', said Doreen, a Full Resident in her thirties. 'In England you couldn't walk ten minutes down the street at night alone. That [the safety] gives you much more freedom.' On the other hand, there was a feeling that the Spanish authorities were untrustworthy and unreliable. I was warned by more than one person not to have my utilities bills paid directly out of my bank account: 'They can take out whatever they want', warned Alice, 'and you have to prove they got it wrong.' Britain is depicted as crime-ridden, but as more honest and trustworthy at the level of officialdom and bureaucracy, while Spain is a complete contrast. 'You can trust the man on the street but you can't trust the authorities in Spain', said Alec, 'which makes you inclined to fiddle and cheat. In Britain you can trust the authorities but not your neighbour.' This distrust of Spanish authorities was quite widespread, and contributed to a feeling of exclusion for some migrants. Even the Anglican vicar felt certain that some of the prisoners he visited were innocent but was quite uncertain whether they would ever be able to prove it.

Timeshare

Though not explicitly expressed as part of the collective representations discussed in Chapter 1, timeshare is part of the image and reality of life in Spain for British migrants and tourists alike. Timeshare touts and companies are a visible feature of life in tourist Spain, and part of life in Spain for the expatriates and the tourists alike is about being stopped in the street by timeshare touts. However, for the migrants timeshare is also about getting to know the timeshare workers, and being accepted by them. It's about being there long enough to look like a resident so that the touts leave you alone, and long enough to stop acting like a tourist and going to the popular tourist places. For some, it is about being a timeshare tout or working in the industry in some capacity.

Timeshare touts are a ubiquitous feature of life on the Costa del Sol. We had been in Spain for less than a week, as I began fieldwork in 1993, when we were 'caught' by the timeshare touts. We had been stopped as we walked around the streets on several occasions and had managed to fob the attackers off, but this one was particularly clever. She asked us questions about ourselves and asked if the girls (my daughters) would like to go for a swim. By now I was beginning to think I ought to experience this as part of fieldwork anyway, so we went. However, the sales representative did not try very hard with us: we were there two hours and came away with free bottles of spirits, and the girls had had a nice swim in the complex's beautiful pool. We had signed nothing and had made no promises to buy. One technique used by the touts to get you to visit the complex and talk to a sales person is to tell you not to sign anything and just to go in order to get 'the freebies' (the special offers, which usually include wines and spirits and sometimes a free holiday). They even tell you what is the shortest length of time you can stay, without upsetting the sales staff and while ensuring entitlement to the free goods. Most of the British migrants I interviewed had been 'caught' by a timeshare tout at least once and some even allowed themselves to be targeted periodically in order to get the opportunity to restock their drinks cabinet.

As time went on and we settled in Spain, several of the timeshare touts learned to recognise us and left us alone. As several of the migrants pointed out, as time goes by you begin to look different and the timeshare people can tell you're a resident. You stop wearing sunglasses all the time, and you stop walking about in shorts when it's only mildly warm. You don't always carry a camera, and you are less likely to be walking in a couple or as a family. Tourists also have a way of looking around them as they walk, and of ambling. Residents go about their business more quickly. They are also less likely to be found on the tourist trails. Timeshare touts know where to hang out to catch the tourists: they wait along the path to the market once a week, or they loiter opposite the beach to catch people as they leave to go back to their apartments. They hang around on street corners near bars and in shopping areas, especially where there is room for them to catch people as they go by without causing a hold-up.

Timeshare is big business in the Fuengirola area, and it has managed to shake off some of its negative image as sales techniques have become less aggressive and packages have become more flexible. For some of the British migrants it provides either a seasonal income, as a timeshare tout whose job it is to get people off the street and into the development, or a more secure income for those who work on the site as sales staff or other personnel. As a result there is a seasonal influx of younger people who work on the streets and a more permanent fixture of people working for the companies all year round.

It seems many people get involved in the timeshare business once they have moved to Spain and when perhaps whatever they had planned to do does not quite work out. It provides the means for many people to stay on. Paul, whose bar in Los Boliches had to be closed down owing to a lack of business, found work with a timeshare company. His wife complained that he worked twelve hours a day and never saw his children. 'But the money's good', she said, 'and we don't want to go home. Kerry is settled in school now, and we like it here.' Sophie, whose husband works as an entertainer, works for timeshare and does very well. 'It helps support the family during seasonal lows, when Gary's money is insufficient', she explained.

Lifestyle: leisure, clubs, social groups

Life in Spain for the migrants as depicted in the representations of them is all about leisure: 'It's one long round of beach parties and cocktail parties', suggested one commentator. 'They spend too much time lazing around, doing nothing, and drinking too much', said another. And it is true to say that at any given time of day or night one can find several British people sitting in bars, drinking, chatting amiably, laughing, and doing little else. But we must not forget that this includes tourists and seasonal visitors as well as more permanent migrants. Most Full and Returning Residents will have a bar that they use frequently as a focal point or a meeting place, in much the same way that a coffee bar might be used in Britain. But they also have other things to do, and few spend all or even part of every day sitting around in bars.

Club life and social groups are a critical feature of life in Spain for the British migrants. There are over fifty British clubs in the Fuengirola area. There is a British club for almost every interest and activity: bowls clubs, a cricket club, an arts centre, a Scottish country dancing club, bridge clubs, a theatre group, Brownie Guides, walking clubs, social clubs, fund-raising groups, healing groups, singing clubs, and many more. Many of those I interviewed take part in the activities of at least one social group. Many are involved in committee work, organising social outings, taking care of fund-raising, doing secretarial work, keeping accounts, organising events and arranging welfare support. For many of the retired migrants this can become a way of life. Many of the British bars are almost clubs in their own right, organising outings, holding bingo nights, serving as information exchanges, holding raffles, organising fund-raising events, and enabling book exchanges.

In addition there are organisations in which the British migrants are critically involved and in which many work as volunteers. One of the largest social groups, with a membership of over 500 is FADS (the Fuengirola and District Society). FADS holds weekly social meetings with jumble stalls, a book stall, a coffee counter (serving tea, coffee, wine, beer and cakes), bingo sessions and quizzes. They also often have visiting speakers. They run bazaars, organise shopping trips to Gibraltar and visits to inland Spain, organise annual holidays, and events from ten-pin bowling nights to a series of Spanish classes. All of this creates a good deal of work for a number of people.

Another large organisation in which lots of British are involved is the Lux Mundi Ecumenical Centre in Fuengirola. The Centre was set up in 1983 by Father Delius (who sadly died in March 1999), a priest in the Jesuit College in Malaga, and is run by the nuns who live there and a group of expatriates. Father Delius explained to me that he saw many foreigners retiring here and living an aimless life, and he thought to himself, 'What do they do? They just sit in bars or stay alone, their life is meaningless.' So he thought of the idea of an Ecumenical Centre. The services provided by the Centre are many and varied, but those most widely used are the weekly coffee mornings, where there is a library, book sale and jumble sale (known as the boutique) and where teas, coffees, cakes and biscuits are sold, and the monthly bazaars, which sell everything from jam to curtains. The Centre thus provides a meeting place and, crucially, a role for many of the volunteers who work there each week. There is often a nurse on duty at the Centre to give advice to people, and to take blood pressure readings. In addition to this, the Centre gives advice on a range of matters from how to find the nearest hospital to how to find out about residence permits. They also rent out items which seem to be in big demand by migrants and tourists, including wheelchairs, cots and walking sticks. The Centre is famous for its fashion shows, which are run by volunteers who model the second-hand clothes from the 'boutique'. These events are incredibly well organised and well attended, raise good funds for the Centre, and are considered very enjoyable by participants and audience alike.

The Lux Mundi Ecumenical Centre, the coffee mornings, the equipment loans, the boutique, etc. are run solely by volunteers, most of them British. Sister Mary (Father Delius's sister, who lives and works in the Centre) told me there is no shortage of volunteers; there is always someone that can help out with things, whatever it is. They also get many donations and gifts, she told me. The whole idea of having nurses came from ex-nurses themselves who now live in the area, and they all give their services free. The library uses donated books and has to have regular tidy-ups, because they get so many donated. The clothes for the boutique are all donated, as is the bric-à-brac. Equipment for loan is also all donated. Other groups use the Centre, like the Brownie Guides, and various choirs and clubs. The nuns run Spanish courses there and Alcoholics Anonymous hold their meetings there. There are church services and prayer groups, and social meetings for the Dutch community. Other than for specific events, the language of the Centre is English. I was quite surprised when I first visited the Centre to note that all notices were written in English, though many of the nuns there spoke no or very little English. Sister Mary, who spoke Spanish and English fluently, told me: 'English is the language of the international community. The Dutch don't like it, they get cross that everything is in English and that's why they don't come as much, but what can you do?'

There is also an English theatre in Fuengirola, *Salon Varietes*, in which many Full and Returning Residents and Seasonal and Peripatetic Visitors (see Chapter 3) are involved. This all began when a small group of people with an interest in theatre formed a small society then later took over the run-down building in Fuengirola which they still use today. They now have a fund-raising wing, an organising committee and several groups of actors willing to put on productions. There are all sorts of people involved. Some are ex-professionals and some are complete newcomers to theatre. The theatre is very popular with people of all nationalities, but all productions are in English. They put on musicals as well as serious plays, and they try to include Spanish people and children. They had Spanish children in 'The King and I', one of the organisers told me. 'The problem is finding Spanish children with good enough English. The lead in "The King and I" was Spanish and spoke no English, yet he learned all his parts', she said. 'You meet different people at the theatre', the mother of one of the committee members told me, 'a different class of people – monied, you know.'

Another crucial institution, for the British migrant is Cudeca (*Cuidados del Cáncer*), a project to build a hospice in the area and to provide palliative care to patients while fund-raising is going ahead. Every British migrant I spoke to had heard of Joan Hunt and Cudeca and many were involved in one way or another. The hospice project encompasses perhaps the majority of the British migrants, who serve in the charity shops, are customers in the shops, are involved in fund-raising activities in other ways, attend the annual bazaar, or are generally made aware of the project through the pages of the local English-language press. Cudeca has changed from being a peculiarly British-focused concern to a very international one. Compare what I heard when I interviewed Joan Hunt, the president, in 1993, with what she wrote to me and what I gleaned from leaflets in the Cudeca centre in 1999.

> Joan began the hospice project a year ago. Her husband died of cancer and this made her aware of the need for a hospice in the area. It is her own project and she manages it all herself. She has managed to get backing from a few companies and has opened a hospice shop staffed with volunteers. The shop is open in the mornings from 10 a.m. to 1 p.m. It is run by British residents. Most of their customers are English tourists and residents, but they are getting more Spanish lately, which Joan says is good because she wants the Spanish involved in the project. As well as the shop, the hospice project is currently running a cancer-care organisation, Cudeca, where volunteers visit terminal patients in their homes and try to help ease their suffering. Joan has twenty-five volunteers at the moment, most of these are ordinary people, she says, who just do some shopping and give company and time to people. Some of the volunteers are nurses. Joan tells me it is very difficult getting good volunteers. 'Many people are away a lot', she says, 'this is such a fluid population.' She tells me some people live here for only part of the year, while others have very long holidays and are away for months at a time, and others are temporary residents. Here she is clearly talking about British migrants to Spain and not people in general.
>
> (Field notes, August 1993)

> Cudeca has helped about twenty-five patients so far, of all nationalities. Joan insists that the hospice will not be only for the British, although most of their referrals so far are British. For one thing they will not get enough financial backing if they keep themselves British. For another thing, they need the involvement and help of local doctors and hospitals and so cannot afford to keep themselves isolated. Joan has managed to get free advertising with a few of the English-language papers, particularly the *Sur*. She has persuaded several companies to put on charity functions, and has got some of them to pledge money for different 'parts' of the new building. She has estimated that she needs about 100 million pesetas to be able to build a Macmillan style 'Green', which is a design she approves of. She would like the hospice to be built between Malaga and Fuengirola because this is 'where there is the highest concentration of people' and because the building must have easy accessibility by public transport. The hospice she is aiming for will have about fifteen beds and will be a purpose-built, well-equipped oasis.
>
> (Field notes, September 1993)

In 1999 Joan wrote to me:

> To the end of last year we have nursed just over 700 patients and this
> week the number we are caring for is fifty-two. This is a heavy load for
> the medical team and to help our doctor we have employed a second
> doctor from the middle of this month . . . The building is going up very
> fast . . . we are now completing one of three floors and before the end
> of the year our medical team and administration will move in.

There are people of all nationalities involved now: a retired Spanish lawyer
is vice president, the legal adviser and treasurer are Spanish, there are Dutch
and American secretaries, and the fund-raising secretary is British.

These are just some of the clubs and organisations which involve a number of the British migrants. Other large groups include the Anglican church,
which holds a coffee morning once a week, and the Royal British Legion,
which now has several branches in the area and a very large branch in
Benalmadena which draws from the populations of Mijas, Los Boliches and
Fuengirola as well as Benalmadena and nearby villages. But there are numerous smaller groups catering for a variety of interests. Many migrants are thus
involved in enjoying club and social life and many are spending a great deal
of their time doing voluntary and committee work. British community life
is therefore very full and can be quite demanding (see more in Chapter 6).
But, for some, life in Spain just means doing those things you would do at
home, but enjoying them more, doing them more slowly and having more
to do in your leisure time (and it's all in the sun). 'I just do the same here
as I would in Wales', Joe told me. 'It's just that here it is all that much more
pleasant. And you tend to take longer over everything. I've just been to the
shops and walked back along the beach. I had to have a look at the sun-
bathers', he grinned.

Importantly, though many of them are working hard in their own businesses or volunteering or as members of club committees, life for British
migrants in Spain is not about work. Life is about living and enjoying, and
work is a means to that end; and spending the money one earns is also about
enjoying life, not about material things. Many of the migrants enjoy eating
and drinking socially. As implied in the descriptions of them in Chapter 1,
alcohol is also a ubiquitous feature of life for British migrants to Spain. Many
people drink alcohol during the day when they would not think to do so
in Britain. But drinking is a social occasion not a solitary indulgence. People
might call into a bar during the day and have a coffee and a brandy, or might
have lunch out and have wine with their meal, and wine and beer were
even served at the Church coffee mornings; however, the people who are
seen drinking heavily are often tourists and holiday-makers. A few of the
permanent migrants are prone to drunkenness, but drunkenness is not what
life in Spain is all about for the majority of British migrants. Alcohol is
cheaper than it is in Britain, and that is part of what makes life in Spain more

enjoyable. It is a problem for some who drink too much, but for most it is merely another and very enjoyable (and ultimately sociable) facet of life in Spain.

'You can be who you want'

A crucial and celebrated feature of life in Spain for many migrants is freedom. Part of that is the freedom from the shackles of the past. Several people told me that it does not matter what you were in the past, you can be who you want to be in Spain. This is picked up in the granting of status or not to people. It was considered bad form to use one's past to demand status or position in this community, though one could draw on one's expertise quite legitimately. Two different people who tried to get positions on club committees were condemned for drawing on their personal histories to try to 'pull rank'. 'He might have been a major in the army but I'm afraid that just doesn't wash here. Anyone can be a committee member, they just have to be voted on. It doesn't matter a jot what he was', complained Edward, of a man who thought he would arrive in Spain and join an organising committee immediately. And Philip, who quickly gained a position in the Anglican church as a result of past connections, was grumbled about bitterly.

This was a bit of a double-edge sword, though. People complained to me that, as Judy put it, 'You can't rely on people here because you will never know much about them, they make up qualifications and experiences and it is hard to check whether they are telling the truth or not.' 'You can't trust them, you don't know anything about them and some of them want you to think they are big-time crooks when all they owe is a TV licence. Then others are really criminals but they act nice. A lot of people who come here are running away from something', said Liz. 'So many British are here illegally', said Mary, talking about her experience of trying to find someone to mend her cooker 'and they tell you they can do a job when they can't. You never know what they were in England. They can tell you anything.' 'People let you down', complained Tony, 'the trouble is people can be whoever they want here, you don't know their background.' This is peculiar when you remember (from Chapter 2) that the first thing people do when they meet for the first time is share a story about why they are here and where they are from. Clearly there is an understanding that some of this story can be fabricated.

On the other hand, people who had done things they would rather forget or had been things they regretted felt they had the opportunity to start again in Spain. There was a sense that you are free from the shackles of the past and that you can wipe the slate clean and start again. This was advantageous to those who had been divorced and wanted a new beginning, like Mary and Michael for whom Spain offered the chance to start again after a messy divorce: 'We both come from the same village, you see, and everyone knows both of us. It's awful, we have all got the same friends and our

Ex's (ex-partners) and everything. We had to get away really.' And then there were those who were not accepted for who they were in their home town (like Andy, who 'came out' to his family and then immediately left for a new life in Spain). There was also a sense in which moving to Spain removed the shackles associated with a given status, such as that of elderly, as discussed above, or of being a woman (see O'Reilly 2000a). Women told me they are less house-bound in Spain, and do not feel the same pressures to be sewing, cooking and inviting people to dinner that they felt at home. Single migrant women told me that back home they felt like social outcasts, whereas in Spain they are able to walk into a bar or a club on their own without feeling uncomfortable or abnormal, and without being stared at. As Denise told me, 'There isn't the same pressure on you to meet a man and settle down. In fact, it is quite normal *not* to be settled down.'

Loneliness and isolation

Despite all the rhetoric about how good life is in Spain and how no-one ever wants to go home, people do get bored. There are inevitably those who suffer from isolation and loneliness, and there are people with problems which are exacerbated by being so far from home. However, any complaints were quickly swept aside with corrective comments about the good life. No-one dwelt on their problems for long, and few people wanted me to think that their problems had anything to do with their migration to Spain as such, or that I should conclude that the migration experience was therefore not a positive one.

Several men told me that they find it difficult to make friends in Spain. For one thing, you know so little about people's pasts that you never know whether you can trust them. For another thing, you never know when someone is going to go home and you are going to lose a friend. On top of that it is difficult to build meaningful relationships when much of the contact between people is superficial and cursory. However, no-one ever told me this without seeming to regret it as soon as they had spoken and then correcting the image they had apparently portrayed by reverting to an emphasis on all the advantages of their new life. Having just descried a good friend of his in Wales, John (a Full Resident in his sixties) went on to tell me, shaking his head with regret, 'You never really make friends here – acquaintances, yes, I've got loads of them, but not real friends.' I looked at him, waiting for him to expand, but he suddenly brightened, tapped the side of my leg playfully and asked, 'Well then, are you going to have a drink?' He would not let me pursue the topic of friends.

Women, on the other hand, needed to have known me for quite a while and needed to feel secure that they were not being overheard before they would confide in me that they sometimes feel terribly lonely and wish they could go home (O'Reilly 2000a). The following excerpt from my field notes gives a good example.

Later on that morning Joan and Beryl sat chatting over a cup of coffee. I heard Beryl say that she is much less bored here now that she has something to do with herself. She said that she used to get very bored and lonely, and people never really understand because they don't think you should.

Joan seemed relieved to hear her say these things and started to tell how lonely and bored she gets, how she misses her family and how she feels she must not admit this to anyone. They said that people do not talk about things like that here, they do not admit that they are lonely.

When they realised I was listening to them they felt uncomfortable and laughed. They do not realise about my study yet. I said that I didn't mean to be nosy and Beryl assured me that I was welcome to listen and join in. Then Joan told me that she has lived here three years and the first two were very difficult. Beryl has lived here longer I think, and says that her husband is ill and would have died long ago if they lived in England still.

They talked about how visitors are always jealous of them but don't realise that everything is not always perfect. 'They expect you to be happy all the time', said Beryl.

(Field notes, June 1994)

Marie, who runs an estate agency with her husband, Derek, confided in me one day that, even after ten years of living in Spain, she felt that she had no real friends. 'You make lots of acquaintances here', she told me, as did many other people, 'but it's hard to make real friends.' Marie misses having someone to call on in times of trouble; someone like her sons or family, she said. She went on to say 'You can tell many people here are lonely because they make excuses to come in here [the estate agency] when all they want is a chat. It's hard to get rid of them sometimes.' She, like all the other British migrants I interviewed, was referring to British people and British friends. None of them even considered trying to make Spanish friends; acquaintances maybe, but not friends. Leslie, with whom I had become quite close friends after one year in Spain, told me that she takes her baby to nursery, comes home, does the cleaning, cooking and shopping, and many days talks to no-one except her husband until she goes to work in the bar in the evenings. 'It gets really lonely some days', she said 'but you can't tell anyone. They don't want to know anyway. My husband just says I am bored!'

People do get bored in Spain, and some do want to go home, but they find it difficult to share this with others. Tony, a 23 year old man, lives in Spain with his parents. He told me when I interviewed him that he wants to go back to England to go to college but he has no-one to stay with there and can't afford lodgings. He has tried to arrange things several times but his parents always just point out the obstacles, the reasons he can't do it, he complained. He has no job in Spain, though he has tried several odd jobs, and he gets very bored. I talked this over with Tony's parents later and his father simply said, 'He'd be bored back there as well. He wouldn't have a job, there's not loads of jobs in England, you know. I don't know what he's thinking.'

There are also people who suffer all sorts of problems associated with being older and far from home, but no-one would want me to exaggerate these. When I interviewed Ann, a Full Resident in her fifties and retired, she told me a very funny story of how she and her husband had helped a woman they hardly knew find somewhere to scatter her husband's ashes. 'She had no-one else, poor dear, so we said we'd take her', Ann told me. She went on to describe how they drove to various different beauty spots and almost decided to scatter the ashes then the woman changed her mind and off they went again to the next place she had in mind. Eventually they were scattered on the golf course, with the woman, Ann and David hurriedly saying a few words of farewell. 'It was hilarious really', Ann said. 'We didn't even know the chap, but you've got to say something. But we didn't really have time 'cos there was this buggy appearing over the hill!' she laughed. 'It was sad, really though, you know. Poor old girl.'

Several people told me, as Peter, a welfare worker did, 'You'll see a lot of loneliness here, a lot of problems.' Indeed, I did witness people with problems. The isolation some people experienced had particularly serious implications for older people with health needs. The following excerpts from my field notes are good examples.

> I telephoned Joan Hunt (hospice project) yesterday and she told me that there is woman in Arroya who has cancer and has been sent home from the hospital as 'there is nothing more they can do for her'. This woman is only 50. Her husband needs to go out and get shopping and go to the bank etc. but cannot leave his wife alone. They have no-one to help them out, apparently, and Joan wondered if I could help in any way. She gave me their telephone number and names.
>
> I tried to telephone them but could get no answer and so I rang Joan back today. She told me the woman has gone back into hospital because her condition has deteriorated.
>
> (Field notes, September 1993)

> An elderly couple were at the desk when I arrived. The man was sitting down and looked a little unwell, I thought. Sister Mary and a Spanish lady were trying to contact a doctor for this couple. Apparently they are Welsh, have lived here seven years and the man has never been to the doctors in that time. The woman has been every month because she suffers with blood pressure, but now the man has some suspicious-looking moles on his head and their doctor advised them to see a dermatologist. They were unable to contact one themselves because they don't speak Spanish and so they had come to Lux Mundi for help.
>
> (Field notes, August 1993)

A gentleman came in during the morning. Sister Mary talked to him and then asked him to wait. She told me he needed to contact the hospital to find out about an operation he is waiting for but he cannot speak Spanish so he had come to ask for help. She asked me to try to get through to the hospital. I was ringing for one and a quarter hours before I got an answer. Sister Mary commented, 'It's a good thing no-one's dying.'

(Field notes, August 1993)

But for all that, when I interviewed people or talked to people in public or in groups, the emphasis was on the advantages of moving to Spain, and possibly the most common phrases I heard were 'No one ever wants to go home' and 'You won't want to go home'. These crucial themes – the loneliness and isolation, and the problems these cause older people in particular; Spain's advantages and the good life for the elderly; crime and criminals; timeshare; the lifestyle and the possibilities for a new start or a clean break when coming to Spain – will be revisited throughout the rest of this book, informing discussions of ethnicity and identity, community and belonging, marginality and escape.

5 Ethnicity and identity

Introduction: ethnicity and identity

This chapter explores the nature of ethnic identity of the British migrants to Spain. Ethnic identity has been defined in terms of associational involvement, in terms of who does what with whom, while for others it stems from a shared blood and soil, or an imagined community of origin. Ethnicity is something that is evoked in symbols of 'us' and 'them'. For all these definitions, the British in Spain can be described as a strongly ethnic group: the British in Spain are essentially British (or Welsh, Scottish, English or Irish). But sentiment, feelings of attachment and belonging are also an important element of identity; and those who do not expect to return home, who have made Spain their (more or less) permanent home, feel as if they belong in Spain and have no romantic memory of or wistful longing for the homeland. There is no claim for territory within Spain, and discreteness from the Spanish hosts is denied or played down.

It seems that for a long time now academics in the social sciences have been obsessed with the notions of integration or assimilation and the maintenance or persistence of ethnic identities in situations of constant culture contact. Atrocities committed as acts of 'ethnic cleansing' have done little to assuage them. Events in former Yugoslavia, especially, have affected thinking about ethnic accommodation elsewhere. Even when authors stress that their interest is purely with ethnic identity, implicitly there is the concern that dual ethnicities in one cultural or geographical space are potentially conflictual situations (Castles and Miller 1993). Such views are equally expressed in the comments of casual observers and reflected in the research focus of the work of many academics. Studies of migration are often static and problem-focused, reflecting underlying assumptions that migration is a deviation from the norm and that it will inevitably be followed by some sort of integration and equilibrium (Benmayor and Skotnes 1994a: 7–8). The Second European Conference for Sociology, held by the European Sociological Society in Budapest in 1995 and attended by several hundred people, took the theme 'European Societies: Fusion or Fission' for its title; and one cluster of working groups combined 'nationalism, ethnicity, migration, social exclusion, racism and genocide' as a unifying theme. One of the 'problems' of migration is apparently that of integration, or lack of it. Immigration societies are often seen as being made up of distinct ethnic/national groups and immigration as a source of disruption. Successful integration apparently depends on policies and principles but also on the actions of the immigrants themselves (see Hutchinson and Smith 1996; OECD 1993). The maintenance of a strong sense of ethnic identity is implicated as a major cause of, or obstruction to, this more desirable result of integration or assimilation of the two or more 'cultures' or ethnic groups involved.

Contemporary discourses of 'European integration', whether referring to political, social or economic integration, conjure in our minds the notion of social integration and of a European identity. However much of a utopian dream that might be, the ideal is implicit in the use of the language. The story goes like this: mass migration leads to a mixing of people, and to a lack of social cohesion. Integration is the desired goal. As Robert Miles points out, integration 'occupies a central place in analyses . . . of the consequences of post 1945 immigration into Europe . . . [I]ntegration was part of the solution to racism' (Miles 1993: 174). The assumption in many studies of ethnicity is that 'plural societies are notoriously unstable because they lack 'a common social will' (Eriksen 1993: 49). The following quote, with its ghostly metaphors, illustrates the fear many people have about the potentially conflictual nature of the 'unmixing of peoples':

> The vision of mass ethnic unmixing remains powerful. Its plausibility is enhanced by the Yugoslav refugee crisis, which resulted directly from the dissolution of a multinational state . . . It is thus understandable that the spectre of an analogous 'unmixing of peoples' in post-Soviet Eurasia . . . haunts discussions of post-Soviet migration.
>
> (Brubaker 1995: 189)

It may be more fashionable, especially since Fredrik Barth's edited collection of essays *Ethnic Groups and Boundaries* (1969), to talk in terms of ethnicity and identity, boundary maintenance and construction, rather than in terms of the assimilation or integration of ethnic groups. However, the concern remains that of explaining the persistence of possibly conflicting identities in situations of ethnic contact, interaction and communication. Barth suggests we think of an ethnic group in terms of a relationship rather than in terms of an entity. 'Ethnic group' once referred, in the anthropological literature, to a population that is biologically self-perpetuating, and that shares a culture, a social space, and a category. Barth suggests that this is similar to the following formula: a race = a culture = a language. What we should concentrate on is not so much the ethnic category as the ethnic relationship: 'the ethnic *boundary* that defines the group, not the cultural stuff that it encloses' (Barth 1969: 10). Ethnic groupings are maintained by a process of continual construction and maintenance of the boundaries; these should be the focus of studies of ethnicity. However, Barth's introduction opens with the following sentence 'This collection of essays addresses itself to the *problems* of ethnic groups and their persistence' (1969: 9, my emphasis).[1] Even in the work of authors describing cultural pluralism; in poly-ethnic situations, where difference is allowed for and perhaps celebrated, there is an awareness that the pervasive myth of the nation state is constantly at work to undermine stability.

> The myth [of the nation state] tells us, as society stabilizes and develops within the framework of a state, ethnicities assimilate, nationalities fuse, and the nation consolidates. Now it often doesn't work this way for reasons of class, racist, and ethnic oppression that is internally structured into various nation states. But it especially doesn't work this way because massive migration is a permanent feature of the world system, constantly *undermining tendencies towards ethnic homogenization* in a given country.
> (Benmayor and Skotnes 1994a: 5–6, my emphasis)

Cultural syncretism is often seen as a source of strength (Battisti and Portelli 1994) and ethnic identity is therefore often discussed in terms of 'the problem of' the persistence of ethnic discreteness in situations of inter-ethnic contact.[2] Arguments which, whether implicitly or explicitly, take assimilation or integration as a given and deviations from this as aberrations are perhaps an inheritance of functionalism in social science (van den Berghe 1981). Assumptions such as these are reflected in accusations of non-integration of Britons into Spanish society by the general public and the mass media.[3]

For Floya Anthias, there is a clear difference between ethnic identity and ethnicity. Ethnic identity merely involves attachment to or acceptance by an ethnic group; it is a matter of subjective identification or of sharing a culture. Ethnicity, on the other hand, is active and involves the establishment of boundaries which exclude others. 'Although ethnic organisation means different things to different people, it is always based on the notion that ethnic origin is a significant arena for cohesion or struggle' (Anthias 1992: 109). This is to take the potential of ethnic discreteness for conflict one step further and to imbue it with an incipient politics, and to imply that if the organisation around ethnicity is not political, then it will be at some time. Much theoretical discussion around ethnicity is concerned with the construction of identities and their subsequent mobilisation. Indeed, for several authors an emphasis by actors on ethnic discreteness has been an active mobilisation directed towards a political purpose (Roosens 1989; Skeldon 1994). Struggles for identity and for the control of cultural and social space necessarily result from the movement of newcomers into previously homogeneous communities (Boissevain 1994).

According to the collective representations discussed in Chapter 1, the Britons in Spain share a strong sense of ethnic identity: their culture, behaviour, friends, dreams and goals reflect an orientation towards rather than against the country of origin and those who share that origin (see Boseley 1993; Hooper 1993). They are accused of mixing only with people of their own nationality, of making little effort to learn the local language or understand the local culture, and of developing an enclave mentality (Champion and King 1993; Kean 1994). They have colonised the coast, and now wish they could go home (Crampton 1993; Fletcher 1994). The implicit accusation is that the British in Spain do not integrate. The Commission of the European Communities maintains that a group which is not involved in the institutions and organisations of the dominant group, nor equally represented in that society's activities and organisation, but which remains culturally distinct, or behaves as if it is culturally different, cannot be described as fully integrated into the wider society (de Foucauld 1992). On the basis of this definition, it can easily be argued that the Britons in Spain are not integrated into Spanish society. But more than simply asserting that they are not structurally part of the wider society, the accusations discussed in Chapter 1 imply *intention* to remain discrete, to construct an identity as ethnically and culturally distinct. Ethnicity plays a very important part in the daily lives of the British migrants to Fuengirola in terms of friendships, activities, and also symbolically. Any outsider looking in, or a short-term ethnographer catching a quick glimpse of community activities and symbols, would perceive a strongly ethnic group in terms of behaviour, networks, symbols and language; but such conclusions amount to ascription and categorisation. To describe the British in Spain simply as an ethnic group is to ignore the subtleties of their own identification with Spanish people and Spanish culture.

A.L. Epstein (1978) introduced the notion of identity into the discussion of ethnicity; 'for every act of identification involves a "we" as well as a "they"' (Epstein 1978: xii). And years later Thomas Hylland Eriksen, following Fredrik Barth, suggested that if ethnicity is so defined – from within – it doesn't matter how different or similar individuals of a group are, or appear to be; if they say they are in group A as opposed to group B, then 'they declare their allegiance to the shared culture of A' and to the symbols of community this group share (Eriksen 1993: 38). However, things are rarely so simple. For these migrants British identity is implied through their actions, rather than stated through their words. By identifying as a 'we', are they implying and constructing another category, namely 'they'? Do the construction and maintenance of such boundaries reflect a desire to remain discrete?

Ethnic Britons

This section examines the evidence of an ethnic identity amongst British migrants and assesses its strength in terms of ethnic association, expressions of shared characteristics, expressions of solidarity, and the symbolising of ethnic boundaries. If ethnicity can be defined, as Sandra Wallman (1986) suggests, in terms of who does what with whom or, as Yancey *et al.* (1976) argue, in terms of frequent patterns of association with a common origin, then ethnicity does appear to be strong among Britons in Fuengirola. We see Britons spending their time with British friends and acquaintances. Chapter 4 described how important club and social group life is to the British in Spain: we see British bars full of British customers and British clubs full of British members. We see leisured Britons, with time on their hands for 'lazing around', spending this time with other Britons in clubs and bars and of course on the beach, taking trips inland, and making visits to Gibraltar. There are over a hundred British-run bars and over fifty British clubs in the Fuengirola area. There is a British club for almost every interest and activity: bowls clubs, a cricket club, an arts centre, a Scottish country dancing club, bridge clubs, a theatre group, Brownie Guides, walking clubs, social clubs, fund-raising groups, and many more. These bars and clubs tend to have a vast majority of British customers and British members. On the other hand, clubs run by other nationalities – Spanish bars, the local pensioners club, and the *Casa de la Cultura* (Spanish arts centre and local centre for culture and adult education) for example – see only a minority of British people as members, visitors or customers. There are even an Anglican church and a British cemetery in the area. There is a British baker's shop, English and Scottish butcher shops, an English grocery store called 'A Taste of England', and an English book shop. For many British, daily life involves talking to and being with other British people and very little interaction with the Spanish. Consider the following case:

Case

Ronnie and Joan get up around 9 a.m. each weekday morning. Joan's elderly mother lives with them and she has to be bathed and dressed first because she always wakes very early in the morning. Joan then takes a leisurely stroll down to a nearby English bar to check if they have any post for her. They used to live above the bar and the postman has not been given a change of address. While she is there, Joan will often have a cup of coffee and a small brandy in the bar. Ronnie, meanwhile, usually goes out to do a bit of shopping, and then returns home to do some ironing or cooking, watch television or sit in the sun on the balcony.

Joan has three part-time jobs: she does ironing for an English woman who owns a restaurant; she cleans the bar of another English couple and cleans the home of a Welsh woman. When she has finished these jobs she might take a stroll along the beach or go home to see her husband.

At four in the afternoon Ronnie and Joan regularly meet two other British couples in a nearby Spanish café-bar. They usually sit outside and drink coffee and maybe wine. Sometimes they will have *tapas* (Spanish snacks). They order their food and drink in English because the barman is fluent, but occasionally they will say a few words in Spanish to his wife, who speaks no

English. Ronnie actually knows no more than a few words of Spanish. Joan is taking lessons but she confesses she is a slow learner.

In the evenings Ronnie often plays cards with some English friends. Joan occasionally goes to a local British bar for a chat and a drink. Once a week they both go to the local British Legion and play bingo, have a couple of drinks and a meal, and meet up with several British friends. Approximately twice a year they return 'home' to visit family in England, and at least twice a year they will have visitors from England staying in their apartment with them.

If ethnic identity is as much to do with associational involvement as it is with either perception or self-perception of a group, as J. Milton Yinger (1986) has also suggested, then Ronnie and Joan have a strong sense of ethnic identity. They spend most of their time with other Britons. They select friends, attend clubs, find work and socialise in their ethnic group. Similarly, many other Britons living in Fuengirola are spending the majority of their time with their compatriots. The above case study was fairly typical. But, ethnic identity apparently stems from the imagination of a shared blood and soil (Bauman 1992); a shared origin, language, religion or race (Eriksen 1993); or from membership of an imagined political community (Anderson 1991).

Britons in the Fuengirola area of Spain draw on these notions of ethnicity and often base friendships and alliances on these imagined shared characteristics alone. When they first meet they will talk endlessly about where they are from in Britain, and two people from the same area seem to delight in exchanging memories of people and places. Certainly, when choosing a bar to go into or a club to join they make their selection on the basis of national identity alone, at least in the first instance. This selection based on nationality becomes even more evident when a Scottish, Welsh or Irish person finds a Scottish, Welsh or Irish-owned bar to frequent. National identity suddenly becomes paramount.

However, the most obvious thing the Britons share is a language. Few British migrants in Fuengirola speak more than a smattering of Spanish, though they often attempt to learn more. Thus an etic perspective reveals a group of people who speak in their own tongue and hardly bother to learn the language of the majority group. The language of their clubs and bars, for example, is British (see Betty and Cahill 1995). When a Colombian woman found she could talk with me in Spanish, she confided in me about her experiences of trying to join a British singing group. She felt an outcast, she said, because her command of English was so poor, and very little Spanish was spoken by the other members. She complained to me that it was obvious she was not really welcome. As a young Spanish woman said of the British: 'The Spanish can't join their clubs and things – it's all in English and they don't feel welcome.' During fieldwork I was often told by Britons that 'it doesn't really matter if you don't speak any Spanish, you can get by', which suggested to me that perhaps the accusations were justified, that Britons actually do have little desire to understand or communicate with the local people; that perhaps they really do just want England in the sun.

Furthermore, these Britons seem to share a sense of solidarity, an attitude that 'we are in this together'. There is a British community spirit, reminiscent of the rhetoric of war-time Britain and conjuring images of patriotism and unity. For example, several social clubs have committee members who are directly responsible for welfare – the welfare of the British in Spain; and the Anglican church keeps a register of British residents in Spain and attempts to secure their safety, health and happiness through regular contact. It is as if one's people were an extension of one's family (see Epstein 1978); they are part of who we were in the past and who we will be in the future, and we have some responsibility for them and for their security and safety: they are us. These welfare committee members and some individuals who have taken this role on to themselves – such as a woman who liaises between the British in Spain and the authorities in London to ease repatriation of those who need it – are working to make things better for the British migrants. When they meet to discuss cases or to plan campaigns, they share nothing more than their ethnic origin, the myth of a shared history, blood and home territory, and their desire to help their compatriots. When they appeal to outside organisations for help in the cause of the British expatriate in Spain, they are expressing this shared identity. During the early 1990s a few of these individuals began appealing to the British government for financial help for older people in Spain. They argued that some expatriates are suffering financial hardship while the British government is not paying certain means-tested or supplementary benefits to overseas residents. The appeal was to their own government, the British one, even though they were appealing for help for people who have moved to Spain to spend the rest of their days. One such meeting which I attended was held in a very traditional British pub (in Spain) and was attended by only British representatives of British clubs and organisations. The following is a quote from a paper that was subsequently prepared for presentation to the Royal British Legion headquarters in London. It can stand alone as a symbol of we-ness (see Bauman 1992), a claim to solidarity based on British identity.

> Those who fought World War 2 to keep Europe free, produced and supported the Welfare State, the envy of Europe, are those who are being repaid with the lowest State Retirement Pension in Europe.
>
> (Brooks 1993: 3)

In Fuengirola there are Royal British Legion clubs, a hospice project with a British woman president, a British animal aid charity, and even a British-run charity group for orphans. These charities are run not only on behalf of their own kind though; the child orphans and the animals in need of help are assumed to be of Spanish parents or owners. Though the Spanish are said to be family-oriented and to love children, some British believe that those who find themselves orphaned are not catered for in this system and therefore 'fall through the net'. And the Spanish are often chided, in the pages of the local English-language press especially, for their very poor treatment of animals. The British appear to be looking not only after their own people and concerns but also trying to change Spain according to their own cultural beliefs and, in doing this, are asserting not only their differences but their cultural superiority – symbolising a 'they-ness'. The hospice project, Cudeca (discussed in Chapter 4) is a very interesting case. It now has Spanish, British and other nationality involvement at all levels, and is expecting to be able to offer support for people of all nationalities. However, in its early days it was quite clear that the concept was a 'foreign' one to the Spanish. The organisers found it difficult to introduce the idea to Spanish people generally, but especially to private health providers, who seem concerned that the project might threaten to steal their businesses.

As one walks around the area one gains confirmation of the criticisms of non-integration and of the persistence of a strong ethnic identification. British bars advertise their traditional British meals of roast beef, Yorkshire pudding, fish and chips, and shepherd's pie. In the construction of a symbolic ethnicity, Britons are cooking and eating traditional British meals which have been removed from the central place in the British diet in modern times. They draw on or construct symbols of Britishness when they visit Gibraltar (a Crown colony) and when they buy tea-bags, pickles, preserves and marmite. A few individuals celebrate St George's Day each year; and there is a huge community meeting in the British theatre on Remembrance Sunday. One year, the Fuengirola and District Society, the largest British social club, organised a trip to Hong Kong (when it was still British), thus drawing on yet another symbol of British Empire. The British in Spain read newspapers from Britain – there is always a queue at the newspaper stand which gets the daily papers from Britain each morning – and they watch satellite television from Britain, especially Sky sports and news, which focuses on British news and events. Interestingly, the locally published English-language press publishes both some news from within Spain and some from Britain. However, the quantitative bias is usually towards the British news.

Favourite trips organised by the social club committees either travel inland to visit quaint, rural Spanish villages as tourists, or to Gibraltar to buy British goods, to exchange sterling to pesetas, and to do one's banking. As I discuss later, Spain is confirmed as Other to the British when they take these trips inland (and act as tourists), but also more overtly when Britons are heard making remarks or jokes about Spaniards and their imagined cultural traits. As Anthony Cohen (1987) found in Whalsay in the Shetland Isles, and K. Dempsey (1990) found in Smalltown, Australia, stereotypes or homogenised images of 'them', the Other, are constructed and used in the maintenance of symbolic boundaries between us and them. And although, as Judith Okely (1983) found amongst the traveller gypsies, these stereotypes and images may not be explicitly articulated as expressing symbolic boundaries, when Britons in Fuengirola talk of slow and backward, or even quaint and friendly Spaniards, they are asserting the boundaries of their own ethnicity. Even statements such as those which follow, which generalise in both negative and positive ways about the Spanish, are marking them out as an homogeneous other:

> I love the Spanish, they are all so friendly. You hardly ever meet a nasty one.
>
> (Dan, forties, Returning Resident)

> The Spanish around here have only learnt to read and write in the last few years you know. They were illiterate when we first came. Most of them have only learned to drive in the last twenty years or so.
>
> (Albert, seventies, Seasonal Visitor)

> You know the Spanish, if they say mañana they could mean anything. You can't really trust them. I never use a Spanish plumber. You never know when he'll turn up!
>
> (Keith, fifties, Full Resident)

> The Spanish are really friendly, and they love to practise their English with you.
>
> (Mary, thirties, Full Resident)

Sojourners

It has been shown that there is evidence of a strong sense of ethnic identity amongst British migrants to Fuengirola. However, as has been argued in previous chapters, one should avoid analysing or categorising British migrants to Spain as one type of migrant. Many of the migrants included in the characterisation above have little orientation towards Spain since they are staying temporarily as Seasonal or Peripatetic Visitors (see Chapter 3). They have no thoughts of Spain as home and no desire to integrate or assimilate, nor to surrender their British identity in favour of a more European or Spanish one. They are sojourners, then, and as such perhaps cannot be expected to want to integrate more fully.

A sojourner status or orientation and an intention (implicit or explicit) to return to the homeland has often been used to explain the persistence of ethnic discreteness or a lack of desire to integrate into the wider society into which the migrant has moved. It is implicitly accepted that a sojourner will have a certain type of orientation towards the receiving country, in that he or she always expects to be returning home and therefore makes no or little attempt to assimilate (Anwar 1979; Uriely 1994). Non-integration has often been explained in these terms – people are retaining a myth of return and an idealised view of home.[4] The assumption in many studies is that 'someone who relinquishes their dreams of the homeland, acts towards integration in the accepting country' (Bonacich 1973) whereas an ideology of return affects the individual's participation in the host society and reinforces ethnic ties (Anthias 1992). Resistance to assimilation or integration goes hand in hand with strong ethnic attachment; strong ethnic attachment in turn attends good memories of and strong ties with home, and a myth of return. As Vaughan Robinson (1984: 235) says of South Asians in Britain, 'The desire for positive association is considerably strengthened not only by religious fervour but also by the existence of a "myth of return"'. This desire for positive association, he says, with reference to an article by Ceri Peach, 'is a factor in the residential and activity segregation of a minority after migration'. And as Uriely (1994: 438) finds of Israeli immigrants:

> The 'settler' type of orientation expressed by the lower-status Israeli immigrants is a central aspect of their adaptation to life in America. The findings of this study show that their notion of a permanent stay in the host country is followed by their readiness to assimilate.

Many Seasonal Visitors to whom I spoke tended not to consider Spain their home, whereas Full and Returning Residents usually considered that they now lived there, as opposed to Britain. Peripatetic Visitors were a heterogeneous group, some of whom thought of Spain as home while others felt themselves to belong in Britain, while others still felt themselves to be betwixt the two 'homes' (see Chapter 3). Many Seasonal Visitors expressed a wish to settle more permanently in Spain one day but often worried that they would miss their families, especially grandchildren. Grandchildren, for older migrants, often symbolised 'home', belonging, and affective ties in general. Seasonal Visitors spoke of their homes in Britain fondly, and of Spain as somewhere they come away to. Though they often said they feel 'at home' in Spain, home remains somewhere you return to for comfort. As Margaret, a 60 year old Full Resident explained, 'In times of trouble, or when you're ill, you want to be at home don't you, and have your family and good friends around you.'

Some migrants who had considered moving to Spain more permanently told me they felt they would get bored eventually. For those with no desire or intention to move permanently to Spain, Britain signified security and Spain the opposite. 'England has the welfare state and all that, and you know what's what', explained Tom, a Seasonal Visitor in his fifties. Mary, a Seasonal Visitor with many Full Resident friends told me: 'We know so many people here who've got themselves in muddles financially – intelligent people who you think would know better.' She believes she is better off not relying too heavily on Spain. Her husband, Tony, went on to tell me, 'You need good private health insurance here, and that costs. And then you never know when you're covered and when you're not.' He then told me of a man who had got the equivalent of a 70 pound bill for an ambulance. He had called the ambulance and then had not needed surgery, so he was not covered by his insurance, Tony told me, shocked.

Those who moved back and forth told me they believed they had got 'the best of both worlds': the best of Britain through families, old friends, familiarity and security, and gentle summers; and the best of Spain in the way of mild winters, new friends, full leisure time, increased health and low winter bills. Sojourners, or visitors, with no intention of moving to Fuengirola more permanently, tend to make friends with others of the same orientation and have little need to integrate fully into wider communities. They behave much more like tourists in Spain, leisure being the main pastime and very few actually working in any capacity, even voluntarily.

The myth of (no) return

The sojourner orientation, however, cannot explain the persistence of a discrete culture and the construction of a strong ethnic identity in all British migrants in Fuengirola. The 'myth of return', which M. Anwar (1979) identified amongst Pakistani migrants in the United Kingdom, cannot be used to explain ethnic attachment in British migrants in Fuengirola. So far this chapter has portrayed ethnic attachment in terms of behaviour, actions and symbols. However, *feelings* of ethnic attachment, or self-ascription – that is, the degree to which a person senses him or herself to be marginal to the larger society and therefore more fervently embraces ethnic identity (Yinger 1986: 27) – have yet to be discussed. In fact, though Britons overtly identify as British and not Spanish, the orientation towards a shared *origin and territory* is not as straightforward as it first appears. Full and Returning Residents, rather than retaining a myth of return to the homeland, identify as committed to Spain. Indeed, many state quite emphatically that they do not want to go back to Britain, ever. These next few quotes demonstrate the extent and strength of this conviction:

> I have no intention of going home and I don't suppose Christopher (his two month old son) will. You can live a better life here.
>
> (Steve, twenties, Full Resident)

> This is home now ... I might not have my family here but they can visit and we can visit them. I don't want to ever go back there to live.
>
> (Carol, thirties, Full Resident)

No-one ever *wants* to go home. That's the truest thing you'll ever hear.
(Derek, fifties, Returning Resident)

People who come here to work or live never choose to go home; it'll be because something went wrong.
(John, seventies, Full Resident)

A few want to go home, but it's not as bad as they [journalists] make out. The trouble is journalists come here and they know what they want to say before they talk to anyone . . . Really it's just that they are having difficulties and they'd be better off in their own country, it's not as if they really *want* to go home.
(Jean, sixties, Full Resident involved in migrant welfare)

Interestingly, this reflects the findings of H. Buller and K. Hoggart (1994: 107), who reported that, amongst British first home-owners in rural France, 'few permanent residents wish to consider returning to Britain'. Though the British in Spain acknowledge that people are returning all the time, to go to university or college, or because of ill health or because they can't afford to stay, it is understood that this is something people have to do but probably would not choose if there were another option. For the younger ones there is always the assumption that 'they will be back one day'. And they often are!

Britons in Fuengirola even expect other people to want to stay: I was told over and over 'You won't want to go home; no-one ever wants to go'. This orientation is overtly stressed as part of their identity: they do not have a longing to return to Britain, there is no myth of return. People are not in fact returning home in the large numbers one might expect. When Russell King and his colleagues (1998) conducted their research on International Retirement Migration (IRM) from north to south European destinations, they had expected to find that many migrants returned home, to families, to familiar surroundings and to good or cheap health service provision, when they became widowed or frail. However, to date there is little evidence that this happens on a large scale. Most Full and Returning Residents I spoke to did not want to return home even when they died. 'This is where my heart is; this is where I want to be buried', said George. 'Who cares where I'm buried; when I'm dead, I'm dead', argued Trudi. When one man, at the meeting between welfare officers discussed above, said he would like to go back home before he dies, Eileen, a Full Resident in her sixties, retorted quickly and angrily: 'Well I don't want to ever go back! Oh no, this is my home now, I've got no desire to go back there.' And the others agreed with her. According to Ronald Elliott (1995), nine out of ten 'expatriates' are not repatriated on death and are buried or cremated in Spain. The vicar at the Anglican church in Los Boliches told me most people are happy to have their last resting place in Spain. He keeps a register of 'expatriates' and their wishes on death – where they want to be buried, contact names and so on. Of 150 people, only three or four want their bodies to be repatriated. This is not because of costs, he said, since they would be about the same either way. 'The British cemetery is the oldest thing the British have in Spain', he told me 'It is over a hundred years old!'

An unidealised view of home

Migrants who do not see their stay as permanent often preserve or create a romantic, idealised view of the homeland. Such an orientation has been identified amongst British colonials in India (Allen 1976) and amongst the Irish in Britain (Holohan 1995), and has become a general theme for migrants and refugees all over the world (Buijs 1993). Some authors argue that migrants invariably strive to preserve an idealised and romantic view of the home society (see Anthias 1992; Buijs 1993; Holohan 1995). For William Safran (1991) a defining feature of a diasporic group is the retention of myths of the homeland. Britons in Spain, however, seek to explode any romantic or positive images of Britain. There is no romanticising of home: 'Britain has changed', they say, 'it is too depressing there nowadays.' Not for them the longing for home which colonial Britons apparently retained, as the following story reveals.

When I had been 'in the field' seven months I decided to make a short trip home, for several reasons. By this time I had made many acquaintances and several commitments: I was working at the Lux Mundi Ecumenical Centre as a volunteer; I was a regular in many daytime bars, at the church coffee mornings, and at Royal British Legion socials and meetings; and I was a volunteer for the hospice project. I told people I would be returning to England for ten days and they looked at me sadly and wished me luck. One woman warned me to 'take plenty of warm clothes'. Several people told me stories of how they once returned to Britain for a holiday or a visit to relatives and that they hated it. Annie told me: 'I went back to England once. Never again. I couldn't wait to get back. Three days and I'd had enough!' Some asked me to post letters for them in England and others asked me to purchase books or goods they cannot get in Spain, like jelly babies and pork pies. People seeing me for the last time before my return kissed me on both cheeks and said: 'Don't worry, we'll keep an eye on the family' or 'Take care'. When I returned to Fuengirola, from Britain, I was asked how I got on there. When I said I had a good time, I received the response 'But it was cold wasn't it?'

On another occasion, when my two daughters had returned to England for a short visit, they were quite irate that they were unable to tell people in Spain of the enjoyable things they had done back home. Laura grumbled to me 'What is it with people here? They won't let you say you had a good time.' And Kelly complained, 'I tried to tell Lucy we went to the beach and sunbathed and she just laughed!'

The community of more permanent migrants is continually constructing and reconstructing a negative image of Britain and a 'bad Britain' discourse. Throughout the year individuals visit Britain for different reasons – for weddings, funerals, visits to relatives. When they return to Spain they often comment on how depressing they found it, or how cold, and how glad they are to be back. The community sees itself as having escaped this 'bad' Britain. Britain is often depicted as signifying any or all of the following: routine; dullness; monotony; greyness; cold; no hope for the future; a miserable old age; misery; modern life; rushing around; no time for pleasure; crime; selfishness; lack of caring; loss of community; lack of trust; poor health; poor education; and a poor welfare state. This is how many permanent migrants talk about Britain, especially when they are in larger groups or when an 'outsider', such as a tourist or temporary resident, is present. As I showed in Chapter 2, in all discussions around 'why we came here to live', the discourse of bad Britain is drawn on. Individuals give their reasons for coming to Spain with reference to unemployment, redundancy, crime, ill health and boredom, using this discourse which constructs a negative future for Britain and a more positive one for individuals in Spain. At the Royal British Legion Christmas dinner (which I discussed in Chapter 2), Trevor and I sat at a table with a group of seven people we had never met before. These seven people all knew each other well. They asked us about ourselves and then spent most of the evening telling us why they came to live in Spain. For all the good things Spain has to offer, the equivalent in Britain is seen as bad or deteriorating. They complained about the British weather and the crime rate, about the fast pace of life and the deteriorating health service. One couple at the table had not moved to Spain permanently but said they intend to. Sharing the discourse and identifying with a wish to leave Britain thus helped them to become part of the group, one of the 'we'.

The 'bad Britain' discourse is supported in several ways. One means is via bad news, which tends to come from Britain. Many people who live in Spain all year round, as well as those who visit for the winters, have access to Sky Television. It is fitted into many apartment blocks and villas and can be viewed in British bars. Many Britons are therefore watching only British news. Britons in Britain often complain that all news is bad, and the bad news this community in Spain is receiving comes directly from Britain. Most people cannot speak enough Spanish to be able to watch Spanish television news and they therefore often do not hear the bad things that might happen in Spain. For example, while I was in Spain in 1994, two teenage girls were kidnapped and murdered in Valencia. I only heard about this from a Spanish woman, though it reached the headlines in the Spanish press. No British person talked about it as far as I heard. The Jamie Bulger case (in which an English child was murdered by two local boys) was, in contrast, discussed by the British at length at many different times and places. 'Bad news' and 'Britain' thereby become associated concepts.

In addition, British tourists tend to mix with resident Britons in the bars, clubs and urbanisations, and in their homes as visitors. As I discuss later, these tourists have more literally escaped Britain for a break away. They complain about the British weather and about work. They are happily drawn into conversations about how bad Britain is becoming these days, to confirm the images which the more permanent migrants are constructing. This 'bad Britain' discourse is incredibly strong and influential. As a thread of significance spun by the migrants, it suspends them quite securely and tightly. When I made the trip home in February which I described above, I had been dreading returning to England in the depth of winter. I was worried that I would be terribly cold; that people would be so depressing that they would get me down; that everywhere would look so grey to me that I would be desperate to get back to Spain. My relief on arriving in England in the sunshine to find people warm, cheerful and welcoming was enormous. For most permanent migrants, Britain is certainly not idealised and there is no 'myth of return' to explain neatly the lack of integration into Spanish society. There is no evidence of a colonial-style pride of British Empire nor a longing for home.

Ethnicity and politics

Contrary to the findings of many studies of ethnicity and nationalism, not all ethnic groups are nationalistic; nor are they always *either* concerned with establishing control over territory *or* aiming to return to the nation state. While many British migrants have a sojourner orientation, others display a strong ethnic attachment which cannot be explained away with reference to a myth of return or a romanticising of the country of origin. The emphasis by migrant ethnic groups on their distinctiveness has often accompanied a demand for recognition of difference or rights, or has been a mobilisation against racism or xenophobia (Roosens 1989; Skeldon 1994). Could this solidarity against a common enemy explain the persistence of discreteness amongst Britons in Fuengirola? It would appear not. The Britons are not, at least yet, making an issue of their ethnicity *vis-à-vis* the Spanish.[5] There is no political arena, no apparent political agenda, nor an overt attempt to assert ethnic difference in relationship to the Spanish. Their ethnicity appears to be more a matter of subjective identification than an active establishment and maintenance of boundaries.[6] What is interesting, in this context, is that this shared ethnic identity is so strong and so taken-for-granted that it is rarely voiced. 'We British' may have been invoked by the Royal British Legion members when appealing to the British government for help (Brooks 1993), or on Poppy Day, or by others on St George's Day, but other than on such occasions, no-one has the need to stress their ethnicity verbally. In fact the British experience no racism against which to rally. In all my time in Spain I have never once heard the words race, racism or racist used by the British towards the Spanish. The British experience of the Spanish is that they are friendly and welcoming. There were times when the people felt that the authorities or certain bureaucratic institutions were not making things easy for them (see Chapter 7) but at the level of daily, personal interaction it was assumed that the Spanish are happy to have them there.

In situations of contact, in interaction with Spanish people, permanent migrants tend to play down their ethnicity; they practise their little bit of Spanish and attempt to minimise differences between the two cultures. At the very traditional annual festival, the *feria*, for example, several British migrants wore traditional Spanish dress and mingled happily with the Spanish, popping into the *peñas* for a drink and a dance, and going home in the early hours of the morning. Some had even learned to dance *Sevillana* for the occasion. Several migrants attended the *Romeria*, a short pilgrimage through the town which marks the start of the *feria*, and during which many participants are on horseback and most wear traditional Spanish dress. They mingled in the crowd by dressing like Spanish people, in smart clothes, rather than like British tourists, in shorts and T-shirts. They brought their picnics and not their cameras, and some again wore Spanish dress. Apparently the more permanent migrants are not in fear of losing their sense of ethnic difference, their identity. Ethnicity is not stressed in interaction because there is no threat of homogenisation, no threat to their discrete identity, and no pressure to assimilate; in short, none of those elements which Anthony Cohen (1985) identifies as incentives to assert ethnicity.

Permanent migrants do not overtly state their ethnic difference to Spanish people. In fact they understate or deny the discrete nature of their communities and groups. Many told me they consider themselves integrated, or, if they admit that they are not integrated, then they at least can talk of their Spanish friends or can tell you that their children are fluent in Spanish and are therefore integrated. They tend to describe at length their acceptance by and friendships with local Spanish people. One man told me what a close community there is in the area in which he lives and I said, 'Do you mean a British community?' to which he replied, 'Oh no, we are integrated here, not like those people in the urbanisations. It is like a village here; one sneeze and we've all got a cold' (Kevin, sixties, Full Resident). This same man speaks few words of Spanish. He owns a bar in which I saw fewer than ten Spanish customers during fifteen months of fieldwork, none of whom was a regular. A woman who spends her time regularly with British people, on a daily basis, told me of her relationship with her Spanish neighbours:

We are ever so close. They invited us to their daughter's christening, you know. They don't come round for coffee or nothing 'cos the Spanish don't tend to do that, but we often see them in the gardens and in the café and we have a chat. Their daughter is really fond of us. She missed us last year when we went back home, you know. They said she kept coming out and looking around for us.

(Beryl, seventies, Returning Resident)

Some British people do have Spanish friends and they love to tell you about them. David, a retired man in his early fifties who does some painting and decorating to boost his income, told me at great length about his Spanish friends. One is a neighbour whom he has coffee with occasionally. One is a man he works with from time to time and whom he also goes out for a drink with on occasions. Neither of these two speaks any English. He is also friendly with a Spanish woman to whom he was introduced by an English woman. He meets her regularly to practise his Spanish and to help her with her English. David speaks Spanish at a conversational level but cannot read or write it very well. He is very proud to have Spanish friends and has learned a lot about Spanish culture from them. However, he once told me that he has no real friends in Spain. The British friends are very superficial, he said, and as for the Spanish ones, 'Well, when you can't really talk to them properly, you can't really call them friends, can you? You can't have a heart to heart or anything – you know, it's difficult.'

It is much more likely that those Spanish people who have at least a smattering of English will get to know British people. The result is that there is a weighting towards better-educated people and people who have some connections with Britain through family or friends. Some get to know one another through the children. Those migrants whose children attend Spanish school are especially convinced that they are integrated within Spanish society themselves. Several migrants talked of their children as Spanish or half-Spanish, emphasising how they (the children) would never go back to Britain. Leslie, a Full Resident in her thirties, told me, 'We're integrated. Debbie, she's got lots of Spanish friends, and their mums come round, you know, and they, some of them, they can speak good English, and they love it . . . 'cos they like their children, to practise, you know.'

Mick, a 41 year old Full Resident, told me he speaks little Spanish himself but his daughter was born in Spain, speaks Spanish fluently, attends Spanish school and has only Spanish friends. He said, 'She'll never live in England. She's Spanish in her mind really.' So, although generally speaking very few people are more than loosely integrated, many British in Spain would like you to think that they are more integrated than they are, and many are making an admirable effort to get to know Spanish people.

Ethnic identification, for British migrants, is with an 'us' rather than against a 'them': British food is prepared for and sold to other Britons, symbolising a shared identity; buying British food is a social occasion or a networking activity (see Shun and Fine 1995 for a discussion of the social meanings of sharing 'cultural' foods). When individuals go to Gibraltar they tell others of their intended trip and are asked to bring goods back; it is a social occasion rather than an individual action. When a company began importing British goods in bulk and made them available for purchase to individuals, this became a social event; the information was shared and telegraphed speedily through the community. I was told by Joan who had heard it from Ted, who had been informed by Jeff at the British Legion social. But more importantly than stressing a boundary between themselves and the Spanish, these social activities confirm the shared ethnic identity of the participants. It contributes to the 'we-talk'; a discourse 'in which identities and counter-identities are conceived and through which they are sustained' (Bauman 1992: 678). But while the '"we-ness" of friends owes its materiality to the "they-ness" of enemies', as Zygmunt Bauman rightly says, for these migrants the 'we-ness' is more of an entity in their daily experience than the 'they-ness', which is a given.

Residential tourists

The first part of this chapter explores migrants' ethnic identity and describes an apparently strongly ethnic group in terms of actions but less so in words and attitudes. It has been seen that ethnic identity does not always entail a commitment to place of origin, nor an overt stressing of difference from the majority group. Ethnicity in this case seems not to involve a conscious symbolising of boundaries between ethnic group and Other. It can, of course, be argued that ethnicity is particularly salient for the permanent migrants, not so much in what they express as in terms of who is doing what with whom and for which purposes. In a very general sense, and at one level of identification, the residents mobilise behind what Anthony Cohen (1987) calls 'the general statement' of ethnic community. But this is not an identification purely with all other Britons everywhere; it is, implicitly, an identification with tourist, holiday Britons. For the more permanent British migrants an identity as 'residential tourists', and as British but different, seems more salient in terms of their daily lives and experiences than attachment to ethnic group *per se*, or to country of origin.[7] Just because ethnicity is so relevant in many cases these days, we should not assume this is always the case; it is an identity which can be invoked, and a very powerful one, but most of the time it is not actively antagonistic.

British migrants are drawing a sense of identity from those with whom they share time and space, rather than against those who have little relevance in their daily lives. As Cohen (1985) has said, identity is concerned with locality and region more than with gross nation; in this context that means with *local* Britons rather than with all Britons. Within Fuengirola, a mass tourist area, it is difficult for an observer to disentangle the more permanent British migrants from the tourists and visitors. As I discussed in Chapter 3, many people return to Britain each year for several months at a time. Several move backwards and forwards between Spain and Britain, owning property in each country. Some have moved to Spain to 'see if things work out' and have not made a decision on permanence; while others have made a commitment to live the rest of their lives there. Many have moved to Spain to live, yet continue to have their British pension paid into a British bank account or their savings held in sterling accounts. Many who have gone there to live will not register with the police as residents and do not appear as resident in Spain in any official statistics. On the other hand, they often told me they are 'here to stay' and exhibited a severing of their emotional and material ties with Britain.

It is an almost impossible task for an outsider to classify between the sojourners, tourists and immigrants of classical migration studies, since for the British themselves the identity as permanent or temporary migrant does not always seem to depend on clear, objective criteria. As a result, outsiders lump the Britons in Spain together and ascribe them an ethnic identity which does not take account of the differences between Britons in terms of orientation to place of origin and to Spain. The ethnic community that outsiders see is a community made up of both permanent and temporary migrants; of Full and Returning Residents; of Seasonal and Peripatetic Visitors; and even of tourists. In fact a simple but useful division that observers should apply is one the migrants often make themselves, between the three categories of more permanent migrants (residents or expatriates); more or less temporary migrants (visitors); and the tourists. While more permanent migrants appear to identify as one with a group of Britons, that is ethnically, it should be remembered that these other Britons are either tourists or temporary visitors to the area in which the permanent migrants have chosen to settle. One difference between the two types of migrant (more permanent and more temporary) is in the intention whether or not to return home; but there are many similarities between them.

As I discussed in Chapter 2, and, incidentally, as seems to be the case with many British home-owner migrants to rural France (see Buller and Hoggart 1994), most permanent migrants in Fuengirola had been tourists first; their initial contact with the area being via a holiday. Even those who chose to settle in the area without having ever been there as a tourist usually visited and holidayed there before buying, moving and settling. Anne, a Full Resident, said 'I had been here several times on holiday and I always said that if anything happened to my parents I would move here for good'. Marie, a Full Resident in her fifties, told me, 'We used to come out each year, for a holiday. We got to know a few people, and then, when Alan was made redundant . . .' Joan, a Returning Resident in her eighties, told me she was looking for somewhere different to live after her husband died, that she went to Spain on holiday and decided to settle. And Gary, a 30 year old entertainer and Full Resident, said, 'I came out on holiday with my friend and never went back – that was five years ago.' As tourists, these people would have visited the tourist areas; they would have seen the sun and the sea; they would probably have spent time with other tourists more than with workers or indigenous people; and they would have employed the tourist gaze – photographing scenery and gazing on exotic others (Urry 1990). For tourists,

Spain is a holiday space – it is what Stanley Cohen and Laurie Taylor (1976) call an archetypal 'free area', a space and activity signifying escape from routine and drudgery.

Not only is it difficult to distinguish between permanent and temporary migrants, but it is also difficult to separate residents, visitors and tourists spatially or with regard to where and how they spend their time. The members and customers of clubs and bars are a mixture of temporary and permanent migrants, and tourists. Even residentially, though they are not living in ethnic ghettos, Britons are not segregated according to whether their migration is a permanent or temporary one. Most migrants live or stay in urbanisations or complexes, in which apartments and villas are rented to tourists on a regular basis. The children of both settled Britons and visitors and tourists will play together, sharing their native language and their common experiences of Britain. If behaviour *reflects* identity, then the time this group of residents spends with other British would suggest that they identify overtly as British; but the British they identify with have escaped from Britain temporarily. If behaviour also *affects* identity, then sharing these spaces, and the social rules by which they are governed, involves sharing an attitude and a certain amount of emotion management. If I ever found myself engaged in a serious or deep conversation with others, I would soon become aware that the conversation was being pulled back to something lighter. On one occasion I overheard a barman telling customers who were involved in a serious discussion: 'Come on, there are tourists here, they don't want to hear people moaning and being miserable, they are here to enjoy themselves.' The space all migrants share in general in the Fuengirola area is a holiday space.

Not only have many migrants to Fuengirola been tourists themselves, but once they are settled as residents they retain contact with tourists in various ways. Most migrants have regular visits from relatives and friends in Britain and so are in constant, close contact with tourists in private as well as public spaces. They are aware that friends and relatives back home consider they live in a holiday space. 'If this wasn't a holiday place you wouldn't get so many visitors. They come here for a free holiday, not to see you', one Returning Resident told me. 'A lot of people get so many people [visitors] in their first year they get sick of it. It's marvellous how many friends you've suddenly got when you live in a holiday area', insisted Gladys, a Full Resident.

Settled migrants often show visitors the local sights, escort them to the beach and socialise with them in bars and restaurants. None the less, even when they are not showing visitors around, they might well be visiting Spanish sights themselves. Many of the British clubs organise regular visits inland where the 'real Spain' provides the authentic experience for the resident and tourist alike (Cohen and Taylor 1992). Permanent migrants also behave more like temporary migrants themselves when they go 'home' for weddings, funerals, Christmas, the summer; their time in Spain providing an escape from these common rituals of life, just as a holiday does for tourists. Even those migrants who state emphatically that they will never go home to live usually have family in Britain and occasionally return for weddings, funerals and christenings. 'I haven't been home in five years . . . except for two weddings', one woman told me proudly.

It is often assumed by others, as well as by residents themselves, that tourists and residents share the same interests and outlook. The newspapers and magazines that are published in the area by and for English-speaking people are directed at tourists and residents alike (a recent addition to the list of publications even has the title *The Tourist and the Resident*). They tend to focus on British club news and entertainment, on places to go and things to do, on eating out, a little bit of local and national Spanish news and a little bit of British news. The emphasis is on having fun and enjoying your time on the Costa del Sol. Serious issues are only occasionally tackled, on the letters pages and in some articles, with special relevance to the expatriate experience.

Spain: the socially constructed space

For British migrants, Spain signifies holiday and escape, not work or refuge or asylum as the host country does for many migrant groups. Spain, especially those coastal areas associated with mass tourism, has been socially constructed, or spatialised. For many Britons it is, at least initially, a marginal site signifying holidays, escape, leisure, fun, liminality, fecundity and new beginnings. For Rob Shields (1991: 31) the term social spatialisation designates

> the ongoing social construction of the spatial at the level of the social imaginary (collective mythologies, presuppositions) as well as interventions in the landscape (for example, the built environment). This term allows us to name an object of study which encompasses both the cultural logic of the spatial and its expression and elaboration in language and more concrete actions, constructions and institutional arrangements.

Fuengirola has been socially spatialised and constructed as a holiday zone, as described in Chapter 2. The space of Fuengirola, similar to other Spanish resorts, has come to signify certain behaviours, actions, relationships, attitudes and myths associated with the beach and with holiday. It signifies via tourist brochures, media, literature, tourism and the constructed tourist gaze, social images, retirement literature and sales, holiday home sales advertising, the soap opera, *Eldorado*, postcards and literature. Spanish resorts, Ibiza currently offering the epitome, with their beaches, sun and fun, have been constructed, both concretely and symbolically, as sites for pleasure, escape and new beginnings. Just as the Orient was almost a European invention

(Said 1978), so the Costa del Sol was almost an invention of package tourism. This part of Spain has been spatialised as a holiday and marginal space and invested with meanings on which individuals subsequently act. These meanings are associated with discourses of holiday and escape. For many migrants the first images of Fuengirola were via tourist brochures and social images of the place as a holiday destination. Brochures focus on the sun and the sea; on getting away from it all; on fun and laughter (Cohen and Taylor 1992; Urry 1990).[8] Even the name has been changed, apparently, from what it was informally known as – the windy coast – to its more attractive 'Costa del Sol' (Holbrook 1994).

As John Urry suggests in his book *The Tourist Gaze* (1990), the tourist attitude and approach to a space and its people have been and continue to be socially constructed. For Urry the gaze of the tourist as it lingers on and photographs foreign scenery, people and surroundings is, he suggests, like Michel Foucault's medical gaze, socially constructed and reconstructed by professional experts. The discourse of tourism, and the signs, symbols, and images portrayed by the media and by travel brochures, construct a sight, an activity or a place so that the consumer sees and 'reads' those signs to which his or her gaze is directed. Tourists are encouraged to 'see' and to gaze upon objects and signs which signify otherness. The form the otherness takes varies from place to place and period to period, and has less to do with intrinsic properties of the place itself and more to do with how it is constructed as a site for either mass or elite consumption. The predominant objects of the tourist gaze in southern Spain were, in the period of package tourism, sand, sun and sea. Now, as we enter a period of selective and nostalgic tourism, the focus or gaze shifts to more cultural signs of bullfights, flamenco and traditional festivals.

'Spain' encompasses diverse signifieds: it is for Britons a mass tourist area; part of Europe; a Mediterranean country; a place to retire to; a holiday home; the California of Europe; sleaze. There is also the Spain of bullfights and passion, quaintness and backwardness, blood and revolution, peasants and traditions. It was interesting to note how many Britons in Fuengirola, Mijas and Benalmadena all tended to talk of Spain, rather than using the village or area name to which they had moved. This tendency is reflected throughout this book when referring to migrants' own attitudes, ideas, thoughts and opinions. It was *Spain* they had moved to or visited; Spain they loved; Spain which was welcoming, friendly, warm, cheap. But for many Britons in Fuengirola, for whom Spain is often one country and one space encompassing all those images above, it is first and foremost a holiday space.

According to Cohen and Taylor, in their intriguing book *Escape Attempts* (1992), holidays are one form of escape from the drudgery and routine of modern living. Indeed, they are created and signposted as such. They overtly offer the subversion of all that is taken as usual and normal. The packaging and the selling of holidays encompass the message of escape: '[G]et away from it all, relax, be yourself, leave your worries at home, enter a new, exciting world' (Cohen and Taylor 1992: 132). This search for escape and for other worlds involves voyages of discovery, including the discovery of one's true self; a theme to which I shall return at the end of this chapter.

Moving to Spain on a more permanent basis is also sold as a voyage of discovery, as an extension of a holiday and new beginnings. Before setting out to Fuengirola to do fieldwork, I attended a sales conference in Colchester for people considering retirement to Spain. A package was being marketed whereby the prospective customers were encouraged to unburden themselves of all possessions and worries, to sell their homes, leave their families and their pasts behind them, and escape to a new world and new beginnings. Based on the modern concept of timeshare-club ownership, where the owner trades his or her two weeks' ownership in one country with people who have ownership in others; they were being sold mobile space in a chain of hotels within which they could move around from area to area within Spain. They would be free of personal belongings and restrictive emotional and financial ties. The retiree would have nothing more to worry about except enjoying life, They were to benefit from lots of sunshine, better health and fantastic leisure opportunities. Nurses and legal advisers would be on call; the disabled would be catered for; and all meals would be provided. Spain was depicted in terms of sea, sand, sunshine, and a chance to begin a new life free from the shackles of the past. Neither Spanish culture, politics, history nor people were referred to during my observation.

Books aimed at those who are considering the move to Spain draw on the same rhetoric of dreams, new beginnings and freedom (see, for example, Reay-Smith 1980; Robinson and Pybus 1991). This literature mainly contains practical and financial advice on buying or renting a home, removals, residence and work permits, taxation, banking and education. Some authors give a brief description of Spain's geography, history, language, culture and government; however, Spain is normally depicted in terms of fiestas and siestas, bullfights, tourists and costas. Rural Spain is painted as quaint and traditional, with a culture strongly influenced by Catholicism.

In summary, while identifying ethnically with other Britons, these other Britons are or have been tourists in Spain and as such have temporarily escaped Britain. The shared common ethnic identity itself is not a straightforward identity with Britain but with escapee British tourists and holiday-makers. British migrant identity, therefore, needs to be understood in the context of Spain's spatialisation as a holiday area, and in terms of the tourist gaze and escape attempts. As A.L. Epstein (1978) argued, ethnicity is but one among a number of alternative identities from which an individual or group can choose: identities are situational and contextual. The social experience for these migrants, since they spend so much time with other Britons, is intra-ethnic rather than inter-ethnic, that is amongst others who share their origins rather than opposed to others of different origin. In their definition of the social situation, for the most part, ethnicity simply does not matter (Eriksen 1993). In characterising these migrants as an ethnic group, we are doing no more than labelling them the way those who used the terms 'race' or 'tribe' attempted to capture the essence or culture or characteristics of apparently discrete groups. Describing them as colonials reconstructing a 'little England' is imputing behaviour to them based on their nationality alone. Even if all the representations are saying is that they are expressing boundaries between themselves and the Spanish in the construction of an ethnic category, this is objectification which ignores the subjectivities of those whom they are categorising or typifying. A social anthropological interpretation attempts to understand the meanings for those actors involved in the construction of their social world. For several of these migrants to Fuengirola, what appears to be ethnic attachment is not simple attachment to origin, but also identification with others who share that origin and also with this particular historical and geographical context, and therefore with holiday, escape and new beginnings.

Residents not tourists

It has been argued above that identities are multiple and contextually displayed. I shall now explore the layers of identity expressed and articulated in migrant contexts. Though Britons implicitly share an identity as escaped Britons, as some form of tourists; permanent migrants *express* an identity in opposition to tourists, especially in the winter, when there are more British migrants in the area and therefore a larger group of people against which to construct a sense of otherness. Further, identity is *with* the Spanish (or an image of Spanish-ness), as committed to Spain, and with a nostalgic British past. For those migrants who identify as having moved to Spain on a more permanent basis, ethnicity seems less important in their daily lives than does identifying against a more present Other – the other Britons. As with individuals, groups gain a sense of self both from and against those with whom they spend time. As Eric Hobsbawm notes at the beginning of his study of nationalism:

> Even today it is perfectly possible for a person living in Slough to think of himself, depending on circumstances, as – say – a British citizen, or (faced with other citizens of a different colour) as an Indian, or (faced with other Indians) as a Gujarati, or (faced with Hindus or Muslims) as a Jain, or as a member of a particular caste, or kinship connection, or as one who at home speaks Hindi rather than Gujarati, or doubtless in other ways.
>
> (Hobsbawm 1992: 8)

By 'in other ways', Hobsbawm no doubt refers to other identities not necessarily based on ethnicity, for example those associated with gender or age.

Britons in Fuengirola think of themselves as Britons and therefore not as Spaniards. But they also think of themselves as Britons who have 'come away'. And when faced with other Britons, they think of themselves as either committed to living in Spain or as staying temporarily. Those who are clearly temporary are labelled 'tourists' or 'visitors'; those who intend to stay label themselves as 'residents' or 'expatriates'. Residents and expatriates are therefore a group within a group; and 'where there is a group there is some sort of boundary, and where there are boundaries there are mechanisms to maintain them' (Nash 1989: 10). Dress, attitude, language, behaviour and knowledge are used to symbolise the boundaries between tourist and resident. While identifying with tourists as British people enjoying the benefits of holiday Spain, residents also identify themselves as different to tourists. Constructing a shared identity as residential tourists,[9] residents share jokes about and construct stereotypes of tourists which symbolise the boundaries between 'them and us'.

> Just for a laugh we went out dressed like tourists, you know, in our shorts and sunglasses.
>
> (Linda, fifties, Full Resident)

> We don't class ourselves as tourists but, um, like, someone will say 'Are you gonna wear your tourist hat tonight?', – 'cos a lot of 'em wear hats – and we'll go down the discos and watch the tourists dance . . . and we'll just look at 'em, amazed.
>
> (Adam, twenties, Full Resident)

> We don't look like tourists any more. My husband doesn't go out topless, I don't go out half-dressed!
>
> (Anne, sixties, Full Resident)

They tell you how unlike tourists they are in their behaviour and habits, to the extent that the timeshare touts can tell a resident from a tourist at a glance (see Chapter 4).

Attempts are made to naturalise the difference between the two groups. Residents often sport deeper suntans than tourists can achieve; suntans which are often worked at with great effort but made to look natural. Few people actually admit to working at a tan; most proudly sport one. I was teased for not having much of a tan: 'You look like a bloody tourist', I was told. Residents also spoke to me of acclimatisation to Spanish weather, complaining that they feel the cold more than the newcomers and the tourists. One man told me, 'Our blood thins, you know. Those of us who've been here a few years couldn't stand the winter in Scotland or England now.' When others complained of the heat in mid-summer, some long-time residents laughingly remembered how they too used to suffer before they got used to it.

Residents make it especially clear in the summer, during the seasonal influx of visitors, that they do not want to be associated with the tourists. They complain at being inundated with visitors. A journalist and 'expatriate', writing in a local English-language magazine, described the regular deluge in the following poetic language:

> Long lost school chums bearing no resemblance to anyone we can remember . . . cousins so distant they're three feet tall, yellow all over and have antennae in the middle of their dome-like heads, who, having used us as free tour guides, leave a trail of devastation behind them.
> (Davis 1993)

Residents share a language that effectively symbolises the otherness of tourists. They adopt some Spanish words, usually a little anglicised, which have particular relevance in their lives as expatriates or foreign residents. Words such as *abogado* (lawyer), *traspaso* (lease agreement), *tinto verano* (red wine with a soft drink like lemonade), *mil* (thousand – only used when referring to pesetas), *ambulatorio* (clinic, health centre) and *tapas* (snacks) are part of everyday conversations between residents. I noticed when my mother visited that one of our friends seemed to be using these words more than usual in her presence. This behaviour was both inclusionary, for us, and exclusionary, for my mother. They also share the language of 'bad Britain' as discussed earlier; and a determination not to 'go home'. When I finally decided that I would be returning to England, even though Trevor would be staying behind, I found it difficult to maintain some relationships. I felt as though I was being dismissed because of my lack of commitment to Spain and the community of residents. These relationships have been strengthened again as I have shown commitment to the community by returning over the years, and my commitment to the 'bad Britain' rhetoric by promising I want to return to Spain one day.

As discussed in Chapter 4, it has become part of the resident community identity to be maverick and different. As Cyril said, 'it's not just ordinary people' that come to live here. Difference is celebrated between the permanent migrants, especially if it marks them out as different to other British who have not committed themselves to the life in Spain. They do not only see themselves as lucky to be living in such a beautiful country but consider themselves brave and deserving of their lifestyles. Even jokes about the criminals (or ex-criminals) within the community mark them out as 'one of us' – as long as the crimes are not violent or aggressive but are crimes against bureaucracy, authority and control. The identification is *with* them rather than *against* them, as individuals admit that they break the law themselves to a small degree here, where they might not have done so in Britain (see Chapter 4). For example, Joan, an 82 year old Returning Resident, told me guiltily but grinning that she drives with no insurance. June, a 70 year old resident who has lived permanently in Spain for twelve years, admitted with a cheeky snigger to having a 'non-resident' bank account so that she pays no tax.

Living the holiday

Identifying with tourists and tourism, as a symbolic community with a 'gloss of commonality' (Cohen 1985: 109) involves sharing the tourists ethos; however, for the permanent migrants this entails making it a way of life: *living the escape*. Permanent migrants identify as committed to Spain, and to a certain way of life which Spain signifies for them. Paradoxically though, this commitment forms part of the identity as 'not tourist'. As with other attempts at a more permanent escape from reality, such as a commune,

> [t]he taken-for-granted relationship between past, present and future is undermined by a determined emphasis upon the irrelevance of the past and future, and a glorification of the present – the here-and-now experience. Time itself is demoted from its central place as an organizing principle within consciousness . . . Standard divisions between work, leisure and hobbies are denied.
>
> (Cohen and Taylor 1992: 161)

By displaying an implicit commitment to the tourist, escapee way of life, individual past histories and their influence on the present are undermined. People often told me things like 'It doesn't matter what he was in the past, none of that counts now' (Meg, eighties) and 'You can be who you want to here, no-one knows your past' (Dan, fifties). Few residents know much about acquaintances or friends' past lives, and are unlikely to know surnames. The Anglican vicar told me people tend not to know each other's surnames or addresses here, and when one man died nearby, he lay dead for days without anyone knowing. Even though he had been involved in the theatre and people were wondering where he was, few people knew any more than his stage name. This denial of past histories was something I experienced for myself during fieldwork. It felt strange to realise that, as I met people for the first time, I had the opportunity to reconstruct my own history and my own identity completely if I so wished. As I discussed in Chapter 4, there was very little chance that anyone would ever find out 'who you really were' or what you had ever done before coming to Spain. This really was the opportunity for new beginnings. For some people this was a very positive thing; Spain was the place for starting afresh, redefining your life and your identity, a place to find yourself. For other people or in other circumstances, this lack of history was a problem. Some tried to stress, often to no avail, how important, how educated or how elevated had been their position before they left home. Some used this denial to wipe out past misdeeds or past sorrows; others were afraid to trust people they knew nothing about.

The future, for many people in Spain, is an empty space too. Few people plan their futures concretely, other than knowing they do not want to return to Britain. 'We might never go back to Wales', said Tony, a resident aged 35, 'but we might not stay around here.' There is a ubiquitous sense of timelessness. For older people this perhaps reflects what Hazan (1994) has defined as an attempt to deny one's place in history and the 'inevitable' future of old age, dependence and death. Perhaps it is an attempt to challenge the concept of time as flowing in a single linear direction. For everyone it lends a sense of living in the here-and-now. It is expressed in behaviour as well as words. If an event is in progress, no-one seems to want to bring it to an end, nor even to know how to end it. On several occasions I attended an event and, often being the last to leave, found myself roped into doing the washing-up or the clearing away because no-one had volunteered or planned for this part. If one goes home during a party they may be teased, even if they have been there for hours and it all seems to be over.

I have already shown, in Chapter 4, the importance placed by migrants on the quality of leisure time. Similarly, there is a shared ethos that time itself is relaxed; no-one should feel pressured nor made to rush, no-one should worry too much about being on time. Walking with the Field Club, for example, was an unpressured and uncompetitive experience since the club ethos strongly insists that no-one should feel they have to cover the route in a given time, if at all. Walks are organised in such a way that participants can turn back or rest at several stages along the way. The British draw on images of a spatialised Spain to support this; for example, they refer with affection to 'the *mañana* syndrome', where tomorrow can mean anything from tomorrow to eternity. The Spanish, for them, are unreliable where time is concerned. In Spain time stands still; it is a little backward and slow, and the pace of life reflects this. This space in Spain allows them to be, legitimately, the same.

In Fuengirola few British people plan things far in advance and they always seem to be free tomorrow. This was something I took a while to get used to: not having to make appointments, being let down at the last minute, taking each day as it came, and making few and flexible plans. Once I turned up to an interview an hour and a half late (I had got lost) and my profuse apologies were met with laughter. The couple I had gone to interview had forgotten I was coming and had been out at the time I should have arrived. On another occasion I arrived to interview a couple at a prearranged time and caught them leaving the building as I arrived, with their towels rolled under their arms. 'Ah, hello', said the man, as he saw me approaching, 'we're just off to Heidi's for a swim. Are you coming? You can talk to us there – or tomorrow?'

As part of the 'residential tourist' identity, worklessness is celebrated and the work/leisure distinction is blurred. Many permanent migrants have *retired* to Spain and are therefore 'leisured' people, while those who work are likely to be doing so within the tourist industry, providing for other British residents, visitors and tourists. They run bars, laundries, letting agencies, property maintenance, hairdressers and other services in which the customers are a mix of resident and visiting Briton. Those who have retired or are living on savings may often need to top up their income with a little extra work but this is likely to be informal and irregular. There is a standing joke about work, displayed in oft-quoted phrases: 'Work, I tried that once and didn't like it' and 'I didn't come here to work'. Sharing an identity as hedonist may have led to the exclamation: 'Many of us have come here to die and we want to have some fun before we go' (Terry, sixties, Full Resident). One barman I interviewed was apparently very angry at news reports (on British television) that people who owned bars in Spain were working long hours and had no time to enjoy the benefits of life in the sun. He told me:

> We only work a few hours a day, and even then it doesn't feel like work 'cos when you're mixing with people who are happy and having a good time, 'cos they're on holiday, they're not miserable like if you go to a pub in England and no-one speaks to you.
>
> (Jack, forties, Full Resident)

Few residents admitted, except amongst themselves, to working hard; it's not what life in Spain is supposed to be about.

Living 'the Spanish way'

As well as identifying with an ethos of holiday and tourism, the residents portray commitment to certain values which they perceive as Spanish. The relationship between the Spanish and the more permanent migrants is not purely based on notions of ethnicity. Although Britons consider they are ethnically different to the Spanish, as a group in opposition to other Britons they believe they share traits with the Spanish. These Britons are not the ethnocentrics that the colonists apparently were. They do not share the 'ruling–class mentality' or the desire to remain intact or unsullied. In intra-ethnic situations, at least, they are keen not to emphasise differences between themselves and the Spanish. They even identify as being like the Spanish to an extent, in that they value certain of their perceived traits.

Resident Britons share symbols of their Spanish identity; they greet each other with kisses on both cheeks, adopt the culture of *mañana*, and adopt community values. Several Britons explained to me their habit of arranging to meet each other in public spaces such as bars and restaurants by suggesting that is what life is like in Spain: 'The Spanish don't pop round like we do (in Britain)', one woman told me.[10] As I described in Chapter 2, they cited the lack of violent crime, feeling safe in the streets, the respect young people show for the elderly, the love of children the Spanish obviously have, the sense of community, and the slow pace of life in Spain all as reasons for moving. Implicit in such statements is another that says 'We are like this too, and not like people in modern Britain.' Spain is not merely a holiday space, it is also a nostalgic place reminding them of how Britain used to be. In a romantic alignment of days gone by and present-day Spain, community is considered stronger and traditional values are still in place. Ken, a bar owner who had lived in Fuengirola ten years explained:

> It's like Britain was in the fifties – like turning the clocks back. Like the time when people knew their neighbours and cared about them, and you could go out and leave your door unlocked, and it was safe to walk the streets at night, and children weren't shut away and hidden like they are now, like some sort of parasites, and families were close.

Spain is portrayed by the British migrants as a place where people still respect their elderly and where family life is valued. Such things are used as justifications for coming to Spain, and yet these people have often left behind their own families, and with them their pasts. Similar findings are reported by Buller and Hoggart (1994: 128) on the British home-owners living in rural France: 'A number of interviewees claimed that France reminded them of rural Britain of the 1950s or even before that, at which time, they maintained, a sense of rural community and local identity still existed.' J. Boissevain argues that this attitude or nostalgia is characteristic of modern capitalist society, in which the past is being commoditised: '[A]nother trend characteristic of today and likely to continue into the future is a romantic longing for the past' (Boissevain 1994: 51). For David Lowenthal (1985) the past is like a foreign country which we visit and gaze upon as exotic; for these British migrants the foreign country suggests the past.[11] It offers 'alternatives to an unacceptable present' (Lowenthal 1985: 49), an alternative which can be constructed from their own imaginings and with which they can identify as part of who they are now (I was therefore I am). For, as B. Curtis and C. Pajaczkowska discuss (1994: 199), 'there is a sense in which a foreign country is always a past – involving both alienation and an act of recovery.'

There is also a sense, amongst more permanent migrants, that the images of 'welcoming community' and 'quality of life' must be upheld. This was revealed when two tourists were discussing a mugging and a resident retorted, 'Oh, but she wasn't attacked was she, that was just a robbery really, not a mugging.' When a British resident in Spain was telling a group of residents that she had been assaulted near her home by a man holding a knife to her throat, it seemed as if either no-one was listening or that they did not really believe her: the incident was dismissed in silence. Complaints about the more irritating aspects of life in Spain (the fact that you apparently cannot rely on a Spanish plumber to come tomorrow if he says he will, for example) are counteracted with comments like 'but that's why we love it here'. Implicit in these statements of Spanish values is the suggestion that Britain no longer shares these values, but that the British residents in Spain do. The construction of a new identity within Fuengirola is therefore involving a reworking of history and an appeal to a core sense of self: a continuity rather than a break. As Cohen has argued (1985: 109), individuals gain their sense of self through a shared 'way of life', a way of life which at the same time differs from the way of life of other groups. Rather than giving up on who they are, losing their core sense of identity or their sense of a continuity of self, their appeal to Spanishness can be interpreted as a continuation of their own feelings of Britishness. Modern Britain thereby represents a break with tradition, and Spain offers an escape from it – an escape to the past. Spain offers a way of life, a lifestyle, or, what Anthony Giddens (cited in Aldridge 1995: 417) describes as: 'A more or less integrated set of practices which an individual [or group] embraces, not only because such practices fulfil utilitarian needs, but because they give material form to a particular narrative of self-identity.'

Conclusion

The Britons in Spain are accused of not mixing with the Spanish, of not learning the language, and of not making any attempt to integrate. They are described by some academics as living in ghettos, with the covert assumption that this is problematic. Such accusations reflect a common concern that migrants should integrate, assimilate or acculturate into the dominant culture, and that if they do not, if they retain a strong sense of ethnic community and identity, then this is potentially a situation of conflict. I learned, through long-term participant observation, that to say that the Britons are not integrating, are constructing and acting on a strong sense of ethnic identity, or that they are perhaps re-creating a 'little England' in Spain is oversimplistic. What is interesting is that it is first necessary to distinguish between temporary and more permanent British migrants (as they do amongst themselves), and having done that we begin to notice differences in their orientation towards Spain. Although they appear not to be integrated into Spanish society in any way, permanent migrants often told me that they are integrated; that they spend a lot of time with Spanish people, do learn about the country and the culture, and do attempt to integrate as far as structural, ideological and language constraints allow.

Difference to Spanish, and ethnic discreteness are not stressed; in fact it is almost taboo to highlight or discuss the lack of integration or communication between the two cultures. British ethnicity is not politically organised, nor is it stressed in interaction with the Spanish. It is not the result of a threat against their ethnic identity or their ethnic discreteness. It seems to be more of a 'we' identification with other Britons than a 'they' identification against the Spanish. Additionally, their ethnic identity, or the persistence of ethnic grouping and ethnic behaviour, does not appear to reflect for the more permanent migrants a lack of desire to integrate, nor a myth of return to the homeland, nor a romantic view of the homeland as is often used to explain the non-integration of other migrant groups into the dominant culture or structures. A more relevant identification is with tourists and tourism; it is expressed in terms of an escapist culture, and reflects a view of Spain constructed via tourism. However, some identification is in opposition to tourists, and with a 'good Spain' which reminds them of a bygone Britain. These migrants identify with certain Spanish traits such as community, responsibility, caring and sharing. But, in this creation of a new culture which borrows from both Britain and Spain, the British in Spain cannot truly create themselves free of the nets that bind most of us, the nets of history and memory (see Ignatieff 1998). The most we can achieve is some distance between what we are expected to be and what we are. The nation's history remains our history, as we shall see in Chapter 7.

6 The construction of community

The British in Spain are not exactly living in ghettos or enclaves, as depicted in the representations of them discussed in Chapter 1. In fact their isolation and discreteness are better conceptualised in terms of networking, exchange and the construction of symbolic boundaries than in terms of residential segregation. This is not so much an ethnic group as a symbolic community. Many British migrants, be they Full or Returning Residents, Seasonal or Peripatetic Visitors (see Chapter 3), are not learning the Spanish language to a level that enables them to interact with the indigenous population on any more than a superficial level. Many spend their leisure and work time with other Britons, and may be considered to lead lives isolated from the wider community; but this is achieved via complex networking and exchange and through the construction of symbolic rather than physical, geographically defined communities.

Following Wittgenstein's advice, Cohen (1985: 12) suggests that rather than attempting to define a community, we consider the word's *use*, in context. In use, he continues, the word implies two related suggestions: that the members of a group of people (a) have something in common with each other which (b) distinguishes them in a significant way from the members of other putative groups. Rather than implying some fixed thing, then, community suggests a relation, a boundary, a distinction between a group and other social entities. The community of British migrants in Spain, which should not be characterised as purely an *ethnic* group for reasons discussed in the previous chapter, is a symbolic one. It exists in the consciousness of its members, but it means different things to different people. In some ways it reflects or establishes structural boundaries but in many ways the boundaries are symbolic, shifting and ambiguous (Cohen 1985). It is a community organised loosely around ethnicity rather than an ethnic group. The term 'community' is more useful than the term 'ethnic group' because it allows for more identifications than merely ethnicity. To label a group 'ethnic' is often no more than to imply a 'race' or 'tribe', no matter how respectable the attempt to move away from such an ascription. An outsider cannot identify where the British community in Spain starts and stops, especially not in terms of individuals and identifiable traits. What can perhaps be shown is that in certain actions, behaviours and words, one of the many things some Britons are symbolising is 'community' and a boundary. However, as John Davis (1992) has argued, symbols evoke rather than denote: sometimes the community evoked is 'not Spanish' and sometimes it is 'not typically British'. Sometimes symbols evoke both segment and community at one and the same time but to different people. Sometimes the community includes other 'foreign nationals' (especially Irish and Americans, who share a language with Britons) and sometimes it does not (as on St George's Day, for example). The boundaries are in flux and can be constructed, reconstructed, deconstructed, imagined or denied according to individual and group needs, according to context, and according to the presence or not of a visible 'Other'.

Ghettos, enclaves and communities

M. Anwar (1979: 11) has said that 'extensive research shows that individuals with similar cultural origins tend to cluster together and thus become *residentially* segregated from the rest of society' (my emphasis). Similarly, authors writing on the topic of retirement to Spain from Britain or other northern European countries hypothesise that migrants are settling in ghetto-style enclaves or in the special tourist developments (*urbanizaciones particulares turísticas*) which are 'like oil slicks rhythmically extending further and further into the coastline demolishing everything in their way' from where they begin a process of colonisation of which they are themselves the victims (Jurdao and Sanchez 1990). 'This has resulted . . . in the implantation of British enclaves in Spain', says Russell King (1993: 196). Tony Champion and Russell King have argued that 'elderly migrants do tend to cluster in purpose-built tourist and residential complexes . . . a kind of enclave mentality develops which has some curious parallels with the quasi-ghettos of labour migrant ethnic communities of the north' (Champion and King 1993: 54). Newspaper journalists and popular sentiment mirror these same ideas, as seen in Chapter 1. My response to these hypotheses is twofold: (a) one needs to be aware of the emotive issues surrounding what have become the pejorative terms of enclave and ghetto; and (b) conceptualising residence in these terms obscures the intricacies of community networking. I shall deal with these responses in turn.

The term 'ghetto' originated with Jewish residential segregation in Venice in the sixteenth century and was later used to refer to all and any Jewish urban residential area. It became used in early twentieth-century America with specific reference to the black, poor, ethnic minority neighbourhoods which grew as a consequence of black, labour immigration and subsequent segregation (Clark 1965). Historically, the concept is linked to power, oppression, segregation policies and practice, and black politics (Meier and Rudwick 1970). Even when used to refer to better-off members of a minority group (as with the phrase 'gilded ghetto'), it continues to imply voluntary or involuntary residential segregation and isolation (Forman 1971: 3). 'Enclave' is an imprecise but territorial term, again with racist connotations – a residential area enclosing an ethnic group. The use of these terms and concepts reflects the source of such assumptions, i.e. 'casual observation, impressionistic newspaper, television and radio accounts, and personal contacts' (Warnes 1991: 55). They are pejorative terms which obscure the real relations between British migrants and Spanish people.

My research in Fuengirola reveals that while there are areas of high concentration of British migrants, these do not warrant the term 'ghetto' or 'enclave' since boundaries are unclear, and since Britons are more likely to reside (be it temporarily or permanently) in mixed neighbourhoods with a distinctly international flavour and culture. While the homes of more affluent Britons are scattered in various areas around the edges of the town, and working-class Britons find themselves in clusters in certain parts of the town itself; migrants of all types are living in close proximity to Spanish and other nationals. Los Boliches is an area of Fuengirola with a high concentration of British residents and tourists. However, within Los Boliches Britons are scattered in apartment blocks, villas, chalets, and urbanisations alongside people of other nationalities.[1] Though King *et al.* (1998) are right to suggest that many British migrants in the Costa del Sol live in purpose-built urbanisations where foreigners are numerically dominant, there are no single, geographically distinct British ghettos. The only ethnic group in this area which could reasonably be described as living in a 'gilded ghetto' or enclave is the Finnish population who have a clearly demarcated residential area named *Avenida de Finlandia*. The presence of this residentially segregated area throws into relief the residential (or touring) arrangements of the Britons and other foreign nationals. As I said above, this chapter argues that the ethnic identity and behaviour of British migrants are better conceptualised in terms of networking and exchange, and the construction of a symbolic community than in terms of residential segregation.

The periphery, informality and exchange

This community, for more permanent migrants, can be characterised in terms of marginality and informality. The construction of informal networks – what M. Anwar (1979) calls inter-linkages between people which they themselves build (and many of the social and economic activities in which they are engaged) – occur on the margins of mainstream Spanish society. They are both informal and undocumented as well as exclusive of Spanish influence or involvement.

There are numerous British-run clubs and social groups. Generally they are not referred to by their members as British groups; indeed, one of the largest even calls itself an International Club, although the great majority of its members are British. The clubs are often not part of or affiliated to formal Spanish structures, and are therefore independent, and can be characterised by their unbureaucratic and relatively informal nature. R. Hedley (1992) has shown that such 'voluntary' organisations blur the definition between public and private spheres; they are in the ambiguous zone between bureaucracy and privacy. The members of these organisations in Spain consist of both resident and visiting Britons, but, with Full Residents often being in a minority in these clubs in terms of numbers, the membership is usually fluid. Individual members frequently return to Britain permanently or seasonally so membership fluctuates (see Chapter 3). The only continuous presence is often a small minority of Full Resident members, who, with a few Returning Residents, form the committees. As C. Rochester (1992) found in a study of community organisations in a village setting, and as is true of such organisations in general, the commitment to the group is voluntary and as such there can be no clear distinction between employer and employee, between statuses or income groups. Relationships within the clubs can thus be ambiguous and open to various interpretations.

Charity groups within the British community[2] are also external to Spanish society in that they are all voluntary and as such cannot be bureaucratised within a formal organisation (see Hobman 1988 on 'the role of the volunteer worker'). They are mainly run by British people and have British volunteers. Even the hospice project, Cudeca (described in Chapter 4), which soon hopes to have raised enough money to build a hospice in the area for people of all nationalities, was set up by a British woman, has a British president, has mainly British volunteers and patients,[3] and the fund-raising is mainly done by British people. People of other nationalities are formally but voluntarily involved within the structure of the organisation as doctors, psychiatrists, nurses and advisers, but many of these are English-speaking professionals with experience of the British experience of hospice care. The organisers of the hospice project are aware that what they are trying to do is at odds with Spanish culture and Spanish health arrangements (in that private health providers feel threatened by the possible loss of revenue) and that they therefore exist on the fringes of Spanish society, at least for now.

Many resident Britons are involved in either club committee work, volunteering or fund-raising in one way or another within their own community. In the winter, when there are more British migrants in Spain in the form of Returning Residents and Seasonal Visitors (see Chapter 3), I became increasingly aware that although the majority of migrants do not work formally, there was a lot of work and activity going on in the form of volunteering, running and organising group activities, and committee work. The English-language newspaper, the *Sur in English*, in 1993 had a clubs' page, advertising foreign clubs and social groups, with the title 'Here to help. All the people on this page are here to make your life easier or more pleasant!' Some of what people are doing in such a situation is working to build a community, working to construct their own world, motivated by feelings of solidarity (Rochester 1992).

Formal work by Britons is often marginal because it tends to be within the service industry providing for other Britons, whether they be tourists, visitors or residents. This is not to say that they do not have Spanish customers – they do, but their business is generally directed towards Britons.[4] These enterprises are often small and peripheral. They are not subject to the same wider economic forces, such as changes in unemployment rates, recession and so on, to which many ethnic economic niches seem vulnerable (see Werbner 1987 for example). In some ways they are even independent of the Spanish economy, except, that is, in its relationship to the British one, and to currency exchange rates. While currency exchange rates remain favourable to the British, visitors and tourists will continue to visit Spain and to provide custom for the 'ethnic' or marginal economy. Similarly, while exchange rates are favourable, tourists (and those migrants whose income generates from within Britain) will have money to spend in the British-run service industries selling laundry care, car rental and so on.

Many people are working informally within the British ethnic community in informal economic activities which 'elude government requirements such as registration, tax and social security obligations, and health and safety rules', to use B. Roberts's (1989) definition. Pensioners and those living on their savings may be topping up their incomes; women might be trying to bring in a little extra; younger men and women are earning what they can where they can rather than going back to England to claim dole. They are involved in all sorts of activities from home maintenance, decorating and ironing, to taxying, pool maintenance and car mechanics. Even those who are working formally (perhaps running their own estate agency, laundry or bar) are often involved in the informal economy in the form of labour or goods exchange. For example, one bar owner manages property for a few British owners who only visit their home once or twice a year and in the meantime rent it out to holiday-makers. She organises the rentals, collects the rent, arranges gas bottle deliveries, meets the tourists on arrival in Spain, pays the utility bills, organises re-decoration, and cleans the apartments for the owners. The same woman also sells videos and birthday cards on behalf of a friend, and tries to raise money for Cudeca. A laundry owner supplements her income by cutting people's hair in their own homes and teaching Spanish to other foreign nationals. A pensioner who retired early from the armed forces does electrical repairs and gardening and rents out two rooms in his home to British tourists.

In addition to the considerable amount of informal work amongst the British there is a lot of networking and exchange of advice, information, help and even goods like videos and books. Cards and letters are posted by people returning to Britain rather than relying on the Spanish postal system; bar owners and regulars give advice about settling into Spain, about the legalities and loopholes; individuals spend endless hours exchanging ideas about where to go and what to do, about good places to eat and where to get certain British or essential goods. Whenever you want to know something or do something, from renting an apartment to getting a watch battery, it is best to ask a settled British expatriate who has found out all the best avenues of help, advice and purchase, as the following excerpts demonstrate.

Alan, a friend of Ken and Jessie's, has been staying here on holiday in an apartment of a friend of theirs. Ken and Jessie got this young man a gas bottle and paid for it. He paid them back in the bar. Jack picked this young man up from the airport and ran him back at the end of his holiday. Yesterday morning Jack had been to the airport three times to meet people.

(Field notes, October 1993)

Trevor was looking for some birthday cards to buy for Justin today. He mentioned this to Nancy and she said that she has some under the bar. She sold him two. Trevor signed them for us all, stuck English stamps on them and gave them back to Nancy so that customers can post them in England for him. There are always people going back, she said, and the mail gets there in a couple of days whereas from here it takes two weeks. She had asked John to bring her stamps when he was going to England. Ken and Jessie often keep a stock of English stamps for this purpose and often send mail back with people and for other people. The Spanish are left out of the whole transaction.

(Field notes, November 1993)

Edward mentioned a book to me, that he thought would interest me. I asked where I can get English books and Ann told me of a good book shop near Barclays Bank. Sheila told me they usually ask someone who is going back to England. 'Why don't you ask Edward to get it for you? He's going back next week.' Joan told me she has friends in Scotland (I think) who post books for her when she needs them. They all agreed that books here are more expensive and take a long while to arrive when ordered. It is quicker and cheaper to ask someone back home to post them for you, apparently.

(Field notes, March 1994)

I noticed that the valet service does all sorts of work over and above the line of duty and not all for money. They loan cots and pushchairs to non-tenants, they give advice, they listen to troubles, they get gas bottles filled, they even loan books, and they are there for people, just to listen and give advice. Sometimes it can get very demanding, Jan said.

(Field notes, June 1994)

The construction of community

The informal economy and exchange

A great deal of this activity, which may or may not be defined by outsiders as economic activity, is defined by participants as 'helping each other out'. The volunteers at Lux Mundi were 'helping out there'. The welfare workers were 'helping people out'. When Jack picked people up from the airport, he was 'helping them out' and when Mary posted letters for someone in England she was 'just helping'. Even Peter, who did a lot of jobs on the side, sometimes referred to this as 'helping someone out of a spot' and sometimes as 'earning a bit of cash'. It is clear that the generally accepted boundary between economic and social, and between formal and informal activity is in some ways an artificial one imposed by those in whose interest it is to regulate some activities and not others. Similarly, behaviour that appears to be essentially profit-motivated and individualistic may not carry these same meanings for the actors involved. It is often social activity, vital to the construction and maintenance of community. As J. Gaughan and L. Ferman (1987: 25) have said:

> A very wide range of informal activity is of the social variety, part of the cohesive force uniting people in all societies founded upon kinship and community . . . A good part of the informal economy, with its emphasis on mutual obligation and reciprocity, forms a nexus of social glue that makes the formation and maintenance of social life possible.

The informal economy – the exchange of market commodities including labour and services which remain unrecorded or unrecognised by the state; and economic activity which is 'off the record' – has caught the attention of academics in recent years. It is a phenomenon which is considered to be growing in 'western' economies, especially since the 1970s. It is often seen as being linked to recession and to mass immigration, and tends to be viewed as the result of survival strategies of the poor and the marginalised (Sassen-Koob 1989). Studies of the informal economy do not usually include voluntary work and social networks of exchange, but I believe they are part of the same phenomenon of the informal construction of social and community life. Though they are more obviously social and less easily characterised as economic, nevertheless the activities involved in volunteering are often seen as 'work'; whilst exchange is often rationalised by the actors themselves as profit-maximising behaviour and can therefore be coupled with informal economic activity. However, informal exchange, reciprocation, and the establishing of informal networks not subject to state formalisation or bureaucracy are more social and communal than the formal economy and formal institutional organisation. Such activities of networking and exchange feature persistently in the daily lives of British migrants in Fuengirola.

So, while informal activity for some social groups is closely integrated within the wider economy, for others it remains confined to their own marginal groups (see, for example, Stepick 1989: 116). The informal activities of the Britons in this part of Spain are marginal, occurring at the edges of Spanish society and outside the regulation of the state. Even more formal activities such as formal work and membership of officially recognised social groups such as the Royal British Legion, are nevertheless peripheral activities within Spanish society, and are therefore British community activities.

Embeddedness in social networks

The *informality* of work, exchange and volunteering is, however, not as complete as it might initially appear: activities are subject to internal regulation and control; they are governed by social rules and implicit taboos. All exchange has social meaning, suggests John Davis (1992). Exchange can include many things from work to volunteering, from giving advice to swapping videos. If a return is expected, whether it be equal or not, then the activity can be called exchange, and is social. Exchange 'enables people to lead a socially integrated life and interact with those around them' – exchange expedites integration, says Marilyn Strathern (1992: 169). Exchange between British migrants contributes to the building of marginal and informal community structures. It both reflects and establishes accepted community values. Settled migrants exchange more with other settled migrants than they do with temporary British visitors, and much more than they do with people of other nationalities. This reflects identification with others of the same ethnic group, but, beyond that, with others with similar tastes and aspirations. They are thus constructing a community drawing on the values they share; values that reflect their culture as permanent British tourists and as escapees of a depressing modern Britain. The culture to which they aspire relies on traditional community values of equality, responsibility, caring and support. The sort of work people do and the rules governing work and exchange in this community reflect the ethos of fun and leisure, but also of community and responsibility.

The goods and information that are exchanged symbolise, on one level, Britishness. Britons exchange English-language videos and books amongst themselves, presuming a shared interest in contemporary cultural symbols including the latest film to be showing in Britain and best-selling books by authors such as Stephen King and Barbara Cartland. National Lottery tickets are sold, pools coupons are collected and sent back to Britain, Grand National sweepstakes are organised and men share information on British sports results.

The work people do voluntarily reflects the community symbols of responsibility and caring, and also the ethos of fun and leisure. The act of doing voluntary work is in itself an expression of commitment and concern: 'Support given within the community by its own members to those who live nearby is a practical expression of a commitment to the creation of a caring society', says Hobman (1988: 137). Volunteers at the Lux Mundi coffee mornings each Tuesday and Thursday admit that they work hard and are committed. However, voluntary work retains the element of choice, autonomy and irregularity: it is not formal work; workers cannot be sanctioned if they step out of line (see Hobman 1988). At the same time the nature of this work is part of making life in Spain enjoyable, comfortable and easy for all migrants. It is not work aimed at rising profits – the gains are social not monetary. A great deal of hard and voluntary (unpaid) work goes into running social clubs and groups and organising the social and leisure aspects of life in Spain. Enjoyment and pleasure are also enthusiastically shared as a great deal of advice and information is exchanged on places to eat out, places to visit and so on.

Embeddedness in social relationships

Exchange also symbolises hidden hierarchies within the overtly egalitarian system. Permanent migrants exchange more with other permanent migrants since they value the others' commitment to staying in Spain. The type of exchange they engage in with more temporary migrants reflects and establishes their own status as settled and knowledgeable. Established residents give advice to new residents on settling in, on residence permits, paying the electricity bill, joining the health centre. They give advice to tourists and visitors on what to do and where to go, thereby establishing themselves as the well-informed party and the newcomer as lower in this particular hierarchy.

Time spent in Spain and commitment to the country are valued in this community. People are more likely to overestimate their length of residence than underestimate it. Those who had been there thirty years told me so with great pride. Many of the people I was told I *must* interview were the long-term residents and therefore established members of the ethnic community. People were shocked, for example, to find that having spent seven months in Fuengirola, I still had not managed to interview a woman who had been living there for thirty years. And a group who play bowls together insisted that the one member I should meet was the man who had been there longer than anyone else. This quote from a local English-language magazine puts it succinctly:

> All foreign residents of Spain have a sin in common. They didn't bring it with them, but began to develop it within weeks after arrival. Within months it had taken hold, though not too comfortably. Within years it had become deeply embedded in the soul, and discomfort had faded with the guilt. The sin is snobbery. We're all snobs in relation to the longevity of our residence.
>
> (Lovell 1994: 21)

Settled migrants have more to bring to the exchange in the way of knowledge, contacts and goods. This establishes their higher status within the networks. Knowledge of the area, of the pitfalls of settling there, of laws and regulations, and of where to go or who to ask to get what, is highly valued. Its use is in its exchange value not in its retention. An 'expatriate' cannot easily find his or her way on to a committee; one's commitment to the club and especially to staying in Spain will have to be proven over time. I offered to act as secretary on behalf of a social organisation which was having problems filling this position. I was not sure I wanted to commit myself to such a time-consuming role but was persuaded by the outgoing secretary that I should just 'give it a try for a while' and see how I got on. During the conversation with this secretary, in which she was trying to persuade me to take on the role, I let it be known that I would be returning to England for good within a few months. The secretary's attitude changed dramatically. She now told me it would not be worth my while taking on the position since I would be unable to commit myself to it for any length of time. Apparently it was not important that I might try the job and give up, what was more important was that I was able to commit myself to staying in Spain and therefore make a commitment to the community. Without this it was not worth my taking the job even for a short period. In another situation, a man challenged the accepted method of self-advancement by being promoted prematurely to a position of authority. As a family member of another official, Philip was granted an influential position within the church organisation very shortly after his arrival in Fuengirola. This created a lot of bad feeling, and several grumbles were quietly heard about the way he just came in and took over when 'several of us have been here for years'. What he had been in the past was in some ways unimportant (see Chapter 4); but more than that, the fact that he had not been a resident long was crucially important.

Community-building

'Community is a matter of mediations and reciprocations', says D. Sabean (1984). Informality, exchange, reciprocation, marginalisation and the building of networks are community-building work. They are not, in this situation, the result of a desperate minority group struggling to survive under conditions of racism and persecution, in the way authors have often attempted to explain the informal economic activity of migrant communities (see Castells and Portes 1989: 12). Rather than helping them *survive*, this community-building 'work' is enabling people to enjoy Spain, to enjoy their stay there, to help them settle and feel part of things, and even to remain in Spain when things do not work out as planned. Migrants are pulling together to make this new mode of life work for all of them. They help each other to make it work and, in doing so, they help make it work for themselves. Community-building is a creative not a static force. Just as Greek Cypriots in Britain developed an ethnic economy which provides employment and services for other Cypriots (Anthias 1992) and Pakistanis in Britain created work for themselves and for other Pakistanis (Anwar 1979), so Britons in Spain provide work for themselves and others who want to stay on. Consider the case of Trevor and Ruth:

Case

Trevor and Ruth moved to Fuengirola when Trevor's landscape gardening business in England began to fail. They sold the business and their home in England and moved to Spain on the proceeds. The intention was to rent a home in Spain, to live off their capital and to stretch it a little further by working casually when they could. They hoped to get by until they reached retirement age in about five years' time, when they could claim their state pensions, saving what was left of their capital for 'a rainy day'. In Spain, they believed, their capital would be worth more than in England, since the cost of living is considered to be cheaper. They would have more for their money and would be able to enjoy the sun and the scenery and the way of life in Spain in their retirement and before.

As it turned out, the cost of living was comparatively more expensive than they had calculated, they found little work to supplement their income, and Ruth desperately missed her grandchildren. They began to talk of return-ing to England. In response, friends and acquaintances passed on little bits of work and recommended Trevor as an odd-job man to anyone they knew. Ruth was encouraged to join the British Legion and to accompany friends to social gatherings. One friend helped them find an apartment closer to the centre of the town so that they would not feel so isolated. They were invited to parties and outings. Trevor was invited to join a darts team.

Eventually Trevor and Ruth decided to go home for a few weeks to make up their minds whether to return to England indefinitely. While they were there, I was told by a friend who heard from them that they were having an awful time in England and couldn't wait to get back to Spain. Apparently it was freezing cold and Ruth was finding British people depressing. Ruth returned to Spain, however, to tell me that she had been very happy in England and couldn't wait to go home. Trevor and Ruth left Spain two months later.

The British migrants work hard to include and retain members, but it is important to note that what is being built is not British and not Britain, although it draws on symbols of Britishness. The way of life they imagine and construct using the rhetoric of community and drawing on images of Spain and Spanishness is constructed and reconstructed in more concrete and experiential terms through the networking and exchange along ethnic lines. All those advantages of living in Spain discussed in Chapters 2 and 4 are made to come true for Britons committed to staying and creating a new life there. For those not committed, like Trevor and Ruth, all the networking and resources available are utilised in order to help them change their minds.

Belonging

The community shares a symbol of equality. As I have said in Chapter 4, there is an explicit agreement that it should not matter what you were in the past, for this is a new life and a new community within which you can, or indeed need, to prove yourself. It should not matter what one was in the past, states the discourse of equality. This involves a denial of personal history and can lead to a disembodied sense of self. People who cannot legitimately draw on who they once were and what they have done in the past have the opportunity to be who they want to but can feel lost without the sense of a continuity of self. R. Voase (1995) suggests that individuals like the British in Spain, who have left their home communities, who have lost the sense of identity once gained through work and social roles, have lost a sense of who they are. This is apparently true, but some of this sense of self is recovered for Britons when they discuss the 'way of life' in Spain and draw on a general identity in terms of 'who we once were' in Britain. A sense of who they are is also sought within the new community, which replaces other affective ties lost through migration.

Place, status and belonging are sought and found within the community of British residents and tourists, within the clubs, bars and organisations, and within the informal economy and the networks of exchange. Residents gain positions on the committees of the various clubs, work as volunteers in the various self-help organisations, exchange work and services within their own networks, and thereby work to construct a sense of community and within this a sense of place for themselves. For Hobman (1988: 13), voluntary work 'makes it possible for countless men and women from all social classes and of different ages to find an effective means of self-expression'. Chapter 4 described the British community in Fuengirola, which includes the following: several Royal British Legion branches; an Ecumenical Centre which runs coffee mornings, church services, bingo, a library and other services for residents and tourists alike; a hospice project with volunteers running charity shops, fund-raising and visiting terminally ill patients; church coffee mornings and bazaars; and numerous social and activity clubs such as the Fuengirola and District Society (FADS). These institutions are generally organised and run by British residents who thereby gain positions of power and status in relation to the other individuals in the community of both residents and tourists. They thereby find effective means of self-expression through their various roles as receptionist, librarian, nurse, jumble sale organiser and so on.

Many of the clubs have huge committees in relation to the numbers of their members. One dancing group has less than a hundred members of which twenty-five are committee members. The Costa del Sol branch of the Royal British Legion at one point had 300 members of which sixty-one were members of one or other committee organising and running the club (RBL 1993). Some of these committee members were also elected to the executive committee. Clubs and social groups thus each have their own hierarchies within which status can be acquired by those individuals who give time and commitment to the community.

Position is slowly earned and jealously guarded, as my own experiences show. I offered my services as volunteer for one group and was asked to make coffees for the 'staff' (other volunteers) at the weekly coffee mornings. When the staff had been served coffee, I initially stayed behind the counter to help serve customers. One morning I stayed on two extra hours and worked very hard. I was quite pleased with myself for being so helpful. However, it was not long before I realised I had almost literally 'stepped out of place'. Women whose role it was to serve coffees were afraid I was stealing their jobs and had made a formal complaint about me. The following week their supervisor spoke to me quietly and asked me to 'please, next week, just serve staff coffees and then leave'. One of the other volunteers, who worked on the jumble sale, later informed me that I had nearly caused a strike: the women had threatened to walk out unless I was made to back off!

A few months later, however, I was offered the opportunity to make coffees for the staff as usual but then to stay on and help with the coffees for customers at a bazaar to be held there that morning. This was a promotion of sorts since it was a more public position: I could now be seen to be a volunteer. Later still, when I had been a volunteer for this group for several months, I was given a job which was much more in the public eye: I worked as receptionist on the club desk once a week. I realised I had at last achieved some status in the group. My commitment to the group, expressed by being there week after week, month after month, had finally been rewarded with a public role.

By slowly granting place and status, the community allows space for permanent residents to replace the feeling of belonging they lost on leaving their homes, their histories, their families, and even a sense of who they are, in Britain. Permanent migrants gradually gain positions of status in relation to newer or temporary migrants. Commitment to the British community is rewarded by position and power, which is then jealously guarded, as evidenced in the story above.

A 'gloss of commonality'[5]

Permanent migrants identify as being equal, as all committed to Spain, as not caring what each was in the past, as egalitarian, as committed to a slow pace of life, but also to community and sharing and caring, to elderly, to family, and to casual informality and so on. However, there are many differences between migrants which become more evident in community spaces such as clubs and societies, but which are glossed over in some situations to give the appearance of commonality. For example, it has already been seen that permanent migrants expect and achieve status over temporary migrants, and that length of commitment to the community is rewarded. One evidence of status is in the use of first and surnames when speaking of people of reputation – most Britons in Fuengirola are familiar with the full names of Joan Hunt (president of Cudeca) and Ken Brown (editor of *Lookout* magazine) for example. The Anglican vicar, the Jesuit priest, Father Delius, who founded Lux Mundi, the British Consul and the chairmen of the Royal British Legion branches are all familiar names and surnames. The use of surnames thus acts as a subtle marker of difference and status.

'Ethnicity is a vehicle for the construction of a difference', says Anthias (1992). It is not necessarily a difference in any more real terms than that; and in fact difference can be constructed using other vehicles. In addition to the accepted hierarchies, other differences between Britons come to the fore within community spaces. People are able to express class, age and gender differences and are, in fact, drawing on their background in their choice of friends and acquaintances. There are many levels of identity, with ethnicity being one, community and commitment to Spain being another, and others informing segmentary and individual difference (see Cohen 1987). 'British' bars are often more specifically Scottish, Welsh, Irish or English bars according to the nationality of the owners. Some club organisers insisted they were not class conscious yet maintained quite selective membership. Club members would not admit to competition between clubs yet competition existed in subtle ways: the two Royal British Legion clubs in the area, for example, reflect a definite class divide. Trevor and I were the only people to go to both branches' Christmas dinners in 1993. In fact someone who asked if we were going to the Fuengirola branch dinner was told 'no, they're going to the posh do' (meaning the other one).

Competition between clubs became apparent during fieldwork:

> I introduced Henry to the others, saying 'He sings with the Barber Shop Singers'. He retorted, 'No I don't, don't ever confuse our group with that lot – we are singers!' Henry is in a different club. I got the name wrong.
>
> (Field notes, March 1994).

> I left Lux Mundi in a hurry so that I could get to the FADS social (three big clubs have their social meetings all on Thursday mornings). Jennie asked where I was going and when I told her she sucked in her breath saying 'Ooh, don't tell people here you're going there, they won't like it!'
>
> (Field notes, June 1994).

These clubs were in such blatant competition with each other that they all held their social meetings at the same time.

Some migrants wanted to disassociate themselves from 'other types' of migrant. Harry, a welfare worker with FADS, told me when I first told him about my research:

> Many people just sit in bars or on the beach and they don't really know what Spain is about. But we're not all like that. There are lots of other places and people and you must see them all.

And Hazel, who works as a volunteer for Cudeca, told me:

> I hope you are not just studying those types who sit around in bars all day. God, I've seen some people ruin themselves with alcohol. There's a lot more going on here than that you know. You should visit our bowls club.

Interestingly, such statements of difference were overt as opposed to ethnicity which was a covert, symbolic statement of difference. What unified permanent migrants was their commitment to stay in Spain over and above their commitment to their ethnic origin.

Change, continuity and unity

In addition to these differences, there are other factors apparently contradicting the symbols of community: some people get bored in Spain; some people get lonely; friends can be hard to keep; and people do go home (see Chapter 4). In fact the community is a very fluid one with people arriving and leaving all the time. The biggest threat to this community is an internal rather than external one: it is the threat of transience. As Peggy, a Full Resident in her seventies, told me one morning at the Church bazaar:

> You don't make many friends here, not friends, just acquaintances; isn't that right [turning to a woman looking at the clothes on the rail]? Well one or two real friends, but mostly acquaintances. It's such a transient society. You never know when someone is going to go home you see, and people you thought were here forever . . . then something happens, like with you [turning to the same woman] and suddenly you have to go back. Last year at Lux Mundi they lost something like thirty-six of their regular people.

Change is something the migrants get used to. In the five months between completion of fieldwork and my next visit to Fuengirola, one English-language newspaper had gone broke and another one had started up; one bar had changed hands twice; three bars had new owners; two others were up for sale; a new bar had opened; and three people I knew well had returned to Britain permanently.

This is a community of networks, of informal structures and of symbols more than a set of identifiable individuals; the individuals that it constitutes are changing all the time. But because individuals are gaining their place, belonging and status from within the British community, and because this depends as much on there being permanent as temporary migrants, continuity within the community is stressed more than change, and sameness is stressed more than difference. The symbols of community are drawn on to mark the boundaries between themselves and Britons in Spain rather than between Britons and Spanish. Britain symbolises the threat to community and so the community identity asserted is not an ethnic one in opposition to another ethnie, but a community one in opposition to other Britons.

When new migrants arrive in Fuengirola they are very quickly drawn into the British community by various means. They are welcomed, offered advice and help, directed to other Britons for certain goods, work and help, and are therefore soon in a position of gratitude or debt. 'Both resident and holiday-maker can ... get good, unbiased advice from a bar catering for expatriates', Ronald Elliott advises newcomers in his booklet *Enjoying Good Health Care on the Costa del Sol* (Elliott 1995: 6). New arrivals quickly become involved in the networks of reciprocation and exchange; external structures within which they are encouraged to act and which they then help construct. Newcomers to the community are not given positions of power and influence, but are nevertheless quickly drawn into the networks if at all possible, especially if they show a commitment to stay and to the community.

Arrivals of new migrants were not celebrated, however, and departures were rarely marked. As with all commonly held beliefs, there is some basis to the suggestion that Britons are unhappy in Spain, are poor, isolated and lonely, and desperate to 'come home'. Many permanent migrants left Spain while I was there, for several reasons: either their money had run out or their business had failed, or they had lost a partner and felt the need to be back with other relatives in Britain. One man told me that he saw seven bars fold in one year (in 1992): 'I lost so many of my good friends that year', he said sadly. 'Four on one plane!' (Don, Full Resident, fifties). These return migrants would leave with little or no ceremony. Indeed, it was not unusual for people just to disappear. One woman who had worked voluntarily in an organisation for twenty years announced quietly that she would be returning to England to live. I had expected there to be an event to mark her leaving but on her last day of 'work' she simply said goodbye quietly, as she always did. A popular bar on the sea-front closed down another day, with no ceremony. The owners had gone home, after seven years, without telling anyone of their plans.

When leavings were marked, as they occasionally were, this was taken as an opportunity to celebrate the expected return (of Seasonal Visitors, for example) and the time spent within the British community in Spain rather than being seen as a farewell. One couple who returned to England after four years in Spain had a farewell ceremony in their local bar. While they drank and ate the mixture of British and Spanish traditional party fare (of *tortillas* and *tapas* and sausage rolls and sandwiches), a video of their wedding celebrations, which was held in Fuengirola the year before, played in the background. Several people took the opportunity to describe the wedding to me. No-one was too sad, because everyone expected the couple to return to Spain quite soon. In fact, such was the expectation that people would return that John and Joan, who had been Full Residents for five years, had the belongings of this and three other couples held in a spare room waiting for their return. On departure, commiserations were usually given rather than wishes of health and future happiness. Phrases such as 'They'll be back' and 'They won't settle' were commonly heard. When the woman discussed above announced her departure, another woman turned to me and said, 'I don't know what she wants to go back for, she's just forgotten what it's like there.' Departures, even when the resident was simply going 'home' for Christmas, were grave occasions. When I left Spain at the end of fieldwork a man said to me as consolation, 'Just tell yourself you are going back to England for your hols. Imagine you're coming back in a couple of weeks.'

This denial of comings and goings lent a feeling of continuity to the community, as did the celebrations of anniversaries and birthdays, which were a ubiquitous part of life amongst the more permanent migrants. Each group and club celebrated the passing of time with rituals and celebrations. Bar owners often celebrated the anniversaries of their move to Spain. Club annual general meetings were well attended. Christmas was marked with annual dinners. Birthdays of long-term residents were occasions for celebration. There was thus a marked difference between public and private discourse of arrivals and departures, of happiness in Spain and discontent. Privately, I was often told that individuals were a little lonely or a little bored in Spain and would perhaps go back if their partners died or if they suffered health problems. They would tell me this tentatively, and vehemently deny it in public. One man chatted to me in a bar about his intention to go home at Christmas and not return to Spain. However, when a few other people joined us at our table and asked this man about his trip home, he assured them he would be buying a return ticket.

A result of there being so many arrivals and departures, marked or not, is that the myths of 'bad Britain' and 'good Spain' are stressed overtly, continually and with great strength. I have already discussed these ubiquitous symbols of community which denote boundaries between those who have a commitment to Spain as opposed to Britain, and those who are still essentially British. In many social gatherings – whether in the company of new migrants, temporary migrants, permanent ones or a mixture – the conversation often centred around the way Britain has changed for the worse and around the many advantages of living in Spain. For established residents there were endless opportunities to stress the conviction never to go home, and for new migrants there were eager audiences to their accounts of why they left. Many temporary migrants would search for justifications for not staying in Spain permanently, while some individuals insisted they would stay on if only the partner would agree to it. In this way all migrants were stressing what they share over and above a history, origin, language and nation: an enchantment with Spain and a disillusion with modern Britain.

Blurring the boundaries

In contradiction to such headlines as 'Shadow over a New Life in the Sun' (*Guardian*, 24.6.89); 'A Place in the Sun Loses its Shine' (*Independent on Sunday*, 23.5.93); 'Gloomy Golden Years' and 'Dreams Turn to Nightmares' (see Mendel 1993), permanent migrants constantly impressed on me how much they love living in Spain, that they have done the right thing to move there and, often, that they will never return to Britain. As I have shown in previous chapters, a 'good Spain' discourse contrasts with the 'bad Britain' one. Spain is a wonderful place to be because of its natural resources of sun, sea, sand and scenery. Spain is a happy place to be because of the wonderful Spanish people with their friendly natures, their ready acceptance of foreigners, the importance they give to family and responsibility, the way they respect their elderly, and their obvious love of children. Spain is also a good place to be because there is less crime here, the migrants told me; there is a sense of community, and of caring for each other. There is more to do here, I was told, and leisure is cheaper or free. There is golf, cricket, bowls, tennis, swimming, snorkelling, sailing (see Davey 1990; Holbrook 1993; Reay-Smith 1980). One can go for long walks in the countryside or along the promenade; eating out is cheaper than in Britain; the pace of life is slower, less hurried. C. Holbrook (1993: 16) enthuses: 'The idea that mañana will be soon enough still flourishes, while the shrug of the shoulders remains the most likely answer when you confront officialdom.' Alcohol and cigarettes are cheaper than in Britain; housing is cheaper and more light and airy; and in addition to all that one usually feels healthier. It was impressed on me that 'People are also happier here because you're mixing with holiday-makers all the time.' And, ultimately, the Andalusian zest for life rubs off on you (Holbrook 1993). Rather than wishing they could go home, most migrants are celebrating their lives in Spain. Rather than trying to recreate a little England, most migrants would emphasise the advantages of living in Spain over and above life in Britain.

However, though many of the advantages of living in Spain are attributable to Spanish society and geography (the sun, the scenery, friendly Spanish people, Spanish culture and society), several of the 'good things' cited as benefits of living *here*, in Spain, are more true of life within a British community in Fuengirola rather than of life in Spain *per se*. But Britons do not seek to draw attention to their marginality in Spain; it is disguised through a rhetoric of integration and socially constructed images of 'Spain'. I was offered many justifications for the decision to settle in Spain, which are worth examining at length, reflecting their significance in people's daily lives. These statements about 'the good life' in Spain generalise the experience for migrants, disguising the specific details of the situation, that is the informality, marginality and even isolation and exclusion of a British ethnic community. With respect to work and income I was told:

> You can live off your savings and they'll go further than they would back home.
>
> > (Mike, fifties, Full Resident)

> If you want to work you can easily find it here. I am a pensioner so I am not supposed to work but people don't dob you in here like they would in England. My pension is not enough to live on but here I can just work when I need to earn a bit for something extra. It's nice to be doing something anyway, and to meet people and that.
>
> > (John, sixties, Full Resident)

> If I was in England I wouldn't earn enough to live off and so I would have to get the dole and then I couldn't work 'cos they would just take it off me, so I would have to sit on my backside all day. At least here I can have a bit of self respect. I can't earn much but you don't need so much here.
>
> > (David, thirties, Returning Resident)

The work these people are referring to is work within the British marginal economy, either informally or formally in small entrepreneurial businesses. The fact that they do not need so much to live on in Spain is related to the British community's ethos of anti-materialism. David, above, does not own a car in Spain; he rents his property and is not on the telephone. He is happy that way – with few overheads and no desire to acquire more material goods. Greg, a young man in his twenties, with no family in Spain, earns a living as a car mechanic. He insists he would have no work in England because there are plenty of people with his skills and too few jobs. He would not be able to work informally as he does in Spain because, he says, someone would find out. He therefore feels that in Spain he has a sense of self-worth and independence he wouldn't have in Britain (being out of work often makes one feel useless and isolated and any work, even informal or casual work, is a remedy of sorts; see Jenkins 1982). Greg's work is all casual (cash in hand) and almost all of his customers are British; they hear of him through friends and acquaintances, by word of mouth. It is, therefore, true to say that people are enabled to work casually and to find some form of employment in Spain where they might not have done in Britain. However, what is not overtly stated is that this is due to the British migrant community and its attitudes rather than to inclusion in the Spanish economy and society.

It is also true to say that the elderly in Spain are more prominent members of society than they would be in Britain; that they experience less ageism and that they are more active (see Chapter 4), but once again it is the British community to which these commendations and praises apply. In Fuengirola older migrants make up the greater part of the British community when both residents and visitors are included in the estimation. They are not a marginal group relegated to the fringes of society: they are running the clubs and the bars; they are on the committees; they are seen in public, drinking in bars and going on day trips. They are not restricted by such strict dress or behaviour codes as the elderly in Britain. They are a conspicuous and powerful part of the community. This is not so true of elderly Spanish people, many of whom wear dark colours or even black, are unlikely to be seen drinking in public bars (especially the women), and have far fewer leisure opportunities than the British create for themselves. 'The old Spanish people, they don't have all the clubs and things the foreigners have', complained a Spanish woman working in the Foreign Residents' Department in Mijas. The ethos of allowing the elderly a place in society, as described by British migrants, is more a symbol and creation of British community than a reflection of reality for Spanish people.

There is also a strong sense of community: 'People are always helping each other out here', said Liz. 'You go in a bar and people talk to you, not like in England where everyone sits in little groups with their backs to everyone else.' Britons told me it is easy to make casual friends in Spain because you get talking to people easily. I found this to be true, but of the British and other English-speaking people. The British appeared to expend a great deal of effort on being friendly to each other and on building community ties, while expectation of relationships with Spanish people was generally low, and satisfaction was high. I was told proudly of a British man who had a lot of Spanish friends: 'Jack is well integrated. He speaks Spanish. In fact he's got quite a few Spanish friends.' Jack was well acquainted with his Spanish neighbours; he would occasionally go to their house for coffee, would chat in the street with them, and was invited to their grand-daughter's first communion party. However, most of this man's time was spent with British people. He worked with and for Britons on a casual basis, he drank in British bars, and was a member of two British social clubs. I heard of a woman who was, apparently, fluent in Spanish. In fact she was only able to converse on a very superficial level in the language, but expectations were low. She had no Spanish friends.

One single woman told me (see Chapter 4):

> A woman on her own is more welcome in Spain. They can go in a bar and sit on their own and someone will talk to them – and they needn't feel as if they are odd because they're on their own. I go out much more here than I did in England.
>
> (June, thirties, Full Resident)

Implicitly this refers to British women in British bars. Single Spanish women do not usually go into bars alone and are possibly more ostracised, if they do, than single women in Britain. As Tina, an English girl who was engaged to a Spanish man, told me:

> We can't go in Spanish bars on our own; the Brits think you can but the Spanish don't do that. They're looking at you and thinking [she makes a gesture, screwing up her nose in distaste]. It's just like back home really.

A further symbol of the British community is the ethos that one creates one's own chances in life. It is through this ethos that community is constructed and reconstructed. 'If anyone is bored or lonely here it is their own fault', said Sylvie, a Returning Resident. An elderly couple, new to the area, on asking if there were any ballroom dancing clubs or groups, were urged to do something about it: 'No, I don't think there are, are there George? Why don't you start one up?' suggested Marie, a Full Resident in her seventies. They did just that, and by the time they had been in the area six months their dancing group was up and running – another British club. The celebration that there is much more to do in Spain is thus made to come true by this very creative British community.

Finally, the ethos of egalitarianism, which many migrant Britons reported proudly, most certainly relates to the British community and to people who have left their pasts and their identities behind them. The words 'It doesn't matter what you were in the past, only what you are now, here in Spain' were said by Britons of Britons. This phrase could not refer to the Spanish – they had not journeyed to a new land and new beginnings – but it was said as if it referred to Spain. The boundaries between a more settled, resident community and Spain and the Spanish were thereby blurred, giving the impression that this was not such an isolated community, that it did not really exist as a peripheral entity on the margins of Spanish society.

Conclusion

This community can be characterised in terms of informal activity – networking, exchange, informal work and volunteering – which occurs on the margins of mainstream Spanish society. These exchange activities constitute the informal construction of social and community life: they serve to draw individuals into the dense networks and symbolically distinguish insiders and outsiders. The rules and norms that regulate social exchange serve to establish and reflect community values, namely the ethos of leisure and the commitment to community, caring and responsibility. Exchange activities also symbolise status, place and belonging within the community and are used to reward commitment and tenacity. But the community is also working hard to blur the boundaries between themselves and Spanish culture and lifestyle. The community that is evoked is in contrast to British society and draws on imagined Spanish traits. Many of the things that are stressed as advantages which Spain has to offer are actually secured and provided by the migrant community itself.

7 British migrants

Betwixt and between

This chapter concludes the ethnography of the previous chapters, pulling themes together in an attempt to throw light on what is going on for these migrants in Spain. It first asks if the Britons in Spain can honestly be depicted as colonials, since they are obviously not 'immigrants' in the now common-sense meaning of the term which imputes powerlessness, minority status, and often colour to immigrant groups (Cashmore 1994: 188). It then shows the British residents in Spain to be living betwixt and between two cultures and two worlds, partly by choice and partly by circumstance, but ultimately maximising their advantage in an inherently marginal situation. The second section discusses how the British in Spain can be considered symbolic of Britain's relationship to the outside and especially to Europe.

Colonisers, expatriates and immigrants

On 27 January 1994 there was a general strike throughout Spain. Andy, who owns a small bar in Fuengirola, told us he had no intention of opening his bar that day because he was too afraid of retribution. He had heard about British bars in the past which had broken strikes and had suffered various forms of abuse and intimidation from Spanish locals as well as the police for a long time afterwards. He even decided, to be on the safe side, to close up at midnight the previous night, and warned all his customers in advance. However, at 11.45 p.m. his bar still had quite a few customers who showed little sign of leaving very promptly. Andy was beginning to wonder how he would enforce the strike when a Spanish man walking past the bar's open doorway, stopped, tapped his watch, and called to Andy in Spanish 'Oy, remember the strike.' Andy asked his customers to finish their drinks quickly and leave but it was just after midnight by the time they had all left. The next day Andy did not go to his bar all day, but on the following day he arrived to find that someone had sprayed 'strike breakers' in Spanish, in huge letters and in bright red paint on the bar shutters. It was very difficult to get the paint off, and Andy felt very afraid about what else was to come.

(Field notes, January 1994)

The Lux Mundi Ecumenical Centre cancelled the bazaar that had been planned for the day of the strike, but no-one knew this until they turned up as usual and had to be turned away. Sister Mary asked me to help her greet people with the news and explain why the Centre was closed that day. There was quite a lot of anger from people who had travelled to the Centre in good time to set up the bazaar, as well as from customers who had hoped to be able to spend a bit of time at the bazaar, shopping and having a coffee and a chat, on a day when the rest of Fuengirola was shut down. I overheard an English woman asking Sister Mary angrily, 'But what's their strike got to do with us? I don't see why we have to stop.' No-one I spoke to that day, either at Lux Mundi or in some of the British bars which did open, seemed clear as to the purpose or cause of the general strike.

(Field notes, January 1994)

Just before Christmas there is a grand lottery held in Spain with such huge prizes that whole clubs or entire communities buy shares in a single sequence of numbers. *El Sorteo de Navidad* is nicknamed *El Gordo*, the fat one. It excites such huge levels of participation that it is more a national event than a lottery. On 22 December 1993, when the lottery was to be drawn, I went into Fuengirola to do some shopping, previously unaware of the magnitude of this event. Shops were shut, no-one was about, the streets were empty. Bars were full, but with every customer's attention tuned to the television set and the doors to the street closed to minimise interruptions. There was an eerie silence broken only by the sound of choirboys singing out the lottery numbers over the airways, seeping out from people's houses and from the bars. I walked around for a while, soaking up the atmosphere, and finally called into a British bar. Here the atmosphere was as usual: no television, people chatting about everyday things. The contrast was dramatic because, as the weather was warm, the bar doors were open wide and the sound of chatter spilled out onto the street. I casually asked if anyone was interested in the lottery and one man told me he had bought a ticket. Someone else asked, 'But can you imagine what would happen if a Brit. won?'

(Field notes, January 1994)

The case studies above depict a minority group living on the margins of society barely interested in the goings-on of the majority group. They seem to confirm all accusations of intentional isolation and ignorance of Spanish culture. However, they hardly depict a powerful group colonising a foreign land, either culturally or politically. Britons in Spain, whether permanent or temporary, do not feel as if they have the choice fully to integrate. The man who asked me what I thought would happen if a British person won *El Gordo* was implying that the Spanish would not like it. For this reason he had not even bought a ticket. There is little real inter-relationship between Spanish society and contemporary British migrants but the Britons are as much marginalised by feelings of exclusion, by lack of information and by bureaucracy as they marginalise themselves by their own actions.

As was discussed in Chapter 1, contemporary British migrants to Spain's coastal areas are often referred to as colonisers, and the areas they inhabit as colonies. To colonise can mean several things. According to *The Cambridge Encyclopaedia*, a colony is: 'An area of land or a country held and governed by another country, usually for the purpose of economic or other forms of exploitation.' Or a colony is a 'group of people who settle in a distant land but under the jurisdiction of their native land' (*Collins Pocket Dictionary*). In ecology, on the other hand, colonisation refers to: 'The spread of species into a new habitat, such as a freshly cleared field, a new motorway verge, or a recently flooded valley' (*Hutchinson Softback Encyclopaedia*). The first two definitions cannot be applied to the British migrants to Spain, since the area of land to which they move is governed neither by the country or state from which they emigrate nor by the migrants themselves; nor are they subject only to British jurisdiction (though this is a complex issue). Neither is the situation one of more subtle economic domination or control, as in the case of a situation often referred to nowadays as 'neo-colonialism'. The economic situation and market activity of the migrants are often marginal and not exploitative of Spanish labour or goods (as discussed in Chapter 6). With respect to the third definition, the loose understanding of which I suspect often informs casual accusations of colonisation, Britons settling in new habitats can only be colonising if they are understood to be a separate species from the Spanish or local inhabitants in the area in question. This is a dangerous assumption resting on notions of pure 'races' and a taxonomy of human beings. To accept this definition is to reify the notion of an ethnic group, hence returning to biological-determinist conceptions of discreteness.

Alternatively, Britons in Spain are labelled 'expatriates', as opposed to the more usual terms of migrants, immigrants or emigrants (indeed they even call themselves expatriates). The term 'expatriate' is a value-laden term implying power, privilege and choice. It invokes a relationship between expatriate and indigenous person in which the expatriate is the more powerful or wealthy. It endows the recipient with status. When one thinks of an expatriate, it is likely one will imagine upper-middle class professionals working in oil-rich countries (Findlay 1995), or the migration of artists, scholars and writers (Earnest 1968), or the migration from richer to 'developing' countries (Öberg 1994). On the other hand, few people in this country would be able to accept the use of the term 'immigrant' as applied to Britons living in Spain. As E. Ellis Cashmore (1994: 188) has said, 'Much political and academic analysis [of migration] operates with a concept of "immigration", which, in turn, tends to stand for "coloured immigration".' 'Immigrant' is again a value-laden term implying lack of choice, lack of power, and low status; consequently a refusal to consider the British *expatriates* in Spain as immigrants endows them with power, prestige and privilege. The implication of the labels of colonisers and expatriates is that lack of integration is through choice, due to the desire to colonise an area and to re-create a patch of Britain.[1]

A marginal minority

Floya Anthias (1992) argues that identity and subsequent actions can only be understood with reference to each historical context and that the same is true of British migration to Spain. As I discussed in Chapter 3, Britons were in fact not attracted to these coastal areas in order either to work or to integrate into Spanish society. They were first invited as tourists when the coastal areas were marketed and 'sold' as holiday places. Then, when it became apparent that tourism only offered seasonal income and when foreign investment was sought as a boost to the Spanish economy, foreigners were encouraged to buy and to settle in these coastal areas – but always as retirees, or visitors, or as entrepreneurs building and expanding their own businesses, not as labour supply, nor for refuge or asylum as many migrants have been in the past. Nor did they come uninvited as imperialists or political colonisers, in the way that Britons (and of course other westerners, including the Spanish) had in the past. It may have been hoped that the cultural mess caused by post-war mass immigration to western countries would eventually stabilise through the melting together of cultures, or the assimilation of one culture by another; but those immigrants were incorporated into the workforce, education system and other institutions of the host society.

Mass migration of Britons to Spain, however, is a very different trend. The British and other northern Europeans represented money, affluence, financial security. Their immigration was generally viewed positively in that they bring wealth and progress to underdeveloped areas. However, it was not expected that they would take anything *from* the economy. One local Spanish official told me resignedly of the British: 'They are good for the area, they bring wealth and prosperity. We want them, of course, but they don't want to mix with us, they don't learn the language.' Later, when it seemed such an influx of British migrants might be a drain on local or national resources because so many were old and not as wealthy as had been hoped, then they were viewed more negatively and still not expected to want to integrate (see Jurdao 1990).

Britons looking for work would not naturally choose Spain. The unemployment rate is one of the highest in Europe, and higher in Andalusia than in the rest of Spain, and the British feel they cannot hope to compete in the Spanish job market. As Soledad García (1994) says, social rights in principle are not the same as social rights in practice, and 'the right to work written into the Spanish constitution does not sort well with the highest unemployment rate in Europe'. Britons believe they stand little chance of being offered a job where a Spanish person is capable of doing it. Furthermore they are usually not fluent enough in the language to be able to compete equally with the local population. As a result, British migrants tend not to look for work within the Spanish economy. If they are attracted to Spain as somewhere to live they might, with knowledge of the local British communities, hope to get work within these but this would usually be informal or entrepreneurial, as has been shown in Chapters 3 and 6. However, it is considered obvious that even entrepreneurial work should not be in direct competition with the Spanish. One man, Graham, whose bar had failed and who was struggling to make ends meet, had an idea to open a Do-It-Yourself (DIY) shop especially for the British customer who might not always know where to buy what, nor how to ask for things that were not usually listed in a standard dictionary. However, he felt on reflection that he would not dare do this since other Spanish DIY shops in the area might lose custom to him, and this would be seen as direct competition. He felt that somehow or other he would be prevented from being successful in this enterprise, not so much by laws but by petty bureaucracy, police harassment or local aggravation. He told me, 'They would tell all their friends not to use my shop, and would report me to the police for things I hadn't done, or plant stuff on me. Whatever they did, they would make sure I didn't make a go of it.' Eventually, this same man bought and sold DIY goods informally through the social networks discussed in the previous chapter. As Hernando de Soto so eloquently demonstrates, legality is sometimes a privilege. The informal economy, rather than reflecting a desire not to integrate, often arises as an on-the-ground solution to an on-the-ground problem (de Soto 1989). Some of these things are changing a bit now, as more and more British migrants buy businesses which serve Spanish and foreign residents, but they are usually new-style businesses that do not compete directly with existing Spanish concerns.

Although it has been shown in the previous chapters that Britons living in Fuengirola cannot be considered to be integrated within wider Spanish society, neither in terms of ethnic identity nor in more concrete actions, it would not be a faithful representation of the situation to label them colonisers. They do not 'integrate' or 'assimilate', but as shown in the previous chapters, nor are they reconstructing a little England in the sun. Nor do they wield political or economic power; in fact, they are excluded from the main Spanish institutions. Britons in Spain have no power to vote in general elections and were slow to be granted the right, in Fuengirola at least, to vote in the local ones. European Union members were to have been given the right to vote in the local elections in 1995 but there were many obstacles to getting themselves registered on the electoral register, and eventually even those few who had managed to gain the correct papers were denied the right to vote at the last minute owing to bureaucratic details and the failure of the two governments involved to reach reciprocal arrangements. By 1999 Fuengirola had got its act together and EU members had the right to vote locally and in European elections, but national elections remain the prerogative of nationals. Yasemin Soysal (1996) points out that this lack of extension of national voting rights to resident foreigners is what differentiates them from national citizens. Full rights of citizenship are further limited by the fact that European residents must prove they are financially independent, or independent in terms of social security, before being granted the right to remain in the host country (Martiniello 1995). No matter how one is accepted in the new country, one remains, in terms of citizenship, a member of one's country of origin first and foremost. This became most evident when, Mike, a retired man in his fifties and a Full Resident in Spain, separated from his wife Jane. Jane went back to England, taking their young daughter, Sarah, with them. When Mike visited them, he discovered them living in squalor in a small flat which they shared with several unemployed and potentially violent (in Mike's opinion) young men. Mike took Sarah back to Spain and fought, and won, custody of her through the Spanish courts. Jane appealed to the European courts and eventually Mike was forced to return to the UK, his home country, return Sarah to her mother and to fight the custody battle from within the country of his birth. This is a reminder that one remains a citizen of one's nation in the eyes of European law.

The Britons in Spain retain a discrete identity in many ways, as discussed in Chapter 5. However, ethnic identification, that is whether or not to *act* on perceived ethnicity, always involves an element of choice (indeed for van den Berghe (1981) it is *purely* a matter of rational advantage-maximising behaviour). This choice is also subject to certain structural constraints (Epstein 1978). The experience for many more permanent migrants in Fuengirola is one of marginalisation and of powerlessness, of lack of control, of unequal access to knowledge, and even of discrimination. Rather than symbolising the boundaries, they are creating the safety-net into which they can fall and within which they can gain their sense of belonging: 'The "we" made of inclusion, acceptance and confirmation is the realm of gratifying safety cut out ... from the frightening wilderness of the *outside* populated by "them"' (Bauman 1992: 679).

Britons feel controlled and excluded by bureaucracy; they are often confused and ill-informed about rights and duties and they are unclear about the law in several areas that affect them directly. 'Although we have lived in Spain for just over four years ... we still do not know our rights, or indeed, if we have any', wrote Mr and Mrs Brook in the *Sur in English* (9–15 July 1993). Residents wanting to become legal, registered citizens, for example, face many obstructions. They often cannot find out what the regulations are and are afraid that once they apply for residence permits they will be on official records, which means if their applications are not successful they can be thrown out of the country. This is a strong restraint against becoming full members of society, and thereby gaining the right to vote. I experienced this set of constraints personally. Having decided to register as a foreign resident in Spain, I set out to discover what were the formal requirements. I asked the local police in Fuengirola, the Foreign Residents' Departments in both Fuengirola and Mijas, the British Consul in Malaga, and several local British residents who had residence permits themselves. Every avenue suggested a different set of criteria: the British Consulate informed us that we would need a full passport, three passport-size photographs, a medical certificate and evidence of health insurance, and evidence of sufficient funds. The Foreign Residents' Department in Mijas listed proof of income in place of 'sufficient funds' and did not mention a medical certificate. Their booklet informed the reader that he or she will require 700 pesetas and a completed request form in addition to those items above. One local woman told us that the whole process had cost one friend 500 pounds sterling and another 1,100 pounds! One said we would need a lawyer, another said to do it yourself. In the end, since we were to apply for these permits from the Fuengirola police, we thought it best to provide whatever they asked for. They requested the following: an affidavit stating that I would provide financially for my partner; new birth certificates for my children from the British Consulate; a translated letter from our bank informing them of my income (the letter from my funders was insufficient); and an official letter from the Consulate stating that we would only be staying one year and that our E111 certificates (state health certificates from the UK) would suffice for that time. The whole process took over five months from application to receiving our permits, many trips to the Consulate and to the local police, and lots of worry and frustration. And ours was not an unusual story. Several Britons suffer trauma as a result of confusion about laws, rules and regulations. The owner of a bar in Los Boliches, for example, was fined the equivalent of 500 pounds sterling for driving a car on English licence plates after he had been registered as a resident, though he had not known this was illegal. He told me angrily that he knows several British and even Spanish residents who drive British plated cars but seem to get away with it. Another couple I interviewed asked me what I could tell them about benefits. They look after their elderly mother on a small income and get no support from either the British or Spanish governments. 'And what do we do when she dies,' they asked me, 'do we ring the doctor or what? If we just let the doctor do everything they might charge us way over the odds. We can't afford top whack.'

It was not uncommon to hear stories of scares and bungles, as reflected in news stories entitled 'Tale of a Tax Scare' (*Sunday Sun*, 18.7.93); 'Wrong Plates!' (*Entertainer*, 24–30 June 1993); and '75,000 peseta fine!' (*Entertainer*, 10–16 March 1994). 'What are they up to now at Sevillana?' one woman asked on the letters page of the *Entertainer* (5–11 August 1993). Several of her clients had their electricity supply cut and were charged reconnection fees because she was late paying the bills for them. She had understood that she had a few weeks in which to pay and would be warned by letter before disconnection took place. However, the regulations had changed without her knowledge and to her huge expense. Even the British Consul believed that in order to find out about laws and regulations in Spain it is best to have some Spanish people on your side. He always employs a few Spanish people so that they have contacts with people in the right offices, and can find out what they need to know. 'Laws are changed so fast, even the police don't know what they are', he told me. 'At the very least you need to speak the language', he said, 'but it is even better if you know someone who has relatives in the right places.'

However, some of the confusion could be due to the fact that national laws are subject to local interpretation. A law was introduced requiring motorcycle riders to wear crash helmets, for example. Unfortunately the word for 'carry' and the word for 'wear' are the same in Spanish (*llevar*), and as a result of interpretation, one often saw motorcyclists driving around town with their crash helmets over their arms – not breaking the law. Britons would tell me things like: 'The Spanish police are a law unto themselves. They make up the rules as they go along and change them to suit themselves without telling anyone so that they can catch them out' and 'They would even defy European laws if it suited them.' One story which circulated amongst British migrants while I was in Spain was used to demonstrate Spanish lawlessness. Apparently the European Commission introduced a new ruling that bar mats were a health hazard and therefore illegal. Officials went round to check, so the story went, but before they arrived in Spanish bars local officials warned the owners of the forthcoming visit, giving them time to hide all bar mats under the counter. Once the officials had left, the bar mats were replaced, to be used freely ever more.

An aspect of Spanish life Britons often found difficult to cope with was the ubiquitous need to employ a *gestor* as a go-between in legal matters. There is no translation for this in English, since there is no equivalent position or concept. According to John Reay-Smith (1980: 42), a *gestor* is a type of administrator who can cope with many financial problems and some legal matters, but above all 'is an expert at completing the multiplicity of documents that so often turn up in Spain'. Legal residents, obliged to convert their cars to Spanish licence plates, for example, would be referred to a *gestor* for advice. Such advice was not cheap. British people, used to understanding the laws of their own country and being able to arrange most official administrative details for themselves (especially those with comparatively small incomes) told me they feel as if 'the Spanish are getting as much money as they can out of us foreigners'. For some Britons, the Spanish just cannot be trusted. When it comes to property purchase for example, Barbara Green (writing in the *Reporter*, a local, English-language magazine) reports: 'Apocryphal stories which range from rip-offs to tax evasion schemes, from cost-cutting tricks to illegal developments are enough to put some people off forever' (Green 1994: 15).

This experience of confusion and ignorance is accompanied by feelings of discrimination and prejudice. 'Discrimination' cried one man whose son was not able to join the local football team because he was 'a foreigner'

(*Entertainer*, 18–24 November 1993). 'Victimised and Defenceless' ran the headline of an article on new tax laws for foreign plated cars (*Sunday Sun*, 18.7.93). Several migrants sensed that they could not get away with things with the Spanish authorities simply because they are foreign: 'It's one rule for them and one for us', said one man. He told me of a couple who ran a successful music bar but had to sell up and go home when their late night music licence had been withdrawn. The police told them they could no longer play loud music after midnight because the bar was situated in a residential area. However, the same bar is now owned by Spaniards, the man told me, and plays loud music until three or four in the morning. Similarly, Andy, who chose not to open his bar on the day of the Spanish strike, did not really feel the strike was his business but thought he would suffer as a foreigner if he broke it. He was sure he was branded a strike breaker as a result of discrimination not objectivity. 'A Spaniard would have been able to explain that he was about to close up. Me, they didn't give me a chance', he complained resentfully.

In our search for an identity we (as individuals and as groups) reflect, to an extent, what people expect of us, as is made known through labelling and interaction. Britons (and other foreign nationals) in Fuengirola are marginalised by Spanish labelling. They are often referred to as 'residential tourists', establishing their status, for Spaniards, as marginal or temporary rather than as fully participating Spanish citizens (see Mellado 1993) and are thus conceptually parcelled off with the tourists. In Mijas, a village near Fuengirola, a Department for Foreign Residents was established within the local council to deal with the specific problems and interests of the local foreign population. This office gives advice to foreigners with regard to residence and work permits, tax liabilities, council fees, services and so on. It also arranges meetings with and social events for foreign residents. Interestingly enough, the same office houses and the same individuals run the tourist office for the area. Tourists and foreign residents are dealt with together. The Foreign Residents' Department, which Fuengirola council decided to provide, was also housed with and shares the same staff as their local tourist office; in fact as a department it comes under the aegis of the Department of Tourism. The building is separate from the main council buildings, positioned in the path of the tourist trail to the local weekly market. Such treatment gives an insight into the way the foreign residents, and especially Britons since they are in the majority, are perceived by the Spanish in this area. They are not viewed as permanent settlers intending to integrate fully into Spanish society; they are tourists who stay on.

In the 1960s, Julian Pitt-Rivers noted the extent of Andalusian hospitality and called it a very noble feature of the Spanish people: the stranger enjoys the special status he was accorded in ancient Greece, where he was protected by Zeus and was welcomed and feasted. However, Pitt-Rivers (1963: 27) suggested this is more than mere hospitality, it is a protection of the community from too much outside influence. Treating a person as a guest maintains his or her distance and checks interference, for 'a guest is a person who, while he must be entertained and cherished, is dependent on the goodwill of his hosts. He has no rights and he can make no demands.' This is an interesting and useful analysis of the marginal status of the guest. It works both ways for the British in Spain who, as we shall see, are both treated as and identify themselves as guests in a foreign land. It is little wonder that they do not bother to mobilise politically: 'mobilization will only be considered legitimate for those groups who are authorized and perceive themselves as legitimate members of the civil societies of their countries of residence' (Wilpert 1989). The British in Spain are constantly reminded, and remind each other, that they are guests.

Spanish people I spoke to about the British migrants tended to share the view that they are generally wealthy, happy and had no desire to integrate with them. My doctor was convinced that the British migrants are all wealthy and intentionally live isolated within their own communities. A woman I practised Spanish with told me she is pleased the migrants have come to the area because they have contributed to the area's economic growth and prosperity, However, when I asked her if she has made any friends or acquaintances of these migrants she replied, 'Oh no, they don't want to get to know us. They have each other.' A policeman I interviewed told me that tourism is good for the area and the British are nice people, so it is OK that their tourism is becoming more like migration, but they could easily become a burden or a problem, he predicted. He was very concerned that people who could not support themselves financially should not be allowed to stay on. As Cohen (1996: xvi) explains:

> Immigrants are often feared; they are perceived as a potent economic threat, as competitors for housing, education, welfare benefits and jobs, and as bearers of an alien culture and religion which undermines the sense of security, well-being and identity of the indigenous population.

It is interesting to note how attitudes towards the British migrants in Spain have moved from welcome to apprehension as the tourism/migration has become more permanent and the migrants seem to be getting older and poorer (Jurdao and Sanchez 1990).

Language is crucial. 'Nothing is likely so palpably to both encapsulate and therefore to isolate a group as linguistic barriers', suggests C. Fried (1983: 4). Although the British in Spain can be accused of not learning Spanish sufficiently well, they feel that the Spanish are not making it easy for them. Police officers who can speak English, for example, will often refuse to do so, forcing the Briton to struggle along. While we were in Fuengirola a hand-written notice was posted in the police station warning foreigners, in English, not to expect to be attended to unless they brought an interpreter with them. This is an area to which British tourists flock every year and in which the second language is English, yet if you are burgled or mugged, you are expected to find an interpreter before going to the police for help! In Torremolinos, a busy tourist spot which has many British residents, the police have recruited translators on to their staff, in order to help with the tourist season, but no mention is made of the resident foreigners' needs. Britons in Spain have the right to use the state health service in line with reciprocal arrangements under European Community legislation, but even in areas where there is a high majority of British and English-speaking residents, there are surprisingly few interpreters or facilities provided for those with language difficulties. Very often no allowance is made for the language or cultural differences. Migrants pointed out that this is very different to the experience in Britain's inner-city areas where there are also high numbers of immigrant minorities. Several permanent migrants (Full and Returning Residents, see Chapter 3) who would normally be entitled to use the Spanish state system make private arrangements, often joining a local insurance scheme which includes doctor's surgery appointments, some minor treatments and English-speaking receptionist and emergency services. Though it costs them more, several people feel that they do not want language misunderstandings to get in the way when it comes to matters of health. 'You don't want mix-ups when it comes to your health do you?', one man explained.

Other public service providers rarely make allowances for language and cultural differences of members of the international community. The Foreigners' Department at the police station in Fuengirola has interpreters, but these are not provided by the police force, they are voluntary and unpaid. In the nearest general hospital in Malaga, the situation is the same; interpreters are voluntary and therefore are not always available when needed. A young British woman who had her third baby in Malaga hospital told me how lonely and isolated she felt during her stay there, mainly because she could not talk to anyone. 'I just wanted to come home', she told me. 'I cried all the time.' This lack of provision, rather than either forcing or encouraging people to learn the language or to integrate, augments the exclusion of minority groups, be they 'expatriates' or 'immigrants'.[2]

Many British migrants to Fuengirola do not learn the local language, for whatever reason. I met people who had lived in the area thirty years and who spoke fewer than twenty words of Spanish. Few are working or spending time with Spanish people on a daily basis in order to acquire proficiency in the language. It is in fact possible to get by quite well without learning Spanish. As this is a tourist area, many local services are provided for the holiday-maker and are oriented towards the tourist. Many locals learn to speak English so that they can compete with other businesses for the tourist custom. Other foreign nationals visiting or living in the area may well have learned English rather than Spanish, knowing they will be able to get by. Thus the second language of the area has become English.[3] English is also becoming accepted as the language of business in Europe.

On the other hand, many permanent migrants do attempt to learn the language but find it difficult to get beyond the practising stage, because when they go into local shops and speak in Spanish, the Spaniard will often reply in English. This can seem rude to the English person, whether it is intended as such or not. I felt quite offended, for example, when a ten-year-old Spanish girl responded to my attempt to talk to her in Spanish by answering me in English. Local Spanish people in Fuengirola often seem more concerned to practise their English-language skills than to teach the foreign visitor any Spanish. Spanish children, especially, seemed to love to learn and to practise their English with the foreign children. Laura, my daughter, became fluent in Spanish but her closest friend insisted in speaking to her in either a very broken Spanish, which Laura found difficult to understand but the girl thought would be easier to interpret than fluent Spanish, or in English (of which the girl spoke only a few words). The Andalusian accent is notoriously strong and there are subtle differences in dialect which can be difficult to master. As Stanley Brandes noted during his anthropological field study in Andalusia in the 1970s: 'Andalusians, scorned and ridiculed throughout the rest of the country for their distinctive accent, are masters of their tongue' (Brandes 1980: 4). British people who learnt the language before coming to Spain would have usually been taught Castilian Spanish; a Spanish quite different in dialect to Andalusian Spanish. Andalusian was spoken by many of the locals in Fuengirola with very strong accents and was difficult to understand until one got used to hearing it. If that person was spending a great deal of her time in the company of other Britons, then the chances of their hearing enough Andalusian to get used to the accent and the dialect were slim.[4] During one discussion about the problems of learning Spanish one woman told me: 'If it makes you feel any better, I met a woman from northern Spain who told me she felt like crying when she came here because she couldn't understand a word. It was like a different language to her.' Joan, a Full Resident in her sixties, echoed these sentiments: 'They speak a different Spanish here to the one you learn.'

Several Britons expressed frustration with their own attempts to learn the language. It was the topic of many a conversation during walks with the field club and whilst whiling away the time in a coffee bar. Some had tried to familiarise themselves with the language by watching Spanish television as much as possible. However, this was not useful since so many programmes were dubbed that the language heard bore no relation to the mouth movements observed. One television programme one could be sure of hearing in Spanish was the news, but this was generally read so fast as to be unintelligible, and employed language usually unfamiliar to the beginner in Spanish.

In conclusion, many Britons who would like to integrate more, who admire and respect the Spanish way of life and Spanish culture, and who want to learn the language, feel in some ways powerless and discriminated against. As discussed in previous chapters, permanent residents share no myth of return and no romantic view of home acting as a constraint against participation in Spanish life. Many like and admire the Spanish people, and even believe they are similar in many ways. Many believe their children are integrated and go to great lengths to deny their discreteness and their ethnic identity in interaction with the Spanish. However, language differences persist in distancing them, enforcing a social exclusion which is further strengthened by bureaucracy, by the control of knowledge, by 'unfair' laws, and by an absence of political representation. Not only are they not *expected* to integrate but neither is participation in Spanish society facilitated or enabled.

Betwixt and between

The above discussion proposes that, rather than being powerful colonisers appropriating a piece of land and reshaping it according to their own designs, these are powerless immigrants relegated to the margins of a society in which they aspire to be fully participating citizens. This is one way in which British migration to Spain could be depicted; it is possibly thicker description than that they are 'colonisers', since it is based on the migrants' own experiences and their own feelings; it reflects some of their own instead of only ascripted desires and intentions. However, this is no more *the* faithful portrayal of the situation than are the labels discussed at the beginning of the chapter. Both external structures and internal actions articulate to make the situation the complex one that it is. While British migrants may complain about bureaucracy and laws, about the lack of knowledge and the difficulties of learning the language, and while they feel discriminated against in some ways, they do little other than complain.

Although British migrants are marginalised by the Spanish, they do not seem to object. Chapter 5 described how their ethnicity is not overtly stressed in interaction; it does not have an organised political element. Britons are not mobilised against a common 'Other' so much as into a common 'we'. The threat of loss of ethnic identity experienced by some ethnic groups is non-existent in this situation and does not need fighting for. They may have no power in Spain, they may not be represented at official level, nor have the right to vote at a national level, but this is not an issue for most. The majority of British migrants to Spain are not registered as residents and therefore do not have their names on the electoral register. Few Britons who were eligible to vote actually registered to do so in the 1995 local elections and so few were disappointed to be denied their rights at the last moment. Registration to vote remained low in 1999, and although things have changed in some areas to the extent that Calpe now has a British woman councillor, one could almost describe the Britons in Spain as politically apathetic. Although they complain endlessly about Spanish bureaucracy, unfair laws, difficulties getting residence permits, and learning the language, they do little to rectify the situation. Complaints such as these are counteracted in conversation by other statements saying how much they love it in Spain, and how they should not complain, and how 'these things are what we like about the Spanish people'.

In some ways the persistent discussions around bureaucracy, residence permits, language difficulties and discrimination are excuses for not integrating. The customers who wanted to attend the Lux Mundi bazaar on the day of the national strike could not understand and perhaps did not want to understand why a strike would affect their essentially leisure pastimes. Britons denigrate the abilities of Spanish workers, which provides a good excuse for not using them when they need to call a plumber or electrician. They insist Spain is all good with regard to crime and family and community but are actually using these myths in the construction of their own community (see Chapter 6). They deny Spain's more negative aspects such as the high rates of petty crime and high unemployment while insisting there is more opportunity for work 'here in Spain'. While they really refer to advantages of being a member of their own community, they do not say as much in so many words. Their lives and identities, their community, all serve to maintain a balance between an imagined Spain and a historical Britain – reality being something they construct there for themselves (as shown in the last chapter). There is a constant contradiction between wanting to integrate and yet doing nothing about it; constructing an isolated community yet pretending they are integrated; loving Spain yet being frustrated by it; living in Spain and being like the Spanish yet not really knowing what that means; feeling marginalised yet doing nothing about it; acting ethnically but denying that too.

The structures around them and the constraints against integration are part of the webs of significance in which they are suspended; the community in which they participate creates structures within the webs of significance that they themselves have spun. The community described in the previous chapter, consisting as it does in symbols of Britishness, in marginality and informality, acts as a constraint on individual actions. Constructed by them as a way of coping in this marginal situation, it serves to marginalise the Britons further. Their sense of status, self-worth and belonging derive from other Britons; if there are not enough of them, or if the networks are not maintained, many people will feel disempowered and disconnected, lost and alone, so it is crucial that they maintain buoyant and exclusive membership. Resident Britons make it difficult for others to return by going on about how bad Britain is, but at the same time they also make it difficult to return themselves. Consequently some are forced to deny their unhappiness or their mistakes, and their desire to return home. At the same time Britons involved in the networks of community are becoming more and more self-sufficient and independent of the Spanish. They are strengthening the boundaries, confirming and reconfirming their marginal status to the Spanish, needing to integrate less and less as they become more dependent on each other both practically and emotionally.

An identity gains reference for validation and inclusion from the locality or local group within which it spends time (Cohen 1985). For the British in Spain, who neither work, nor share a routine or any affective ties with

Spanish people, the local reference point is the foreign, English-speaking community. Britons are unlikely to have that feeling of belonging in Spain which is an essential component of identity with a group (see Fried 1983). This is demonstrated most clearly in their ambiguous orientation towards Spain. Some vehemently insist that they are guests in this country, while others angrily insist that they are not. The letter pages of English-language newspapers are filled with individuals complaining about things like postage rates, noise in Spain, taxes, crime and so on. This inevitably elicits a deluge of responses from angry residents telling the moaners to put or shut up, stressing that they are 'guests' in a foreign land. 'As I am a guest in this country I don't like to criticise it', says Henry Home, a resident of eight years, commenting on bullfighting in the *Sunday Sun* (22–28 August 1993). A British journalist in Spain sums it up:

> There are a number of *Lookout* readers, born and bred north of the Pyrenees, who have settled in Spain and apparently become more Spanish than the Spaniards. Any half-way critical comment about their adopted country . . . triggers a salvo of angry letters to the editor.
>
> (Burns 1993)

Many Britons expect nothing of the Spanish, rarely suggest Spain owes them anything, are grateful for the way they are received into the country, and are flattered to be accepted as friends by the Spanish people: 'We are fortunate that the Spanish welcome so many foreigners amongst them', insists one man in a letter to the *Entertainer* (25 Nov.–1 Dec. 1993). Britons also do not feel they can, or should, turn to the Spanish in times of trouble. The appeals for help on behalf of the elderly and poor migrants (discussed in Chapter 5), which came from welfare officers of British organisations, were directed to the British rather than the Spanish government. Moreover, many of the more practical needs of residents are addressed from within the British community, which offers welfare assistance and advice as well as the provision of goods and services and the exchange of information.

Explaining liminality

When I had been in Fuengirola for one year I decided to conduct a sample survey in order to gain quantitative support for general findings, to verify typicality. I designed a questionnaire that asked for background details on household size, age, income, work, class background, and duration of stay in Spain.[5] The questionnaire then had more open-ended questions on lifestyle, attitudes, health and language learning. Replies were to be anonymous. I conducted a pilot study, requesting seven individuals of various ages, both men and women, to complete the questionnaire for me in order that mistakes or problems might be revealed prior to its being disseminated more widely. Each respondent was pleased to do this, but some were less than happy about the idea of a survey in general; they worried that people would not want to 'be bothered' or to answer personal questions. One man voiced concerns:

> Many questions will possibly create misgivings. Why do you have to ask questions on income? As soon as people see questions like that they are going to think you are from the tax. I have already heard people asking 'Do you think she's from the government?' They think you're a tax inspector or something.
>
> (Charles, thirties, Resident)

He recommended that I ask no questions on name, address, date of birth, income or work, as these would worry people – they made the questionnaire's anonymity doubtful, he thought. Several other questions, for example those about health insurance schemes, should not be asked since they are too personal, he thought: they are about people's free choices, and asking questions about them compelled people to defend such choices. One of the women in the pilot study told me:

> A lot of people here don't want to be answering questions on their finances and such like, they just want to be left alone. I don't know how you'll get on [shaking her head slowly]. The older people get, the less they want to be answering questions . . . and if they've got no residency or pay no tax or something – and rumours are rife.
>
> (Ellen, seventies, Resident)

As a result of these concerns, I adapted the questionnaire and added a cover-note to make it more clear that respondents would remain anonymous. It was distributed, using stratified and network sampling procedures, via a selection of clubs, bars and social groups. However, only 14 per cent of the total number of questionnaires distributed (21 of 150) were ever returned and I was unable to draw representative conclusions. Several people cheerfully took questionnaires home to fill in but never returned them to me. I would initially ask them when they would be returning their questionnaires but eventually abandoned this approach.

There are several explanations for this poor response rate to the survey, and a great deal to be learned from it. First, those people who took part in my pilot study were correct in supposing that few migrants wanted to be bothered, or to be asked personal questions. Several of the reasons for not registering as residents apply to not filling in questionnaires: many British migrants in Spain do not want to be recorded on official records; some do not have the required residence permit; some are tax evaders; some have left debts in Britain; some are working illegally or informally; and some simply want to escape bureaucracy. Of course there are many migrants who are neither clandestine, illegal, informal nor undocumented, but even these seemed to feel, as I have discussed above, that life in Spain is about freedom and escape rather than supervision, documentation and control. During the time I was doing fieldwork a couple in their fifties, with grown-up children living in England, sold their villa in Mijas and moved into a rented apartment in order that the man could work informally (off the record) and so that they could disappear from Spanish figures. He told me: 'We haven't come here to be bothered by paperwork and journalists, we just want to get on with it' (Terry, fifties, Resident).

Another reason for the low response to the survey lay in my reluctance to damage the delicate relationship I had established with migrants, a relationship based on trust and friendship, and which depended on my role as researcher being understated, almost covert, in certain situations. This factor is related to the attitude I felt the majority of migrants had towards officialdom and journalists; to anyone trying to pin them down. I wrote the following thoughts in my notebook at this time: 'This community is living a fantasy life – and the authorities try to force reality onto them, that's why they object to this sort of thing.' Aware of this widespread antipathy to bureaucracy, I was almost apologetic in my request for respondents, and was reluctant to challenge those who chose not to respond. Indeed, several individuals were more guarded towards me for a period after my attempt at a survey than they had been previously.

One way to explain why the Britons do little to rectify their liminal status in Spain gains reference from their relative wealth in Spain. Britons in Spain are better off financially than they would be in Britain. One of the main factors attracting people to Spain was the comparative cheapness, the lower cost of living. Everyone I spoke to referred to Spain's cheapness as one among many justifications for their migration (either temporary or permanent). However, the cost of living is only cheaper in comparison, and can only stay that way while much of the migrants' income is not paid at the local level. Britons are bringing money into Spain in the form of capital, income from pensions and statutory state benefits, and income from earnings (especially the more temporary migrants). This money is exchanged into pesetas and is spent in Spain. While the exchange rate is favourable, they are well off. When it is not favourable, those with savings can transfer their capital into a different currency, but those with income coming from Britain in the form of pensions and earnings are less well off. Temporary migrants and tourists can then buy fewer pesetas with their expendable income, and therefore have less to spend in Spain. Those who are earning money within Spain (as opposed to bringing it in from outside) often derive their income from other Britons and need the tourists and migrant customers to be wealthier than the Spanish in order to encourage them to keep visiting Spain and to keep spending. One couple told me quite plainly, if the peseta gets any stronger they will just have to go home.

As a result, the liminality of the British migrants is to their advantage. Their existence and lifestyle in Spain depend to an extent on this liminality, and on this relationship between Britain and Spain where they are still British and still retain links with Britain but live and spend their money in Spain – a poorer country. It is not to their advantage if the Spanish economy blossoms, since a strong peseta diminishes both their spending power and their earning potential. Neither is it to their advantage if Britons use the services of Spaniards, for repairs, hairdressing and so on, since this would take work from migrants wishing to earn a living in Spain.

An attempt to explain the reluctance to apply for residence permits also refers to economic advantage. Many Britons who are not legal residents in Spain (that is, those who have not registered as resident there) believe they are not liable to pay tax on earnings in Spain; and believe they can draw on British state benefits, and health and social services in Britain in times of trouble as long as they retain British residential status (Svensson 1991). Non-residents in Spain apply for tax-exempt bank accounts. Many hold their capital in off-shore accounts which they can easily access from within Spain. They really do try to have the 'best of both worlds'. They live in an economic niche. Those who have gone to Spain to live on capital raised through various means, including redundancy payments (such as Tom, Linda and Terry, whom we met in Chapter 3), and who need to work a little to supplement this, are usually not legal residents.

A further attempt to explain the maintenance, by Britons, of a liminal status draws on the notion of tourism, escape, holiday and spatialised Spain (as discussed in Chapter 5). To return to the issue of choice, as opposed to structure and constraint, ethnic identity is as much about 'interest' as 'affective tie' (Yinger 1986). In other words, the individuals involved in constructing an ethnic group may share an interest in common more than, or as well as, an affective tie. The interest this group shares is in tourist Spain and in escaping from modern Britain, either temporarily or more permanently. Full integration into Spanish society would shatter the illusions of holiday, escapist Spain, of crime-free Spain and of backward Spain. Otherness or abnormality is what makes the holiday, tourism or escape the pursuit it is, says R. Voase (1995). Getting involved in formal structures would shatter escapism and freedom from routine. It would also mean paying taxes, social security, and declaring all earnings. Many people said these were the benefits of living in Spain – being free and left alone, even for the elderly. Consider, for example, the response to my attempt at a survey, as discussed above. Respondents wanted to be left alone, to be undocumented and unrecorded, to be free. It is as if they were still travelling because, as Curtis and Pajaczkowska suggest (1994), travelling is 'time out' from the mundane, it takes one to a new space where time stands still; in other words, travel is displacement.

Britons in Spain enjoy being marginal, being difficult to count, difficult to pin down, difficult to essentialise. Many of them make it difficult for anyone to chart or predict their movements, to describe or categorise them. As I said at the end of Chapter 4, it is easier to describe Britons in Spain in terms of what they are not than what they are. They were obstructive when I tried to survey them. They like to be so fluid and flexible, it is another attraction of Spain and part of the escape. As I said above, these migrants never saw Spain as signifying routine and drudgery. It never meant hard work. However, it did mean all the opposites of what Britain is, namely crime, greyness, drudgery, routine, certainty, scripting – those aspects of modern living from which we all, according to Cohen and Taylor (1976), try to escape. Spain signifies light and hope. New migrants arrive in Fuengirola every year following their dream of running their own business in the sun, away from the pressures of fast living, crime and recession in England. Being a holiday area, Spain still represents happiness, light heartedness, hope and dreams. Even with the unemployment rates so high, the British feel there is hope for them to succeed in a business that provides for the local British migrants and tourists. Spain for them is not the modern Spain of some commentators; they are unaware of the super-slick Eurostate, the centres of top fashion, modernist buildings and high-tech industries (Graff 1993; Punnet 1990; Richards 1992; Stradling and Vincent 1994). Britons actually need very little integration to achieve their goals, since what they want involves integration in the British community, and involves keeping the Spanish as 'Other'. Their aspirations are towards the good life, and they get angry if anyone suggests they are not having a good time or are working too hard. Most insist that they are successful in their move and that they are integrated.

A British diaspora?

Maybe it would be useful to conceptualise this movement of British people as part of a wider movement and to draw on the notion of a diaspora. Diaspora traditionally meant dispersal, and has been associated specifically with the banishment of the Jews from their homeland and thus with catastrophic, forced dispersal, with oppression, with degradation, and with a shared, bitter longing for home. However, the Jewish experience was far from homogeneous, and other mass dispersals have demanded conceptualisation. The notion of diaspora has undergone a series of changed meanings, the broadest of which was perhaps offered by W. Conner (1986), who suggested that a diaspora is 'that segment of a people that lives outside the homeland'. The concept has since been applied to the movement of peoples of many nations and ethnies for a variety of reasons and with diverse experiences (see Cohen 1997). But a concept has to be defined in something of a restricted sense in order to be applied usefully. Safran (1991) in the first edition of the journal *Diaspora*, argues for a restricted definition in which the concept of diaspora is applied to an expatriate minority with at least some of the following characteristics:

- they or their ancestors have been dispersed from a specific origin to two or more peripheral or foreign regions

- they retain a collective memory or myth about their homeland, which includes notions of location, history and achievements
- they remain partly separated from their host society and perhaps believe they can never be fully accepted
- they regard their homeland as their true, ideal home and as the place to which they or their descendants should eventually return, when conditions permit
- they believe they should retain a collective commitment to the maintenance, restoration, safety and prosperity of their homeland
- they continue to relate, practically or vicariously, to the homeland in one way or another.

Since this definition relies so heavily on memory of and commitment to the homeland, the British in Spain, as described in the pages of this book, hardly warrant the label of a diaspora. Furthermore, Safran has insisted that gypsies, for example, cannot be considered a diaspora since there is no shared awareness, for themselves, of a gypsy problem. Tölölyan (1996), writing in *Diaspora* a few years later than Safran, again argues that the concept of diaspora has become too vague to be useful. For him, consciousness of a 'problem' is also crucial; diasporans tend to be 'citizens of one country who also think of themselves as members of a transnational political and cultural community, sometimes even a transnational nation or a "transnation".' He talks of a *diasporic consciousness* which arises as a result of the awareness of other ethnic groups, like ourselves, in other parts of the world. The British in Spain, as I showed in Chapter 5, have no myth of return to the homeland, and though they do identify as British, there is no awareness of a British diaspora or transnation.

Cohen (1997) argues that too much emphasis on myths of return is not helpful. He adds memory of a traumatic event and the possible creation of a homeland to Safran's list above. This still does not allow us to include the British in Spain in the definition of diaspora. However, Cohen also allows for trade, labour and imperial diasporas, and here we begin to think of the British in terms of diaspora generally. Certainly there is an argument that the British Empire constructed a British diaspora, with a diasporic identity, with an awareness of the eventual return home (though sometimes temporarily) and with a consciousness of others in the scattered transnation. The British migrants to Spain in modern times are not part of this tradition, but are nevertheless British and are at some level very aware of their Britishness. The Britain they have left behind is one they do not identify with much, but the historical nation remains part of who they are. They do not expect to be allowed to integrate into Spanish society, and they retain a strong dependence on their home society, sometimes financially and sometimes emotionally, but always with the secure knowledge that if all else fails, they can (and do) just go home. In these ways, the British in Spain can be conceptualised as a sort of diaspora, without (as yet) a diasporic consciousness.

The crucial thing about the concept of diaspora is that it links members of ethnic groups with others of the same or similar origins. Without wishing to sink into biologism, writers on diaspora seem to rely heavily on the notion of nation, or homeland, and certainly on imagined community (see Anderson 1991) as the crucial element which distinguishes a diaspora from an ethnic group. The British in Spain, regardless of their overt denial of their pasts and of their shared, national history, identify as British citizens first and foremost, and in many of their attitudes and behaviours they symbolise Britain's historical and ambivalent relationship to other nations. They continue to receive pensions from Britain, many retain the right to vote in their home countries, and they retain a multitude of emotional, historical, familial and economic ties.

The British and the others

These British migrants in Spain are not integrating into Spanish society, there can be no doubt about that. They are not successfully learning the language and therefore cannot communicate with Spanish people. They spend most of their work and leisure time with other Britons. They have even constructed a marginal, informal community and economy. However, the permanent migrants, those who are settled in Spain, do not retain a myth of return to the glorious homeland. Their ethnic identity is neither overtly stressed nor politically organised; it is not emphasised in order to stress discreteness or to claim rights. In fact differences from Spanish people are made to appear less than they are at times of interaction, while similarities with Spanish are highlighted in conversations with less permanent migrants. On the other hand, neither are these Britons colonising the areas to which they migrate. They have no political or economic power in Spain, and their experience is of marginalisation rather than advantage. British migrants live on the margins of Spanish society, not residentially but economically, socially, structurally and ideologically. They take what they want from each culture – their own and their host's – enjoying their marginality to its full advantage. They are neither expected nor do they need to integrate (Rodríguez *et al.* 1998).

Above all their situation is fraught with contradictions. They don't integrate yet say they do, or that their children do. They construct and reconstruct strong community boundaries yet talk of community as if it includes the Spanish as well as other nationalities. They deny their isolation. They live fun and leisured lives, often denying or understating the work which goes into the construction of community. They insist that their lives in Spain are good and that no-one ever wants to go home, while individuals are choosing to go home every day. They deny their boredom and suppress their loneliness as this contradicts the image they wish to portray of a happy, friendly and exciting experience. This marginality is to their advantage in economic terms and in terms of their escapist way of life. But these Britons are accused by other Britons of colonising parts of Spain, of the lack of integration or assimilation, of neither learning from or taking an interest in the culture of their hosts. It is as though integration were the accepted norm in situations of culture contact, yet contemporary Britain, as a nation state, continues to exhibit ambivalence in its dealings with the outside world and with other cultures and societies.

The more recent history of Britain is the history of Empire and power; of colonisation and Commonwealth; of racism and multiculturalism; of relative superiority and decline; of nationalist pride and national despondency. Colonisation and the spread of Empire sought and found justification in biologically determinist theories of race with their implicit racial hierarchies. Exploitation of other cultures and peoples was excused with reference to these racial hierarchies and to the poverty the people were suffering. Colonisation, it was believed, would bring wealth, health, happiness and education to these backward peoples, who would then be able to join in the general march towards progress aided by the benevolence of the superior civilised races. Britons, like the members of other colonising nations, were helping improve the lot of poor peoples around the world.

British migrants in Fuengirola were occasionally heard to use similar rhetoric when referring to the changes they and other migrants had effected in the poorer parts of Andalusia. The notion of improving a poor economy, of teaching a backward culture, is evident in several situations. The area of Fuengirola, it was generally agreed, had been a poor, tatty fishing village before modernisation and progress. Foreigners, rather than exploiting the area for their own profits, had brought wealth to the area and to the welcoming and grateful peasants whose lot had changed dramatically thanks to tourism and investment. Locals might be complaining now about the spoilt environment and the overcrowding but, it is argued, they were glad enough, and continue to be content, to extract what money they can from betteroff foreigners either by selling their land at exorbitant prices or by increasing the taxing of incoming foreign nationals. The general, though quietly spoken, consensus of opinion is that without tourism, migration, and the foreign investment which led to increases in these, locals in Andalusia would still be backward and poor; they should be grateful to the foreigners for helping them catch up with the rest of Europe (see Rodríguez *et al.* 1998).

In the same way the actual presence of such foreigners is considered to contribute to progress in the realm of ideas and culture: 'The Spanish should learn as we have that strikes help no one', one woman told me as we discussed the general strike referred to at the beginning of this chapter. 'They are so backward in so many ways . . . if only they would learn from us. Some expats have been very important people in their own countries. They could teach these youngsters a thing or two', said a man after a meeting with representatives of the local Partido Popular. But, these expostulations are countered with reminders that 'we are guests in their country; it is not our business to try to change or influence the local people and their culture', as

Joan insisted through the pages of the *Sur in English*. Such expressions of national discreteness, and respect for the otherness of people of other nations, are perhaps a reflection of the critique of colonialism (Gledhill 1994) and Britain's changing but still ambivalent attitude towards the outside world.

The history of British migration is one of an unequal relationship between the British traveller and the indigenous people; the Briton being superior in each case. Before mass tourism and the rise in expendable wealth of the lower classes, Britons abroad had traditionally been colonisers or wealthy travellers. The image is of the wealthy, socially advantaged, superior, arrogant traveller of past centuries who creates a 'Little England' in each area in which a group settles. Representations of the colonialist and privileged traveller appear in both historical works of fiction and non-fiction and in modern critiques of Empire. Academic historical works on colonialism discuss 'the ubiquitous nature of the military and hierarchies, the omnipresence of "Home" in the layout and furnishings of "the bungalow", and the importance of The Club for the reaffirmation of British cultural identity' (King 1976) in colonial cities in Africa, Asia and middle America. Other authors, I suspect in response to the critique of colonialism which describes racism, elitism, ethnocentrism and exploitation, attempt to give 'white men and women' the voice in their telling of colonial histories. These both reflect and challenge stereotypes of an isolated British society, and of ubiquitous protocol and elitism. Everywhere the image is of British superiority and discreteness but also of embarrassment at the same and, more subtly, of the mixing of cultures and a little acculturation.

Fictional literature of the colonial period depicts a life of power, prestige and privilege, of English elites and native servants, of parties at the club, of golf, English gardens, of children attending boarding school in England and of course the military (Lessing 1996a, 1996b; Scott 1976). However, a lot of this same literature depicts children as the link between 'natives' and imperialists, just as British migrants in Spain consider their children to be the link between themselves and the Spanish. Maybe this is where the label 'colonisers' has come from: the 'expatriates' in Spain are seen to reconstruct and relive the colonial lifestyle which has since been denigrated. Notions of childish innocence, of the 'noble savage', and challenges to the natural basis of race abound in this literature, reflecting these debates within British society. The children, who form firm bonds with servants and native children, are shown to censure their parents' racist attitudes. Innocent and inquisitive youths are able to question the taken-for-granted more freely than the older Britons, just as 'young' Britain can shake off the stereotypes associated with 'old' ideas.

However, the cultural contact of the colonial encounter did not lead to overt acculturation by the British of foreign cultural expressions, traits or habits. Britons have traditionally worked at remaining intact. While British culture was transported abroad, the culture of the colonies was not brought back 'home'.

Englishmen did not walk the streets of London in turbans or even pith helmets like Africans were supposed to sport top hats in Africa . . . The British exerted themselves to make sure they were *not* contaminated by other cultures, which was what all that nonsense about dressing for dinner in the African bush was about.

(Porter 1984: 350)

Similarly, in Fuengirola, certain elements of British society, that are contemporaneously considered valued, are adopted, retained, revered and respected. Punctuality, professionalism, experience in the wider world and respect for animal rights, for example, are considered peculiarly British. Some British migrants are more literally remnants of Empire. Having worked in the colonies for a great part of their lives, civil servants reconstruct the 'old world' to a small extent in little corners of Europe. Some retain delusions of superiority in relation to the indigenous peoples, symbolised in their choice of servants (like Dolly, whom we met in Chapter 2, with her Spanish cleaners and gardeners) as opposed to friends (other British ex-civil servants). But the Empire is dead and colonialism has been discredited. These old colonials, who are in a minority in Fuengirola, are living a myth of power and prestige. Other permanent British migrants move slightly towards acculturation by absorbing some of what they imagine to be typical Spanish culture, but actually remain discrete both culturally and structurally.

While Britons in Spain retain discreteness but feign integration, Britain itself continues to resist acculturation, loss of sovereignty, and to delude itself with a myth of superiority in the face of relative decline and interdependence. Reaching out to the outside world is always accompanied by a drawing back from it. The long, protracted process of decolonisation entailed in Britain two (of many) opposing elements: the acceptance of the equality of other cultures and a revival of nationalism. 'Commonwealth studies' was established as a branch of knowledge both celebrating and exploring ethnic/national discreteness and difference. While encouraging acceptance, this also enforced separateness. At the same time the loss of Empire was blamed for Britain's subsequent economic decline. Britain gradually became aware of its own smallness both literally and politically/economically in relation to the rest of the world. Conscious of its need to strengthen relations with the outside world in general, it was torn between whether to direct its energies towards the Commonwealth, the Atlantic Alliance or the promise of European union. At the same time the collapse of Empire precipitated an influx of immigrants in the form of ex-colonial subjects but Britain was unprepared for multi-racialism. Contradictions between thinking of these incomers as either 'British subjects' or 'foreign immigrants' reflected fears that British cultural and racial integrity was being threatened by this movement. In a similar way Britons in Spain now are content to be Europeans, free to move unhindered within the countries of the Union, but complain, albeit quietly, about the way 'foreigners' are able to enter *our country* and draw on our welfare system for aid while Britons in Spain are struggling to be paid what would be their due if they still lived in their home country (in the way of supplementary and means-tested benefits).

British pride is a legacy of Empire, and post-Empire Britain was slow to give up on the self image of being a superpower. Britons thought for a long time that their nation still 'ruled the world' (Low 1991). That this attitude of superiority still lingers is evident in the anti-European stance of some nationalists. To help cope with the post-colonial and post-industrial depressions, nationalism and little Englandism were revived; our traditions were turned to for respite. Isolation led to nationalism and to nostalgia. Margaret Thatcher, during her years as Prime Minister, attempted to foster a return to the Victorian values which would help Britain regain its pre-Empire glory. Rather than turn outwards, we were urged to turn inwards to our own British values and traditions. These traditions were listed as 'honesty, thrift, reliability, hard work and a sense of responsibility' (Porter 1984: 357). These values are reflected and drawn on in the construction of the British migrant community in Fuengirola: values which are seen by these migrants to be synonymous with the Britain of the 'good old days'. As Lowenthal (1985: 49) says, 'The past offers alternatives to an unacceptable present.' And since national pride was considered a 'casualty of the empire's demise' (Porter 1984), so patriotism was added to Thatcher's list of those values to which we must return. The Falklands War served as a symbol of patriotism, of unity in the defence of our subjects and our territory.

Implicit in this call for a return to traditional values was the accusation that contemporary Britain was suffering from a malaise, a disease which attacked our economy but stemmed from our lack of community values and national spirit. Thus finding fault with contemporary Britain was the first step on the way to its recovery, both spiritual and economic. So Britons who have migrated to Spain in the last thirty years, and who denigrate contemporary Britain as depressing and depressed, have not so much abandoned a sinking ship as moved, spatially and temporally, in order to reconstruct the old world with the traditional values which Britons once shared. These values are traditionally associated, for the English at least, with relaxation, slowness and the quiet life of our island garden.

Many of the more permanent migrants to Spain have established a community which shares the symbols of a historical Britain. I discussed in Chapter 5 how the community spirit was reminiscent of war-time unity and pulling together. The culture of the community as expressed through music, through theatre, is the culture of Britain past rather than Britain present. The Royal British Legion meet in The Shakespeare pub, which is a dark bar with wooden beams and soft furnishings. This same pub hosts a regular Old Time Music Hall sing-along. The past for these migrants is any time that is not present; that is not technology, modernisation, youth, energy, speed or rapid change. Many musicians who sing in the local British bars have established repertoires of old songs from any of the decades prior to the 1980s. Occasionally they would like to try something different, something new, but are afraid it might not be accepted. Many observers of the community (visitors to the area) commented on the way the British there 'live in the past'. Teenage migrants joked about the way they themselves were so 'out of touch' with what's going on in the world. It is as if Spain (especially Andalusia, as a rural and undeveloped area), being a relatively backward country, symbolises the golden, romantic past of community and caring, of traditional values of family and responsibility.

Britain's entry into and subsequent involvement in Europe have continued to be sullen, to lack enthusiasm, and to be rife with diversity. This relationship with Europe can stand alone as a symbol of British nationalism, of a history of ambivalence towards the outside which we need, admire and value but also protect and isolate ourselves against. David Marquand (1988: 11) hypothesises that it is our 'possessive individualism' which has marked our relations with the outside world. The individualism which enabled early industrialisation in Britain contains the 'assumption that society is made up of separate, atomistic individuals, pursuing only their own private purpose'. When this is transposed on to the nation state, it is as an autonomous sovereign power reluctant to relinquish individuality for some imaginary common good. Britain has gained the reputation of being Europe's 'awkward partner' (Brivati and Jones 1993). The fact of Britain's victory in the Second World War separated it from the rest of Europe and lent a feeling of superiority which it took to relations with European countries. Britain had aspired to sustaining a major world role independently of Europe and so came reluctantly to 'the Community', as it was then. From the outset of the application to join, and ever since, there have been both Euro-enthusiasts and Euro-sceptics. Public views with regard to membership of the European Community were apparently weak, again reflecting ambivalence, and while some Britons remain reluctant to surrender national sovereignty, politicians and the mass media, especially the tabloids, sporadically fuel the nationalist smoulder.

Meanwhile Britons in Spain argue for their rights to be European citizens; to move freely within Europe without the need for residence and work permits; to live in a European country and claim reciprocal health and social security benefits. On the other hand, they consider themselves 'guests' in Spain, and are grateful for being accepted and welcomed as foreigners into the host community. They spend their time in ethnic niches yet consider themselves to be absorbing some elements of Spanish culture. They joke about Spanish backwardness and slowness while celebrating the relaxed way of life. They construct discrete communities and call them international ones.

Conclusion

These British migrants to Spain are not colonisers in any sense other than perhaps the purely ecological. They have little political or economic power, except for the fact that the Spanish economy as a whole, particularly in some regions, is dependent on the vagaries of the tourist industry, on giant package tour companies, and on exchange rates remaining favourable to would-be visitors. The migrants themselves do not have direct experience of this power, however, and cannot directly exercise local control or influence. The experience is one of marginalisation more than of inclusion and acceptance. British permanent migrants are not expected to integrate, are not enabled to learn the language, are not included in local structures of control, and are not included through either work or family. They are even labelled 'residential tourists'.

However, the migrants themselves construct and maintain a marginal community, and even an economy, which serves to marginalise them further within Spain. They do not expect to integrate to any great extent and neither do they try to do so. Their ethnic identity is not threatened, their discreteness is certainly not threatened, nor are they a poor, exploited immigrant minority. Their marginal status is a result of a complex interplay between history, circumstance and aspirations; between structure and action.

They perhaps have something to gain from being marginal, in the guise of those things which tourism, escape, Spain, community and nostalgia can offer; those things the relationship between a historically backward and a leading nation can offer. The shared culture of the migrant community is a constant contradiction between the symbols of holiday and escape; the symbols of community and sharing, responsibility and commitment; and between symbols of entrepreneurialism, informality, maverickness, difference and of Britishness. They identify as being committed to Spain, but they are not really integrated; they are marginal but deny it. They identify with other Britons but are covert about it. They identify overtly with Spanish people but not in their relationships and networks, only in symbols. In the construction of a community they draw on symbols of community: equality, commitment, responsibility, and those things community in the past is supposed to have meant (Cohen 1985). They portray these to be associated with what Britain once was and what Spain is now. They draw on symbols of holiday and escape and demonstrate that, for them, Spain is somewhere to escape to, and Britain somewhere to escape from. They apply to Britain for help and draw on Britishness while doing so. They spend time with other Britons but run Britain down and identify as different. They symbolically dangle betwixt and between two cultures and two countries; two economies and two social spaces. But all the time they remain essentially British; they are symbols of lost Empire, of national pride, of ambivalence towards the Other, of disaffection with modern individualistic aspirations, of the call to return to community (and nation), and even of the loss of a diasporic consciousness. For while the collapse of Empire and the evolution of a multi-racial Commonwealth (including Britain itself) have fragmented the unquestioned loyalty, and dissolved the essence, of the British imperial diaspora (Cohen 1997: 81), these Britons abroad both remind Britain of its past and intimate its future.

Notes

1 Introduction: the 'Brits in Spain'

1 I accept that for some groups the word 'British' is a contested category and that it is not immediately apparent who is British and who is not. As Benedict Anderson (1983) so eloquently demonstrates, the modern nation state is merely an imagined community. In this book, as in the research on which it is based, I use 'British' to apply to those English, Scottish, Welsh and Irish people who are identified, either through their actions or words, as British nationals. I would have used another word had there been a satisfactory one available. An Irish woman, having enquired about my research, asked 'Does that include the Irish?' I told her it does if she wants it to.

2 Setting the scene

1 'First home' refers to the home one would live in if possible, rather than being seen as secondary to the home in Britain.
2 Data on recessions and periods of growth in Britain are collected from the *National Institute Economic Review*. See especially no. 139, Feb. 1992.
3 But this is a problematic assumption, as discussed more fully in Chapter 4.
4 The N340 is renowned in Spain as having once been Europe's most dangerous road, with an average of thirty accidents per kilometre per year (Ritchie 1994).

3 Migration

1 I based my research in what I call the Fuengirola area, which is covered by the two councils of Fuengirola and Mijas.
2 Figures I am quoting from the Fuengirola and Mijas census data are taken directly from figures given to me by officials in Mijas and Fuengirola and not from published data.
3 This is a typology of British migrants in Fuengirola, rather than a typology of migration *per se*. I have changed the names of the various groups since - writing on this topic previously (see O'Reilly 1996a, 1996b). I have avoided the use of the term 'expatriates' here for reasons discussed in Chapter 7. The label 'returners' has been changed to 'peripatetic visitors' to concur with the distinction between visitors and residents as the two main groups of migrant.
4 Borrowed from Warnes (1993: 55), who refers to this type of migration as peripatetic residence.

5 I say 'legal status' because those migrants spending more than six months of the year in Spain are legally obliged to register as official residents and to apply for residence permits (see Chapter 3).
6 According to Kochan and Whittington (1991), many British pensioners who had retired to Spain had deposited their small nest-eggs with the Bank of Credit and Commerce International (BCCI), attracted by higher than average interest rates and a friendly service. Their combined savings of 83 million pound sterling were wiped out overnight when BCCI was closed amidst allegations of huge fraud. While I was in Fuengirola this topic was energetically discussed amongst migrants, many of whom had invested in the bank or knew someone who had.
7 None of whom has yet completed or published findings of their research.
8 These are estimations based on observation over a long period of time. I refuse to make sophisticated calculations on age using unrepresentative data, especially since I did not ask people actual ages but only age 'group'.
9 Retirement migration now applies to all social classes and not just the better-off (Victor 1987).

5 Ethnicity and identity

1 This obsession with ethnicity and boundary maintenance and construction directs an ethnographer's gaze towards the boundaries between ethnic and larger groups to the neglect of other boundaries invoked by communities and to the neglect of historical and wider social factors in the construction of an identity. For this reason this study is not of ethnicity: theoretical discussions around ethnicity have insufficient scope (Stanton 1994) and insufficient complexity.
2 Consider, for example, the title of the book by Manning Nash (1989): *The Cauldron of Ethnicity in the Modern World.*
3 I do not mean to suggest that everyone thinks integration, to the extent of cultural homogenisation, to be a good thing – many people celebrate poly- or multiculturalism. However, there is a ubiquitous and almost taken-for-granted fear that ethnicity amongst migrant or minority groups inevitably leads to nationalism, which leads to political claims for territory, which leads to conflict. In other words, that ethnicity = dysfunction.
4 It is called a 'myth' of return because, for many, economic circumstances prevent such an event at least in the short term (Anwar 1979).
5 Although their organisation is not overtly political, Abner Cohen (1969) has argued that the relations between one group and another, as between individuals, are always relations of power and may at any time become political.
6 Floya Anthias (1992) argues that this type of 'cultural identity' cannot be defined as 'ethnicity' since ethnicity is active – exclusionary or usurpatory – and always has a political element. This is not to reduce ethnicity to politics, but is an acknowledgement that purposive, political action is implicit in the establishment of boundaries based on ethnic origin (Anthias 1992). A problem with Anthias's analysis is that it is limited by the fact that her attention is always directed towards traditionally oppressed and powerless 'immigrants' and not 'migrants' in general.
7 This is the point at which I most clearly depart from the expressed identity of migrants themselves. It seems to me that tourism is an important factor in the meanings of life in Spain for British migrants, but many migrants, as will be seen, expressly identify as 'not tourist'. Charles Betty, a returning resident and academic in the field of social policy research, makes a simple, but for him crucial, distinction between 'expatriates' (including himself) and 'tourists' (see Betty and Cahill 1995).

8 I pulled four brochures covering Spanish resorts from travel agents' shelves early in 1999. They all focused on sunshine, sea, swimming pools and bright blue skies (especially pictorially) more than on history or culture.

9 I have borrowed the term 'residential tourists' from the Spanish, but am unsure of its origins. A Spanish lawyer, who works on behalf of many foreign residents and who writes for a local English-language newspaper, uses the term in his articles and advertisements. I use it to invoke the relationship between migrants and tourism in the Costa del Sol. I find this phrase useful here but realise there are problems with it, especially as for residents it conflicts with their identity as committed to Spain (see Chapter 7 for further discussion of the term).

10 Interestingly, a Spanish woman told me the opposite. 'The British here, they drink so much because they always meet in bars', she explained. 'We don't do that, we go to people's homes. A Spanish woman always cooks extra in case anyone visits unexpectedly.'

11 Stradling and Vincent (1994) suggest that the 'Spain is different' tourist slogan of the 1960s drew on (and shaped) foreign perceptions of a sun-soaked land where life continued as it had for centuries.

6 The construction of community

1 It is not only the British who are moving to and buying property in Spain in increasing numbers since the 1960s and 1970s: Germans, Scandinavians, Dutch and Americans are well represented in this area too (Svensson 1991). I refer to these as 'foreign nationals' in Spain.

2 When I refer in this chapter to the British community, I am referring to an experience shared by Britons, but also by some other foreign nationals, which is 'other' than Spanish. Life in Fuengirola for German migrants, for example, may be similar in many ways to the experience for British migrants. What I call a British community is not labelled thus by its members, who are more likely to refer to the international community and to their members as foreign residents in Spain. However, my research focused on British migrants and those groups I studied and those networks I traced had a majority of British members.

3 The situation here is changing as the project attracts more Spanish volunteers and an increasing number of Spanish patients.

4 Those Britons who have businesses appealing to all nationalities tend to be more successful in terms of growth and endurance. None the less it is difficult to set something up which is in direct competition with Spanish services or industry. Many British are afraid to try, and there are rumours preventing them further, as I discuss in the next chapter.

5 From Cohen (1985); also see Chapter 5.

7 British migrants: betwixt and between

1 Some authors suggest they have transported a bit of Britain abroad; see Svensson (1991) and Champion and King (1993).

2 As I completed my fieldwork, things were beginning to change in the area. In the council offices an English-speaking official was installed to help foreigners with problems related to local administration. However, the new mayor of the Socialist Party (PSOE) cancelled this provision soon after he was elected in 1995. He believes such actions increase encapsulation. Now the mayor of the People's Party (Partido Popular) is overtly trying to make Fuengirola Spanish again.

3 Interestingly, though, the first foreign language my daughters were taught at school in Fuengirola was French.

4 One theory which circulates as explanation for the persistence of such strong local dialects is that, post-Franco, Spanish regional dialects, which he attempted to suppress, are experiencing a revival throughout the country as a whole.

5 Since I had hoped the survey would reach a large sample, including people to whom I had not otherwise gained access, I decided that questionnaires would be quicker, cheaper and less time-consuming than to interview respondents.

References

Age Concern. 1993. *Growing Old in Spain*. London: Age Concern.

Aldridge, A. 1995. 'The English as they see others: England revealed in Provence', *The Sociological Review*, August, pp. 415–34.

Allen, C. (ed.) 1976. *Plain Tales from The Raj*. London: Futura Publications.

Anderson, B. [1983] 1991. *Imagined Communities*. London: Verso.

Anderson, J.M. 1992. *Spain 1001 Sights. An Archaeological and Historical Guide*. London: Robert Hale.

Anglican Church 1993. 'Expatriate Community Service'. Leaflet advertising 'register of information on expatriates: names, addresses, next of kin, family doctor etc.'

Anthias, F. 1992. *Ethnicity, Class, Gender and Migration*. Avebury: Aldershot.

Anwar, M. 1979. *The Myth of Return*. London: Heinemann.

Ayuntamiento de Mijas 1993. 'Mijas Town Hall Foreign Residents' Department answers your questions about: work and residence permits'. Malaga. Leaflet.

Baird, C. 1995. *Spain. The Versatile Guide*. London: Duncan Peterson.

Barth, F. 1969. 'Introduction' in Barth, F. (ed.) *Ethnic Groups and Boundaries*. London: George Allen & Unwin, pp. 9–38.

Battisti, F. and Portelli, A. 1994. 'The apple and the olive tree. Exiles, sojourners, and tourists in the university' in Benmayor, R. and Skotnes, A. (eds) *Migration and Identity*. Oxford: Oxford University Press, pp. 35–51.

Bauman, Z. 1992. 'Soil, blood and identity', *The Sociological Review*, November, pp. 675–701.

BBC TV. (6.7.92–9.7.93) *Eldorado*. A Cinema Verity/J DY T production. Producer: Corrine Hollingworth.

BBC TV. 1996. *The Tourist*. (See MacCannell 1996.)

Beard, R. 1994. 'The cost of keeping a home in paradise', *Daily Mail*, 17 August, pp. 28–9.

Beckford, J. 1982. 'Beyond the pale: cults, culture and conflicts' in Barker, E. (ed.) *New Religious Movements. A Perspective for Understanding Society*. New York: Edwin Mellen Press, pp. 284–301.

Bedarida, F. 1991. *A Social History of England 1851–1990* (2nd edn). London: Routledge.

Bel Adell, C. 1989. 'Extranjeros en España', *Papeles de Geografía*, no. 15, pp. 21–32.

Benmayor, R. and Skotnes, A. 1994a. 'Some reflections on migration and identity' in Benmayor, R. and Skotnes, A. (eds) *Migration and Identity*. Oxford: Oxford University Press, pp. 1–18.

Benmayor, R. and Skotnes, A. 1994b. *Migration and Identity. International Yearbook of Oral History and Life Stories*, Vol. III. Oxford: Oxford University Press.

Betty, C. 1994. 'An investigation of the lifestyles of elderly British expatriates on the Costa del Sol'. Proposal for PhD research, University of Brighton, Sussex.

Betty, C. and Cahill, M. 1995. 'British expatriates' experience of health and social services on the Costa del Sol'. Unpublished paper, University of Brighton, Sussex.

Boissevain, J. 1994. 'Towards an anthropology of European communities' in Goddard, V.A., Llobera, J.R. and Shore, C. (eds) *The Anthropology of Europe*. Oxford: Berg, pp. 41–56.

Bonacich, E. 1973. 'A theory of middleman minorities', *American Sociological Review*, 38, 583–94.

Bonnett, A. 1993. *Radicalism, Anti-Racism and Representation*. London: Routledge.

Boseley, S. 1993. 'A sour taste of paradise', *Guardian*, 4 June, p. 12.

Brandes, S. 1980. *Metaphors of Masculinity. Sex and Status in Andalusian Folklore*. Pennsylvania: University of Pennsylvania Press.

Brein, M. and David, K.H. 1971. 'Intercultural communication and the adjustment of the sojourner', *Psychological Bulletin*, 76, 215–30.

Brivati, B. and Jones, H. (eds) 1993. *From Reconstruction to Integration: Britain and Europe since 1945*. Leicester: Leicester University Press.

Brooks, G. 1993. 'Ex service pensioners living abroad in the European Community'. Unpublished paper prepared for presentation to Royal British Legion HQ, London.

Brubaker, R. 1995. 'Aftermaths of Empire and the unmixing of peoples: historical and comparative perspectives', *Ethnic and Racial Studies*, 18 (2), 189–218.

Buechler, H.C. and Buechler, J.M. 1987. 'Introduction' in Buechler, H.C. and Buechler, J.M. (eds) *Migrations in Europe. The Role of Family, Labor and Politics*. London: Greenwood Press, pp. 1–7.

Buijs, G. 1993. 'Introduction' in Buijs, G. (ed.) *Migrant Women: Crossing Boundaries and Changing Identities*. Oxford: Berg.

Buller, H. and Hoggart, K. 1994. *International Counterurbanization: British Migrants in Rural France*. Aldershot: Avebury.

Burkart, A.J. and Medlik, S. 1974. *Tourism, Past, Present and Future*. London: Heinemann.

Burns, T. 1993a. 'Foreigners in a friendly land', *Lookout*, March, pp. 33–7.

Burns, T. 1993b. 'Like it or leave it. No country is perfect. Not even Spain', *Lookout*, October, pp. 8–19.

Bytheway, B. 1995. *Ageism*. Buckingham: Open University Press.

Cashmore, E.E. 1994. *The Dictionary of Race and Ethnic Relations* (2nd edn). London: Routledge.

Castells, M. and Portes, A. 1989. 'World underneath: the origins, dynamics and effects of the informal economy' in Portes *et al.* (eds) *The Informal Economy*. Baltimore: Johns Hopkins University Press, pp. 11–37.

Castles, S. and Miller, M.J. 1993. *The Age of Migration. International Population Movements in the Modern World*. London: Macmillan.

Champion, T. 1995. 'Internal migration, counterurbanization and changing population distribution' in Hall, R. and White, P. (eds) *Europe's Population*. London: UCL Press, pp. 99–129.

Champion, T. and Fielding, T. 1992. 'Editorial introduction' in Champion, T. and Fielding, T. (eds) *Migration Processes and Patterns. Volume I. Research Progress and Prospects*. London: Belhaven Press, pp. 1–14.

Champion, T. and King, R. 1993. 'New trends in international migration in Europe', *Geographical Viewpoint*, 21, 45–57.

Chapman, M. and Prothero, R.M. 1985. 'Themes on circulation in the Third World' in Prothero, R.M. and Chapman, M. *Circulation in Third World Countries*. London: Routledge & Kegan Paul, pp. 1–29.

Clark, B. 1965. *Dark Ghetto. Dilemmas of Social Power*. London: Harper & Row.

Coffey, A. 1999. *The Ethnographic Self. Fieldwork and the Repression of Identity*. London: Sage.

Cohen, A. 1969. 'Political anthropology: the analysis of the symbolism of power relations', *Man*, 4, 217–35.

Cohen, A.P. (ed.) 1982. *Belonging. Identity and Social Organisation in British Rural Cultures*. Manchester: Manchester University Press.

Cohen, A.P. 1985. *The Symbolic Construction of Community*. London: Routledge.

Cohen, A.P. 1987. *Whalsay. Symbol, Segment and Boundary in a Shetland Island Community*. Manchester: Manchester University Press.

Cohen, R. 1996. 'Introduction' in Cohen, R. (ed.) *Theories of Migration. The International Library of Studies on Migration* (Vol. I). Cheltenham: Edward Elgar Publishing, pp. xii–xvii.

Cohen, R. 1997. *Global Diasporas. An Introduction*. London: UCL Press.

Cohen, S. and Taylor, L. 1992. *Escape Attempts. The Theory and Practice of Resistance to Everyday Life* (2nd edn). London: Routledge.

Collinson, S. 1993. *Europe and International Migration*. London: Pinter Publishers (for the Royal Institute of International Affairs).

Concise Oxford Dictionary of Sociology 1994. Edited by Marshall, G. Oxford: Oxford University Press.

Conner, W. 1986. 'The impact of homelands upon diasporas' in Sheffer, G. (ed.) *Modern Diasporas in International Politics*. London: Croom Helm, pp. 16–46.

Crampton, R. 1993. 'Costa del Sunset', *Times Magazine*, 28 August, p. 6.

Creffield, D. 1995. '10,830,000! That's the number of Britons living abroad', *Overseas Jobs Express*, 15 November, p. 1.

Crick, M. 1989. 'Representations of international tourism in the social sciences: sun, sex, sights, savings, and servility', *Annual Review of Anthropology*, 18, 307–44.

Curtis, B. and Pajaczkowska, C. 1994. '"Getting There": travel, time and narrative' in Robertson, G., Mash, M., Tickner, L., Bird, J., Curtis, B. and Putnam, T. (eds) *Travellers' Tales. Narratives of Home and Displacement*. London: Routledge, pp. 199–215.

Damer, S. 1995. 'Bitter Lemons. A proposal for a sociological research project into British ex-patriates in Cyprus'. Unpublished paper, Dept. of Sociology, University of Glasgow.

Davey, P. 1990. *Long Stays in Spain*. Newton Abbott: David & Charles.

Davis, B. 1993. 'The Locust Eaters', *Entertainer*, 19–25 August, p. 19.

Davis, J. 1992. *Exchange*. Buckingham: Open University Press.

de Foucauld, J.B. 1992. 'The scale of the problem' in Johnson, T. (ed.) *Combating Social Exclusion, Fostering Integration: report of a conference hosted by the Commission of the European Communities*. Brussels: Commission of the European Communities, pp. 8–142.

de Soto, H. 1989. *The Other Path. The Invisible Revolution in the Third World*. London: I.B. Taurus.

Debelius, H. (1989) 'Too hot on banana beach; wanted Britons in Spain', *The Times*, 4 August.

Dempsey, K. 1990. *Smalltown*. Melbourne: Oxford University Press.

Dictionary of Human Geography 1994. (3rd edn). Edited by Johnston, R.J., Gregory, D. and Smith, D.M. Oxford: Blackwell.

Durkheim, E. 1982. *The Rules of Sociological Method and Selected Texts on Sociology and its Method* (introduction and edited by S. Lukes). London: Macmillan Press.

Earnest, E. 1968. *Expatriates and Patriots. American Artists, Scholars and Writers in Europe*. Durham, NC: Duke University Press.

Ellen, R.F. 1984. *Ethnographic Research. A Guide to General Conduct*. London: Academic Press.

Elliott, R. 1993. *Enjoying the Costa del Sol*. Malaga: Bookworld España.

Elliott, R. 1995. 'Enjoying good health care on the Costa del Sol'. Booklet. Free edition available from BUPA International, Malaga.

Epstein, A.L. 1978. *Ethos and Identity*. London: Tavistock Publications.

Eriksen, T.H. 1993. *Ethnicity and Nationalism, Anthropological Perspectives*. London: Pluto Press.

European Commission. 1995. *Tourism in Europe*. Brussels: EC.

European Commission. 1996. *Tourism and the European Union: A Practical Guide*. Brussels: EC.

Facaros, D. and Pauls, M. 1992. *Cadogan Guides. Spain*. London: Cadogan Books.

FADS, *Fuengirola and District Society Yearbook 1994*. Malaga: FADS.

Fassman, H. and Munz, R. 1994. 'Patterns and trends of international migration in Western Europe' in Fassman, H. and Munz, R. (eds) *European Migration in the Late Twentieth Century*. Aldershot: Edward Elgar, pp. 3–34.

Fennell, G., Phillipson, C. and Evers, H. 1988. *The Sociology of Old Age*. Milton Keynes: Open University Press.

Findlay, A. 1995. 'The future of skill exchanges within the European Union' in Hall, R. and White, P. (eds) *Europe's Population*. London: UCL Press, pp. 130–41.

Fletcher, D. 1994. 'Life in the sun is not so hot for elderly', *Daily Mail*, 6 May.

Fodor's Spain 1994. New York: Fodor's Travel Publications.

Forman, R.E. 1971. *Black Ghettos, White Ghettos and Slums*. Englewood Cliffs, NJ: Prentice Hall.

Fraser, R. 1973. *The Pueblo. A Mountain Village on the Costa del Sol*. London: Allen Lane.

Fried, C. 1983. 'Introduction' in Fried, C. (ed.) *Minorities: Community and Identity*. Berlin: Springer-Verlag, pp. 1–8.

García, S. 1994. 'The Spanish experience and its implications for a citizens' Europe' in Goddard, V.A., Llobera, J.R. and Shore, C. (eds) *The Anthropology of Europe*. Oxford: Berg, pp. 255–74.

Gaughan, J.P. and Ferman, L.A. 1987. 'Towards an understanding of the informal economy', *Annals of the Academy of Political and Social Science*, 593, 15–25.

Geertz, C. [1973] 1993. 'Thick description: toward an interpretive theory of culture' in Geertz, C., *The Interpretation of Cultures*. London: Fontana Press, pp. 3–30.

Geertz, C. 1988. *Works and Lives. The Anthropologist as Author*. London: Polity Press.

Gledhill, J. 1994. *Power and its Disguises. Anthropological Perspectives on Politics*. London: Pluto Press.

Goward, N.J. 1984. 'The fieldwork experience' in Ellen, R.F. (ed.) *Ethnographic Research*. London: Academic Press, pp. 87–118.

Graburn, N.H.H. 1978. 'Tourism: the sacred journey' in Smith, V. (ed.) *Hosts and Guests*. Oxford: Basil Blackwell, pp. 17–32.

Graff, M.L. 1993. *Culture Shock! Spain*. London: Kuperard.

Green, B. 1994. 'Buying a property in Spain? It's only common sense', *The Reporter,* February, p. 15.

Hall, R. and White, P. (eds). 1995. *Europe's Population. Towards the Next Century*. London: UCL Press.

Hammersley, M. and Atkinson, P. [1983] 1995. *Ethnography. Principals in Practice*. London: Routledge.

Hampshire, D. 1995. *Living and Working in Spain*. Harmondsworth: Penguin.

Hay, T. 1993. 'A great time to buy', *Lookout*, September, p. 47.

Hazan, H. 1994. *Old Age: Constructions and Deconstructions*. Cambridge: Cambridge University Press.

Hedley, R. 1992. 'Organising and managing volunteers' in Hedley, R. and Davis Smith, J. (eds) *Volunteering and Society. Principles and Practice*. London: Bedford Square Press, pp. 93–119.

Hobman, D. 1988. 'The role of the charitable and volunteer organisations' in Wells, N. and Freer, C. (eds) *The Ageing Population. Burden or Challenge?* London: Macmillan Press, pp. 131–41.

Hobsbawm, E.J. 1992. *Nations and Nationalism since 1780* (2nd edn). Cambridge: Canto.

Holbrook, C. 1993. 'A chance to run with the bulls', *Sunday Sun*, 5–11 September, p. 10.

Holmes, E.R. and Holmes, L. 1995. *Other Cultures, Elder Years* (2nd edn). London: Sage.

Holohan, A. 1995. *Working Lives. The Irish in Britain*. Hayes: Irish Post.

Holy, L. 1984. 'Theory, methodology and the research process' in Ellen, R.F. (ed.) *Ethnographic Research*. London: Academic Press, pp. 1–34.

Hooper, J. 1992. 'Shadow over a new life in the sun', *Guardian*, 22 April, p. 21.

Hooper, J. 1993. 'A hard lesson in Spanglish', *Guardian*, 4 June, p. 13.

Hudson, R. and Williams, A.M. 1989. *Divided Britain*. London: Belhaven Press.

Hutchinson, J. and Smith, A.D. 1996. 'Introduction. Concepts of ethnicity' in Hutchinson, J. and Smith, A.D. (eds) *Ethnicity*. Oxford: Oxford University Press, pp. 1–16.

Ignatieff, M. 1998. *The Warrior's Honor. Ethnic War and the Modern Conscience*. London: Chatto & Windus.

Jenkins, C.L. 1991. 'Tourism policies in developing countries' in Medlik, S. (ed.) *Managing Tourism*. Oxford: Butterworth-Heinemann, pp. 269–77.

Jenkins, R. 1982. 'Work and unemployment in industrial society: an anthropological perspective' in Laite, J. (ed.) *Bibliographies on Local Labour Markets and the Informal Economy*. London: SSRC.

Jurdao, F. 1990. *España en Venta*. Madrid: Endymion.

Jurdao, F. and Sanchez, M. 1990. *España, Asilo de Europa*. Barcelona: Planeta.

Karn, V. 1977. *Retiring to the Seaside*. London: Routledge & Kegan Paul.

Kean, G. 1994. *Costa del Sol. Essential Travel Guides*. Harmondsworth: Automobile Association.

Kearney, M. 1986. 'From the invisible hand to visible feet: anthropological studies of migration and development', *Annual Review of Anthropology*, 15, 331–61.

Kemp, J.H. and Ellen, R. 1984. 'Informal interviewing' in Ellen, R.F. (ed.) *Ethnographic Research*. London: Academic Press, pp. 229–36.

King, A. 1976. *Colonial Urban Development: Culture, Social Power and Environment*. London: Routledge & Kegan Paul.

King, M. 1992. *AA Tour Guide Spain*. Harmondsworth: Automobile Association.

King, R. (ed.) 1993. *The New Geography of European Migrations*. London: Belhaven Press.

King, R. and Rybaczuk, K. 1993. 'Southern Europe and the international division of labour: from emigration to immigration' in King, R. (ed.) *The New Geography of European Migrations*. London: Belhaven Press, pp. 175–206.

King, R., Warnes, A. and Williams, A.M. 1998. 'International retirement migration in Europe', *International Journal of Population Geography*, 4 (2), 91–111.

Klein, G.D. 1990. 'Sojourning and ethnic solidarity: Indian South Africans', *Ethnic Groups*, 8, 1–13.

Kochan, N. and Whittington, B. 1991. *Bankrupt: The BCCI Fraud*. London: Victor Gollancz.

Lanfant, M.F. 1995. 'Introduction' in Lanfant, M.F., Allcock, J.B. and Bruner, E.M. (eds) *International Tourism, Identity and Change*. London: Sage.

Larner, D. 1993. 'Retiring on the Costa could cost you dear', *Sunday Times*, 29 August.

Lessing, D. 1996a. *Going Home*. London: HarperCollins.

Lessing, D. 1996b. *In Pursuit of the English*. London: HarperCollins.

Let's Go. The Budget Guide to Spain and Portugal 1993. London: Pan Books.

Lloyd, B. 1992. *Reflections of Spain*. London: Thames and Hudson.

Longino Jr, C.F. 1982. 'American retirement communities and residential relocation' in Warnes, A.M. (ed.) *Geographical Perspectives on the Elderly*. London: John Wiley & Sons, pp. 239–62.

Lore, D. 1994. 'One million expatriates can't be wrong', *Entertainer*, 24 Feb.–2 March, p. 7.

Lovell, D. 1994. 'The time snobs', *Reporter*, 1 April, p. 21.

Low, D.A. 1991. *Eclipse of Empire*. Cambridge: Cambridge University Press.

Lowenthal, D. 1985. *The Past is a Foreign Country*. Cambridge: Cambridge University Press.

Luard, N. 1984. *Andalucia. A Portrait of Southern Spain*. London: Century Publishing.

MacCannell, D. 1996. *Tourist or Traveller?* London: BBC Educational Developments.

MacKinnon, I. 1993. 'A place in the sun loses its shine', *Independent on Sunday*, 23 May, p. 11.

Malinowski, B. 1922. *Argonauts of the Western Pacific*. London: Routledge & Kegan Paul.

Marquand, D. 1988. *The Unprincipled Society: New Demands and Old Politics*. London: Cape.

Martin, P. 1993. 'The migration issue' in King, R. (ed.) *The New Geography of European Migrations*. London: Belhaven Press, pp. 1–15.

Martiniello, M. 1995. 'European citizenship, European identity and migrants' in Miles, R. and Thränhardt, D. (eds) *Migration and European Integration: The Dynamics of Inclusion and Exclusion*. London: Pinter Publishers, pp. 37–52.

Marvin, G. 1990. *Coping with Spain*. Oxford: Basil Blackwell.

Mayle, P. 1989. *A Year in Provence*. London: Alfred Knopf.

Mayle, P. 1991. *Toujours Provence*. London: Pan Books.

Meier, A. and Rudwick, E. 1970. *From Plantation to Ghetto*. London: Constable.

Mellado, V.M. 1993. 'The Chamber of Commerce requests measures to reactivate residential tourism', *Sur in English*, 26 November–2 December, p. 5.

Mendel, J. 1993. 'Growing old in Spain', *Lookout*, November, pp. 38–58.

Miles, R. 1993. *Racism after Race Relations*. London: Routledge.

Misiti, M., Muscara, C., Pumares, P., Rodriguez, V. and White, P. 1995. 'Future migration into Southern Europe' in Hall, R. and White, P. (eds) *Europe's Population*. London: UCL Press, pp. 161–87.

Montanari, A. and Cortese, A. 1993. 'South to north migration in a Mediterranean perspective' in King, R. (ed.) *Mass Migrations in Europe. The Legacy and the Future*. London: Belhaven Press, pp. 212–33.

Mullan, C. 1993. *The Problems of the Elderly British Expatriate Community in Spain*. London: Help the Aged.

Nash, M. 1989. *The Cauldron of Ethnicity in the Modern World*. Chicago: The University of Chicago Press.

Newland, K. 1994. 'Involuntary migration. Refugees in the new Europe' in Hamilton, K.A. and Hunter, R.E. (eds) *Migration and the New Europe*. Washington DC: CSIS, pp. 56–71.

Öberg, S. 1994. 'Factors in future south–north migration' in Lutz, W. (ed.) *The Future Population of the World*. London: Earthscan Publications, pp. 361–87.

OECD. 1993. 'Chairman's conclusions' in *The Changing Course of International Migration*. Paris: OECD, p. 257.

Okely, J. 1983. *The Traveller Gypsies*. Cambridge: Cambridge University Press.

O'Reilly, K. 1996a. 'Using surveys and quantitative data in field research', *Sociology Review*, 5 (3), 6–9.

O'Reilly, K. 1996b. 'A new trend in European migration: contemporary British migration to Fuengirola, Costa del Sol', *Geographical Viewpoint*, 23, 25–36.

O'Reilly, K. 2000a. 'Trading intimacy for liberty: British women on the Costa del Sol' in Anthias, F. and Lazaridis, G. (eds) *Gender and Migration in Southern Europe*. Oxford: Berg.

O'Reilly, K. 2000b. 'Blackpool in the sun: images of the British on the Costa del Sol' in King, R. and Woods, N. (eds) *Media and Migration*. London: Routledge.

Ortega, O. 1993. 'Reportaje' in *Feria y Fiestas del Rosario 1993 Official Programme*. Malaga: Ayuntamiento de Fuengirola.

Overbeek, H. 1995. 'Towards a new international migration regime: globalization, migration and the internationalization of the state' in Miles, R. and Thränhardt, D. (eds) *Migration and European Integration: The Dynamics of Inclusion and Exclusion*. London: Pinter Publishers, pp. 15–36.

Papademetriou, D.G. 1994. 'At a crossroads: Europe and migration' in Hamilton, K.A. and Hunter, R.E. (eds) *Migration and the New Europe*. Washington DC: CSIS.

Pascual Vegas, J. 1993. 'El turismo: nuestro medio de vida' in *Feria y Fiestas del Rosario 1993 Official Programme*. Malaga: Ayuntamiento de Fuengirola.

Peacock, J.L. 1986. *The Anthropological Lens: Harsh Light, Soft Focus*. Cambridge: Cambridge University Press.

Pearce, D. 1995. *Tourism Today. A Geographical Analysis* (2nd edn). Harlow: Longman.

Pearce, M. and Stewart, G. 1992. *British Political History 1867–1990. Democracy and Decline*. London: Routledge.

Pitt-Rivers, J.A. 1963. *The People of the Sierra* (2nd edn). Chicago: Phoenix Books.

Pooley, C.G. and Whyte, I.D. 1991. 'Introduction. Approaches to the study of migration and social change' in Pooley, C.G. and Whyte, I.D. (eds) *Migrants, Emigrants and Immigrants. A Social History of Migration*. London: Routledge, pp. 1–15.

Porter, B. 1984. *The Lion's Share. A Short History of British Imperialism 1850–1983* (2nd edn). London: Longman.

Portes, A., Castells, M. and Benton, L.A. (eds) 1989. *The Informal Economy. Studies in Advanced and Less Developed Countries*. Baltimore: Johns Hopkins University Press.

Powdermaker, H. 1966. *Stranger and Friend*. New York: W.W. Norton.

Prus, R. 1997 *Subcultural Mosaics and Intersubjective Realities. An Ethnographic Research Agenda for Pragmatizing the Social Sciences*. Albany: State University of New York Press.

Punnett, N. 1990. *Travel and Tourism*. Oxford: Basil Blackwell.

RBL. 1993. Royal British Legion, Costa del Sol Branch, Newsletter.

Reay-Smith, J. 1980. *Living in Spain Today*. London: Robert Hale.

Reig, M. 1995. *Costa del Sol, Spain*. Madrid: Ministerio de Comercio y Turismo.

Richards, R.A.C. 1992. *How To Live and Work in Spain*. Plymouth: How To Books.

Ritchie, H. 1994. *Here We Go. A Summer on the Costa del Sol*. Harmondsworth: Penguin.

Roberts, B.R. 1989. 'Employment structure, life cycle, and life chances: formal and informal sectors in Guadalajara' in Portes *et al.* (eds) *The Informal Economy*. Baltimore: Johns Hopkins University Press, pp. 41–59.

Robinson, R. and Pybus, V. 1991. *Live and Work in Spain and Portugal*. Oxford: Vacation Work.

Robinson, V. 1984. 'Asians in Britain: a study in encapsulation and marginality' in Clarke, C., Ley, D. and Peach, C. (eds) *Geography and Ethnic Pluralism*. London: George Allen & Unwin, pp. 231–57.

Robinson, V. 1996. 'Introduction: the geographical contribution to the study of human migration' in Robinson, V. (ed.) *Geography and Migration. The International Library of Studies on Migration, Vol. 2*. Cheltenham: Edward Elgar Publishing, pp. 6–24.

Rochester, C. 1992. 'Community organisations and voluntary action' in Hedley, R. and Davis Smith, J. (eds) *Volunteering and Society. Principles and Practice*. London: Bedford Square Press, pp. 120–31.

Rodríguez, V., Fernández-Mayoralas, G. and Rojo, F. 1998. 'European retirees on the Costa del Sol: a cross-national comparison', *International Journal of Population Geography*, 4 (2), 91–111.

Rogers, A. 1992. 'Elderly migration' in Rogers, A. (ed.) *Elderly Migration and Population Redistribution*. London: Belhaven Press, pp. 1–15.

Roosens, E.E. 1989. *Creating Ethnicity*. London: Sage.

Sabean, D.W. 1984. *Power in the Blood*. Cambridge: Cambridge University Press.

Safran, W. 1991. 'Diasporas in modern societies: myths of homeland and return', *Diaspora* 1 (1), 83–99.

Said, E.W. 1978. *Orientalism*. London: Routledge & Kegan Paul.

Salt, J. 1992 'Current and future international migration trends affecting Europe', *People on the Move: New Migration Flows in Europe*. Strasbourg: Council of Europe Press, pp. 41–81.

Salt, J., Singleton, A. and Hogarth, J. 1994. *Europe's International Migrants: Data Sources, Patterns and Trends*. London: HMSO.

SALVA (Salon Varietes). 1993. Promotional paper about, and appeal for funds for, the international theatre in Fuengirola. Unpublished paper: The Salon Varietes.

Sassen-Koob, S. 1989. 'New York City's informal economy' in Portes *et al.* (eds) *The Informal Economy*. Baltimore: Johns Hopkins University Press, pp. 60–77.

Scott, P. [1976] 1984. *The Raj Quartet*. London: Heinemann.

Shaffir, W.B., Stebbings, R.A. and Turowetz, A. 1980. *Fieldwork Experience*. New York: St Martin's Press.

Shaw, G. and Williams, A.M. 1994. *Critical Issues in Tourism. A Geographical Perspective*. Oxford: Blackwell.

Shields, R. 1991. *Places on the Margin. Alternative Geographies of Modernity*. London: Routledge.

Shun, L. and Fine, G. 1995. 'The presentation of ethnic authenticity: Chinese food as a social accomplishment', *Sociological Quarterly*, 36 (3), 535–53.

Siu, P.C.P. 1952. 'The sojourner', *American Journal of Sociology*, 58, 34–44.

Skeldon, R. 1994. 'Reluctant exiles or bold pioneers' in Skeldon, R. (ed.) *Reluctant Exiles? Migration from Hong Kong and the New Chinese Overseas*. Hong Kong: Hong Kong University Press, pp. 3–18.

Skypala, P. 1988. 'Pitfalls in expat haven: problems of expatriates living in Spain', *The Times*, 11 June.

Sleater, M. 1993. *Heart of Clubs '93*. Malaga: TV Image.

Smith, V. 1978. 'Introduction' in Smith, V. (ed.) *Hosts and Guests. The Anthropology of Tourism*. Oxford: Basil Blackwell, pp. 1–14.

Solé, C. 1995. 'Portugal and Spain: from exporters to importers of labour' in Cohen, R. (ed.) *The Cambridge Survey of World Migrations*. Cambridge: Cambridge University Press, pp. 316–20.

SOPEMI. 1990. 'Trends in international migration: continuous reporting system on migration'. *Annual Report 1990*. Paris: OECD.

SOPEMI. 1993. 'Trends in international migration: continuous reporting system on migration'. *Annual Report 1993*. Paris: OECD.

Soysal, Y. 1996. 'Changing citizenship in Europe: remarks on postnational membership and the national state' in Cesarini, D. and Fulbrook, M. (eds) *Citizenship, Nationality and Migration in Europe*. London: Routledge.

Speare Jr, A. 1992. 'Elderly migration, proximity of children, and living arrangements' in Rogers, A. (ed.) *Elderly Migration and Population Redistribution*. London: Belhaven Press, pp. 57–118.

Spradley, J.P. 1980. *Participant Observation*. Fort Worth: Harcourt Brace Jovanovich Publications.

Stanton, G. 1994. 'The play on identity: Gibraltar and its migrants' in Goddard, V.A., Llobera, J.R. and Shore, C. (eds) *The Anthropology of Europe*. Oxford: Berg, pp. 173–90.

Stepick, A. 1989. 'Miami's two informal sectors' in Portes *et al.* (eds) *The Informal Economy*. Baltimore: Johns Hopkins University Press, pp. 111–31.

Stradling, R.A. and Vincent, M. 1994. *Cultural Atlas of Spain and Portugal*. Oxford: Andromeda Oxford.

Strathern, M. 1992. 'Qualified value: the perspective of gift exchange' in Humphrey, C. and Hugh-Jones, S. (eds) *Barter, Exchange and Value. An Anthropological Approach*. Cambridge: Cambridge University Press, pp. 169–91.

Sur in English 1994. 'Cultural tourism', *Sur*, 17–23 June, p. 2.

Svensson, P. 1989. *Your Home in Spain* (2nd edn). Longman: London.

Svensson, P. 1991. *Buying and Selling Your Home in Spain* (3rd edn). London: Longman.

Theroux, P. 1992. *The Happy Isles of Oceania*. London: Hamish Hamilton.

Tölölyan, K. 1996. 'Rethinking diaspora(s): stateless power in the transnational moment', *Diaspora*, 5 (1), 3–36.

Touch Productions. 1992. *Coast of Dreams*. Documentary for Channel Four (re-shown in 1994).

Ullman, E.L. 1954. 'Amenities as a factor in regional growth', *Geographical Review*, 44, 119–32.

Uriely, N. 1994. 'Rhetorical ethnicity of permanent sojourners: the case of Israeli immigrants in the Chicago area', *International Sociology*, 9 (4), 431–45.

Urry, J. 1990. *The Tourist Gaze*. London: Sage.

Valenzuela, M. 1988. 'Spain: the phenomenon of mass tourism' in Shaw, G. and Williams, A.M. (eds) *Tourism and Economic Development. Western European Experiences*. London: Belhaven Press, pp. 39–57.

Valero Escandell, J.R. 1992. *La Inmigración Extranjera en Alicante*. Alicante: Instituto de Cultura, Juan Gil-Albert.

van de Kaa, D. 1993. 'European migration at the end of history', *European Review*, 1 (1), 87–108.

van den Berghe, P.L. 1981. *The Ethnic Phenomenon*. London: Praeger.

Victor, C.R. 1987. *Old Age in Modern Society*. London: Chapman and Hall.

Vincelli, S. 1994. 'Prefatory remarks' in Hamilton, K. (ed.) *Migration and the New Europe*. Washington DC: Center for Strategic and International Studies, pp. xiii–xvi.

Voase, R. 1995. *Tourism: the Human Perspective*. London: Hodder & Stoughton.

Wallman, S. 1986. 'Ethnicity and the boundary process in context' in Rex, J. and Mason, D. (eds) *Theories of Race and Ethnic Relations*. Cambridge: Cambridge University Press, pp. 226–45.

Warnes, A.M. 1991. 'Migration to and seasonal residence in Spain of Northern European elderly people', *European Journal of Gerontology*, 1, 53–60.

Warnes, A.M. 1992. 'Elderly migration: motivations and causes' in Rogers, A. (ed.) *Elderly Migration and Population Redistribution*. London: Belhaven Press, pp. 16–21.

Warnes, A.M. 1993. 'Demographic ageing: trends and policy responses' in Noin, D. and Woods, R. (eds) *The Changing Population of Europe*. Oxford: Blackwell, pp. 82–99.

Weller, S.C. and Romney, A.K. 1988. *Systematic Data Collection*. London: Sage.

Wells, N. and Freer, C. 1988. 'Old myths: frequent misconceptions about the elderly' in Wells, N. and Freer, C. (eds) *The Ageing Population. Burden or Challenge?* London: Macmillan Press, pp. 3–15.

Werbner, P. 1987. 'Pakistani traders in a British city' in Eades, J. (ed.) *Migrants, Workers and the Social Order*. London: Tavistock, pp. 213–33.

Whyte, W.F. 1984. *Learning from the Field. A Guide from Experience* (with the collaboration of Kathleen King Whyte). London: Sage.

Williams, A.M., King, R. and Warnes, T. 1997. 'A place in the sun. International retirement migration from northern to southern Europe', *European Urban and Regional Studies*, 4 (2), 115–34.

Wilpert, C. 1989. 'Ethnic and cultural identity: ethnicity and the second generation in the context of european migration' in Liebkind, K. (ed.) *New Identities in Europe*. Aldershot: Gower, pp. 6–24.

Wiseman, R.F. and Roseman, C.C. 1979. 'A typology of elderly migration based on the decision making process', *Economic Geography*, 55 (4), 324–37.

Yancey, W.L., Eriksen, E. and Richard, J. 1976. 'Emergent ethnicity: a review and reformation', *American Sociological Review* 41, 391–403.

Yinger, M. 1986. 'Intersecting strands in the theorisation of race and ethnic relations' in Rex, J. and Mason, D. (eds) *Theories of Race and Ethnic Relations*. Cambridge: Cambridge University Press, pp. 20–41.

Yinger, M. 1994. *Ethnicity. Source of Strength? Source of Conflict?* Albany: State University of New York Press.

Index